PRAISE FOR *THE CURSE OF CASH*

—

"[A] fascinating economic manifesto.... [An] absorbing exploration of the uses, and misuses, of currency, and its intractability in controlling modern economies."
—PUBLISHERS WEEKLY

"Rogoff is always worth listening to.... [He] is on very solid ground... when he says the process of weaning us further off cash should begin with the abolition of high-denomination notes."
—DAVID SMITH, *Sunday Times*

THE
CURSE
OF
CASH

THE CURSE OF CASH

KENNETH S. ROGOFF

WITH A NEW AFTERWORD
BY THE AUTHOR

PRINCETON UNIVERSITY PRESS

PRINCETON AND OXFORD

Requests for permission to reproduce material from this work should be sent to
Permissions, Princeton University Press

Published by Princeton University Press, 41 William Street, Princeton, New Jersey 08540

In the United Kingdom: Princeton University Press, 6 Oxford Street, Woodstock,
Oxfordshire OX20 1TR

press.princeton.edu

Cover design by Faceout Studio. Cover image courtesy of Shutterstock.

Excerpt from *The Collected Writings of John Maynard Keynes* copyright © 1931, 1972,
2010, 2013 The Royal Economic Society. Reprinted with the permission of Cambridge
University Press.

Second printing, and first paperback printing, with a new afterword by the author, 2017

Paperback ISBN 978-0-691-17836-3

The Library of Congress has cataloged the cloth edition of this book as follows:

Names: Rogoff, Kenneth S., author.
Title: The curse of cash / Kenneth S. Rogoff.
Description: Princeton : Princeton University Press, [2016] | Includes bibliographical
    references and index.
Identifiers: LCCN 2016014943 | ISBN 9780691172132 (hardback : alk. paper)
Subjects: LCSH: Paper money. | Money. | Currency question. | Monetary policy.
Classification: LCC HG350 .R64 2016 | DDC 332.4—dc23 LC record available at
    https://lccn.loc.gov/2016014943

British Library Cataloging-in-Publication Data is available

This book has been composed in Sabon LT Std with DIN Pro Display

Printed on acid-free paper. ∞

Printed in the United States of America

10 9 8 7 6 5 4 3 2

To my parents,
June and Stanley Rogoff

—

CONTENTS

PART III: *International Dimensions and Digital Currencies*

PREFACE

This book deals with an issue that might seem stupefyingly mundane, more of a minor irritant than a curse. Yet, as I will try to persuade the reader, paper currency (cash) lies at the heart of some of today's most intractable public finance and monetary problems. And getting rid of most cash could help more than you might think.

The reader can be forgiven for thinking that monetary economists must worry about paper currency all the time, and that there must be endless scholarly tomes about it. Nothing could be further from the truth. Indeed, most academic and policy economists tend to think of physical paper currency as an irrelevant sideshow in today's world of high-tech banking and finance. Modern Keynesian macroeconomic models either marginalize the role of cash or banish it entirely; it is just too inconvenient to deal with. Most monetary policy experts can't be bothered with paper currency, as they believe it to be thoroughly uninteresting and unimportant.

Even central bankers don't care all that much about cash, even though their institutions make tens of billions of dollars supplying the stuff. Board members happily devote endless hours to discussing the minutiae of interest rate policy, and how it will affect inflation and unemployment. But don't bother them with any discussion of cash issuance except when it comes time to think about profit and loss statements. Even then, they are not going to get too excited. Deep down, most central bankers believe that their main objective in life is to help guide the economy along a path of stable growth and prices, not to make money.

Yes, cash has gotten slightly more attention in recent years, as central bankers worry more about how far they can push interest rates below zero, as debt-laden governments' national treasuries become increasingly desperate for tax revenues, as security agencies try to forestall terrorist threats, and as justice departments try to deal with growing national and international crime syndicates. But most policymakers still take paper currency as an immutable fact of life and restrict their ambitions to mitigating any problems it causes. Even academics, who are supposed to think outside the box, have concentrated their attention on complex and risky policy ideas for dealing with the impotence of monetary policy once interest rates are zero, rather than asking how the issue might simply be swept off the table.

And that is precisely what I aim to propose here. Why not just get rid of paper currency? Or, to be precise, why not phase out most of it, taking care to execute the transition extremely slowly and gradually, dealing with financial inclusion issues through subsidized debit cards, retaining small notes indefinitely, perhaps eventually to be replaced by a coins-only system.

This solution might sound simple, and one might well ask why it takes an entire book to discuss it. But tackling the idea seriously takes us on a wide-ranging journey across all the ways that paper currency touches our lives, some concrete, some practical, some extraordinarily abstract. Though there are ever so many ways this topic can be sensationalized and politicized, I try to take a balanced tone throughout, highlighting both the advantages and the risks. This is not an easy task, as many topics are highly emotional. For example, what one person sees as illegal immigration, another might see as an escape mechanism for those fleeing from persecution and extreme poverty. Where does one draw the line between the government's right to enforce tax laws and the public's right to privacy? Regardless of readers' initial prejudices, I suspect many will find the facts presented in this book sobering, and many of the arguments for preserving paper currency in its current form more superficial and less compelling than they might seem.

My hope is that most readers will find the book quite accessible. Where it has been essential to tackle somewhat more esoteric issues, I have kept the discussion as clear and simple as possible, with any absolutely necessary technical material relegated to endnotes and topics in the appendix. The future role of cash in our society is simply too important a topic to leave in a small dark corner of monetary economics. I trust that by the end of this book, the reader will see the topic of paper currency as far from mundane and certainly not a minor issue.

THE
CURSE
OF
CASH

CHAPTER 1

——

Introduction and Overview

Has the time come for advanced-country governments to start phasing out paper currency (cash), except perhaps for small-denomination notes, coins, or both? A huge number of economic, financial, philosophical, and even moral issues are buried in this relatively simple question. In this book, I argue that, on balance, the answer is "yes." First, making it more difficult to engage in recurrent, large, and anonymous payments would likely have a significant impact on discouraging tax evasion and crime; even a relatively modest impact could potentially justify getting rid of most paper currency. Second, as I have argued for some time, phasing out paper currency is arguably the simplest and most elegant approach to clearing the path for central banks to invoke unfettered negative interest rate policies should they bump up against the "zero lower bound" on interest rates. Treasury bill rates cannot fall much below zero, precisely because people always have the option of holding paper currency, which at least pays zero interest.[1]

Although in principle, phasing out cash and invoking negative interest rates are topics that can be studied separately, in reality the two issues are deeply linked. To be precise, it is virtually impossible to think about drastically phasing out currency without recognizing that it opens a door to unrestricted negative rates that central banks may someday be tempted to walk through. After all, even today when the door to negative rates is cracked only slightly ajar, several major central banks (including the Bank of Japan and the European Central Bank) have already shoved a foot through. Thus it is important to think about phasing out cash and developing negative interest rate policy in an integrative fashion.

The idea of sharply scaling back the world's mountain of paper currency seemed like pure fantasy when I first proposed eliminating large bills almost two decades ago, an idea that traces back to

Henry (1976).[2] It was an obscure academic paper on an obscure topic in a relatively obscure journal, yet something about the crazy offbeat idea of getting rid of $100 bills caught the eye of *New York Times* writer Sylvia Nasar[3] (author of *A Beautiful Mind*). Her article, in turn, caught the attention of then–US Treasury Secretary Robert Rubin, who raised the issue with his staff. To my chagrin, I was later told that the main thing that Rubin focused on was not my argument for getting rid of all large-denomination notes (say, equivalent to $50 and above). Rather, it was my conjecture that the planned new 500-euro notes (about $570) might challenge the dominance of the United States' $100 bill in the global underground economy. So much for policy influence.

I still think my focus was the right one.[4] The "profits" governments reap by blindly accommodating demand for cash are dwarfed by the costs of the illegal activity that cash, especially big bills, facilitates. The effect of curtailing paper currency on tax evasion alone would likely cover the lost profits from printing paper currency, even if tax evasion fell by only 10–15%. The effect on illegal activities is probably even more important.

There is little question that cash plays a starring role in a broad range of criminal activities, including drug trafficking, racketeering, extortion, corruption of public officials, human trafficking, and, of course, money laundering. The fact that large notes are used far more for illegal activities than legal ones long ago penetrated television, movies, and popular culture.[5] Policymakers, however, have been far slower to acknowledge this reality.

Cash also plays a central role in the illegal immigration problem that bedevils countries like the United States. It is incredible that some politicians talk seriously about building huge border fences, yet no one seems to realize that a far more humane and effective approach would be to make it difficult for US employers to use cash to pay ineligible workers off the books and often below the minimum wage. Jobs are the big magnet that drives the whole process. More generally, cash is an enabler for employers who would skirt employment regulations and avoid making Social Security contributions.

Of course, any plan to drastically scale back the use of cash needs to provide heavily subsidized, basic debit card accounts for low-income individuals and perhaps eventually basic smartphones as well. Several countries, including Sweden and Denmark, already do so, and many other countries are contemplating similar steps. A simple idea to jump-start the process is to create debit accounts through which all government transfer payments are made. Financial inclusion would be good public policy with or without phasing out cash. In any event, the blueprint I propose in this book leaves small notes in circulation for a long time (perhaps indefinitely), which should cover most concerns about everyday payments for most people. Leaving behind small bills (ideally eventually converting these to slightly weighty coins) also addresses some of the most visceral concerns about security, privacy, and emergencies.

Anyone who thinks that debit cards, cell phone payments, and virtual currencies are already burying cash could not be more wrong. Demand for most advanced-country paper currency notes has been rising steadily for more than two decades. Believe it or not, as of the end of 2015, $1.34 trillion worth of US currency was being held outside banks, or $4,200 floating around for every man, woman, and child in the United States. The orders of magnitude for most advanced-country currencies is broadly similar. Incredibly, the vast bulk of this mass stash of cash is in high-denomination notes, the kind most of us don't carry in our purses and wallets, including the US $100 bill, the 500-euro note (about $570 at present), and the 1,000–Swiss franc note (a little over $1,000). Almost 80% of the US currency supply is in $100 bills. How many people have 34 of them in their purses, cookie jars, or cars, as each individual would need to account for his or her share? And this is for every man, woman and child, so a four-person family would need to be holding $13,600 just in $100 bills, and that is not counting smaller bills. Treasuries and central banks routinely make billions from printing large-denomination notes, yet no one quite knows where exactly most of it lives or what it is used for. Only a minor fraction is in cash registers or bank vaults, and surveys of consumers in the United States and Europe don't begin to explain the rest. And it is not just the United States that has a gigantic currency supply dominated by big bills. The problem is nearly universal in advanced economies.

Even central banks are starting to see their reverse money laundering operations as a mixed blessing. I use the label "reverse money laundering" to capture how central banks effectively take clean large-denomination notes, ship them out to banks where, after a series of intermediate transactions, cash—and big notes especially—often end up as dirty money in the underground economy. Traditional money laundering, of course, takes proceeds from illicit activities and filters them through seemingly legitimate enterprises to produce clean money.

The main motivation for central banks to rethink the role of cash does not so much seem to be a moral awakening as a realization that paper currency has become a major impediment to the smooth functioning of the global financial system. How can something as antiquated as paper currency really matter for a global economy in which the total value of all financial assets dwarfs the total value of cash? The reason is so utterly banal it will shock anyone who hasn't thought about it.

Paper currency can be thought of as a zero-interest-rate bond. Or to be precise, it is a zero-interest anonymous bearer bond: it has no name or history attached to it, and it is valid no matter who holds it.[6] As long as people have the choice of paper money, they are not going to be willing to accept an interest rate that is significantly lower on any kind of bond, except perhaps for a modest compensating differential because cash is costly to store and insure. As trivial as the problem seems, the zero bound has essentially crippled monetary policy across the advanced world for much of the past 8 years since the financial crash of 2008. If unconstrained negative rate policy were possible—and all the necessary financial, institutional, and legal preparations were made—central banks would never "run out of bullets" (i.e., room to keep cutting interest rates). A good case can be made that open-ended negative interest rate policy would have been extremely helpful in the depths of the financial crisis.

Few policymakers had really been worrying about the problem until the financial crisis struck. The zero bound constraint simply had not been that much of a concern since the Great Depression, outside post-bubble Japan. Since 2008, the situation has changed dramatically. Indeed, over the past 8 years, virtually every major central bank has wished it could have set significantly negative interest rates at one time or another. A few, including those of Denmark, Switzerland, Sweden, the Eurozone, and Japan, have tiptoed into negative rate territory, probing the boundary where a flight from corporate bank accounts and government debt to cash would make the policy ineffective or even counterproductive. But even if the lower bound on policy interest rates is a little less than zero, it is still a constraint.

The idea that negative interest rates might sometimes be good policy, and that paper currency stands in the way, is hardly new. At the height of the Great Depression, leading economists from across the spectrum, including Yale's Irving Fisher and Cambridge's John Maynard Keynes, reached a remarkable consensus. If only there were some way for governments to pay a negative return on cash, monetary expansion just might be able to push the world out of depression. The problem back then, as in many countries today, is that with short-term policy interest rates already at zero, monetary policy was stuck in a "liquidity trap," with nothing more to do. Inspired by the maverick German thinker Silvio Gesell, Fisher penned a short 1933 book *Stamp Scrip*, exploring the idea of requiring people to periodically put new stamps on the back of their paper currency notes to keep them valid. This, of course, was a very primitive way of paying a negative interest rate on cash. Keynes praised the idea in his 1936 *General Theory* but rightly came to the conclusion that it was utterly impractical.[7] Rejecting Gesell's solution to the liquidity trap helped lead to Keynes's famous conclusion that government spending was the key to propelling economies out of the Great Depression.

Yet Keynes might have reached a very different conclusion in a world like today's, where transactions have already increasingly migrated to electronic media, including credit cards, debit cards, and cell phones. There is nothing impractical at all about paying negative (or positive) interest on electronic currency, such as banks hold; as already mentioned, several central banks are doing it! The main obstacle to introducing negative interest rates on a larger scale is legacy paper currency, particularly the large-denomination notes that would be at the epicenter of any full-scale run from Treasury bills into cash.[8] Of course, other institutional obstacles impede full-on negative rate policy, for example, arranging for the payment of negative coupons on debt, proscribing excessive prepayment of taxes, and ruling out long delays in cashing checks. However, as I shall argue in chapters 10 and 11, all these issues can be dealt with, given a long enough lead time.

Phasing out paper currency, or charging negative interest rates on cash, is an emotionally charged issue. Modern-day Silvio Gesells have met with unbridled hostility from some quarters. In 2000, Richmond Federal Reserve official Marvin Goodfriend published a purely academic paper suggesting that one possible way to pay negative interest rates was to put magnetic stripes on currency. Rather than receive praise for his creativity and prescience, Goodfriend quickly became subject to a barrage of hostile and threatening emails, and he was pilloried on conservative radio talk shows. In 2009, Harvard economist N. Gregory Mankiw wrote a whimsical *New York Times* op-ed, where he discussed the zero bound problem, and he mentioned that one of his graduate students suggested the idea of holding periodic lotteries based on the serial numbers on currency. After each lottery, currency with the losing serial numbers would be declared worthless. This unorthodox way to pay a negative rate on cash was put forth tongue-in-cheek for purely illustrative purposes. It is thoroughly impractical. After all, how can people be expected to keep track of all the losing numbers over time? To Mankiw's surprise, he too was immediately subjected to a barrage of hostile emails and commentary, including letters to the president of Harvard demanding that he be fired on the spot.

Not all those who seek to protect paper currency represent End of Days cults or see a connection between a cashless society and the Mark of the Beast. (Although as someone who has long written on sharply reducing the role of paper currency, I can attest that some of those types are in the mix.) Most people who want to protect paper currency have perfectly legitimate reasons for hoping to preserve the status quo. After a lecture I gave at Munich University in 2014, former European Central Bank board member and chief economist

Otmar Issing strongly took issue with my views and commented that paper currency is "coined liberty" (a nod to Dostoyevsky's *House of the Dead*)[9] that must never in any way be compromised or surrendered. My aim in this book is to take these objections seriously, seeking where possible to ask how one might mitigate them. Some prefer the relative convenience of cash, though its advantages persist in an ever-smaller range of legal transactions. Others value the anonymity, a far more complex issue to deal with. How does society balance an individual's right to privacy with society's need to enforce its laws and regulations?

Deciding where that line should be—and how to implement and enforce it—is perhaps the single most critical question that any future task force on ending cash will need to consider. The issue of privacy encompasses much more than cash policy; it raises issues about cell phone records and browsing histories, not to mention the security cameras that are now nearly ubiquitous throughout the world's major cities. Cash, though, is still an important part of the mix, and if one wants to contemplate phasing it out, it is critical to have a hard look at both the goals and the alternatives (e.g., prepaid cash cards with strict limits). Maintaining the convenience and privacy of paper currency in small transactions are important reasons that any path toward phasing out paper currency needs to begin with large-denomination notes and possibly leave small-denomination notes circulating indefinitely or until fully satisfactory alternatives are in place.

———

Organizing a book around a theme that touches on so many diverse topics has been a formidable challenge, especially if one wants to take seriously both the practical and philosophical concerns raised by phasing out paper currency. I have tried to design a structure that makes it easy for the reader to navigate directly to specific topics she is interested in, or simply to read the entire book straight through. A lot of material, particularly citations, has been put into endnotes. These do not necessarily need to be read in detail on a first pass. There are also a few topics that seemed a bit too technical for the text; these have been ganged in a short appendix.

The main text is divided into three parts. Chapter 2 begins with a selective history of currency, highlighting a few key points that I draw on later. An absolutely critical point is that paper currency really comes in two flavors, backed and unbacked. Under a gold-backed paper currency standard, for example, central banks fix the value of the currencies in terms of gold by standing ready to buy and sell currency for gold at the official price. As we shall see, they can run into trouble if they don't have enough gold to back all the currency they print. Under an unbacked or fiat money regime, the only thing that makes paper currency valuable is a mix of social convention and government decree. In modern times, all major currencies are pure fiat monies, a device that traces back to the Mongol emperors in China.

Absent any need to back paper currency, modern-day governments have pumped out vast piles of it. Chapter 3 lays out the basic facts about the huge paper currency supply outstanding, with a focus on advanced-economy currencies, albeit including some facts about emerging markets. Then in chapters 4 and 5, I trace out the different sources of demand. Who could be holding so much cash? Sources of demand include the legal tax-paying domestic economy, the not-so-law-abiding domestic underground economy (including both tax evasion and crime), and the global economy, including both legal and illegal demand.

Chapter 6 explores a fundamental plus for paper currency, which is the considerable income governments earn from exercising their monopoly. It looks at different measures of the profits from paper currency and develops estimates of how much would be lost if a substantial share of the demand migrated to electronic payments. An important issue is not only the lost future profits but also the cost of retiring a large part of the extant supply, which in the first instance would involve issuing government debt to soak up the cash as it is turned in. The actual cost would likely depend on the extent to which anti-money-laundering laws and cash deposit reporting requirements were suspended during the phaseout period, since that would affect how much dirty money was turned in. I conclude that the overall social benefits to phasing out currency are likely to outweigh the costs by a considerable margin.

Of course, a lot depends on just how much lower tax evasion and criminal activity would turn out to be in a "less-cash" world. This is an unknown, though I speculate that the effects are likely to be substantial, provided the government is vigilant about playing Whac-a-mole as alternative transaction media come into being. The key instruments that the government has are the ability to make it impossible for financial institutions to accept an alternative currency and the ability to make it difficult to use in ordinary retail establishments. Yes, there are always end-arounds: gold coins, uncut diamonds, and virtual currencies. But if one looks into the practicalities of it, and the considerable restrictions already in place (e.g., on licensed diamond and gold dealers), it quickly becomes apparent that the alternatives to cash are likely to be costlier, riskier, and less efficient. We specifically look at virtual currencies in the penultimate chapter of the book.

Chapter 7, the final chapter in part I, contains a concrete plan for phasing out paper currency, up to small notes and coins. The long timeline is intended to give people and institutions time to adjust and to help policymakers navigate unforeseen problems. An important general principle is that an ideal system should create obstacles to large and repeated anonymous transactions but not to small ones; it should also ensure financial inclusion. By leaving small bills or coins in place indefinitely, the blueprint deals with many of the concerns that might arise if cash were completely eliminated, such as blackouts after natural disasters. How quickly paper currency can be eliminated altogether depends on experience and the evolution of technology. Toward the end of chapter 7, I discuss the case of the Scandinavian countries (especially Sweden), which for a variety of reasons have moved further and faster toward being less-cash societies than perhaps any other country so far. It is far too soon to draw any firm conclusions from these early experiences, but they do appear to show that a lot of the more superficial objections to sharply reducing the use of cash can be navigated.

Part II of the book deals with negative interest rates. As already noted, it is hard to seriously study phasing out paper currency without recognizing the possibility that it could fundamentally impact central bank policy.[10] After an introduction and overview, chapter 8 explores what is known about just how serious the zero bound on interest rates is in practice. There is a growing and evolving academic literature, but it is based on limited data and experience. Moreover, the models themselves have internal limitations, for example, the crude way in which they treat financial markets. The bottom line is that even though most central bankers intuitively believe the zero bound is likely to be an important and recurrent problem, the academic research is still in its early days, and the results so far are mixed.

Chapter 8 also details some of the efforts central banks have undertaken to mitigate the zero bound without appealing to negative rates. Chapter 9 goes on to look at other ideas for dealing with the zero bound, such as raising central bank inflation targets from 2% to 4%. Chapter 10 takes up alternative approaches to allowing for (open-ended) negative interest rate policy without phasing out paper currency. One interesting and important idea is for the government to issue separate electronic and paper currencies and to manage an exchange rate between them. Chapter 11 explores other frictions and barriers that might prevent negative rate policy from being effective and how to address these frictions. I then turn in chapter 12 to concerns that negative interest rate policy will unhinge monetary stability, and that it will create too much temptation for departures from modern rule-based policy.

Part III of the book takes on topics that span both parts I and II, including international dimensions and digital currencies. Is coordination necessary (chapter 13)? Are there spillovers from negative interest rate policy? Does the dawn of digital currencies make this all irrelevant anyway (chapter 14)?[11] I also consider the case of developing countries and emerging markets; for most it is too soon to contemplate phasing out paper currency, though phasing out large-denomination notes is likely still a good idea. The Final Thoughts chapter concludes the book.

Finally, a few words on terminology. Throughout, I use the term "paper currency" broadly to encompass other transaction media with similar form and function as paper currency, but not literally made from paper. Of course, early Chinese currencies were made from leather and tree bark, and the relevant alternative today is polymer plastic, which is already being adopted by a number of countries, including Canada and the United Kingdom. Plastic currency notes are definitely more durable than paper and are supposedly more difficult to counterfeit. However, for most purposes here, these are not first-order issues. Aside from a few other small details, which will be highlighted where relevant (e.g., it is potentially easier to scan individual serial numbers on the plastic notes), the reader should think of paper currency and plastic currency as the same thing throughout this book. I will use the term "paper currency" to refer to both.

Relatedly, I drift sometimes into using the terms "paper money" or "cash" instead of saying only "paper currency," just to avoid being monotonous. They all mean the same thing here. Colloquial usage of the term "cash" sometimes extends to include all forms of liquid wealth, but here in context it should be clear enough that I am always using "cash" to mean "paper currency." In 75 years, if paper currency is still being used by isolated tribes in the Amazon or East Texas, they will probably have their own words to describe it anyway.

PART I

The Dark Side of Paper Currency: Tax and Regulatory Evasion, Crime, and Security Issues

CHAPTER 2

The Early Development of Coins and Paper Currency

In a book that presages the death of paper money, I would be remiss not to include a long and glowing eulogy. The evolution of modern money will also help us understand some important nuances about the role of government and technology that will prove useful in analyzing the scope for alternative currency systems in the future.

The long legacy and storied history of paper money in our psyche and culture is a formidable artifice in itself, not to be taken lightly. For Westerners, the history begins with Marco Polo's insightful account of paper currency in China, a revelation that stunned Europeans as some form of alchemy. This suspicion is echoed in Johann Wolfgang von Goethe's *Faust*, when the demon Mephistopheles tempts the emperor, who is in severe financial distress, to introduce paper money to increase spending and pay off state debt. The device works in the short run but ultimately leads to inflation and ruin. Goethe, writing early in the nineteenth century, was nothing if not prescient. Without paper money, there might have been no German hyperinflation, and perhaps no World War II.[1]

Failed paper money may be cursed, but successful paper money has long been a cornerstone of the world's most successful economies. A century and a half before the founding of the Federal Reserve in 1913, American Benjamin Franklin arrived in London, planning to suggest that the British allow the American colonies to create a universal paper money to help pay their share of costs from the Seven Years' War; the idea did not materialize.[2] Ironically, the very American currency Franklin envisioned 250 years ago has now not only come into existence, it has also far surpassed its British counterpart in global import and now constitutes what is perhaps the greatest symbol of American power. Franklin's picture, of course, adorns the $100 bill. The significance of "the Benjamins" is not lost on China's leaders, who are already thinking ahead to the day when large-value renminbi notes might supplant US $100 bills in the global imagination. It might be a while, though.

The history of paper money is immensely fascinating and deeply interlinked with the development of technology and society. Many marvelous theoretical and historical treatises have been written on money since Polo.[3] My purposes in this brief historical tour are, however, sharply circumscribed. Three points are critical.

First, the history of money is anything but static, and there should be nothing shocking about the idea that the medium of exchange can evolve from paper to electronic, from Benjamins to, say, a government-run version of the virtual currency Bitcoin. Second, although a great many items can serve as money, the best technology tends to win out, eventually. It is no accident that metal coinage trumped other commodity currencies, and that paper currencies eventually trumped coins. And it will be no accident when the paper era fades. There is nothing in the modern economic theory of money that precludes an electronic currency.[4]

Third, in many instances currency innovations begin in the private sector and are then appropriated by a government. Like it or not, a strong central government has huge advantages in providing a safe guaranteed asset, if only because any private money is ultimately vulnerable to government interference. These lessons are well worth bearing in mind for assessing the future of digital currencies (or, more narrowly, encrypted or "cryptocurrencies") and other attempts to use new, possibly superior, technologies, to leapfrog private currencies ahead of publicly issued money. There have been such cycles before, as this chapter illustrates.

Every advanced civilization, with the debatable exception of the Incas of South America, has required a solution to the problem the great nineteenth-century monetary theorist William Stanley Jevons famously termed the "double coincidence of wants." This is simply the challenge of designing a system that, at a minimum, relieves the necessity of doing all trade by barter. Money is not so important in small nomadic or tribal societies with only a few goods and a strong social order governing allocation. As societies become more developed, however, with diverse goods and large populations, achieving allocation without some form of money has long proven nearly impossible. Even if it is really true that the Incas were able to reach a relatively high level of development without a currency system, the idea that this might be feasible in more technologically advanced modern societies remains unthinkable. The centrally planned economies of the former Soviet bloc used input-output matrixes to try to map out every detail of production in their economies, yet even they still found it indispensable to have a currency system.

The most interesting part of the story for us starts with the development of metal coins. The reader should understand, however, that there have also been a plethora of commodity currencies, including whale's teeth in Fiji, rice in the Philippines, feather money in Santa Cruz, grain in India, cowrie shell money in large parts of Africa and China, cattle in Colombia, and wampum beads in the United States. Paul Einzig devotes a chapter in his classic book on primitive monies to "The Slave Girl Money of Ireland," an abhorrent practice not restricted to ancient Ireland.[5] Even after modern currencies were invented, commodity currencies have continued to be used in times of duress, and it could happen again. Cigarettes and gasoline were used at times as currencies in Europe after World War II, as war-torn economies struggled to regain basic functions.

EARLY COINAGE

The true invention of modern metallic coinage is generally thought to have started in Lydia (in modern Western Turkey) in the seventh century BC. Made of electrum, a naturally occurring alloy of gold and silver, Lydian coins were hand struck and stamped with an image on one side (for example, a lion), leaving a punch mark on the other side. The idea of having a relatively uniform transaction medium, with the government standing behind it as the guarantor of quality, can be listed as one of the quantum breakthroughs in the history of civilization. Standardized coins may now seem obvious, but at the time it was pure genius. Many economic historians assume the technology of coining arose in the private sector and was then largely taken over by the king, but it is hard to know for sure.[6] Although many of some 300 issues of Lydian coins that have been identified are private, it is difficult to establish whether these came first.[7]

Even though the birth of standardized coinage is something we now recognize as a transformative technology, it took almost eight decades to radiate outside a few neighboring Greek states. The real explosion in coinage came after another technological breakthrough, as the Lydians learned to separate electrum into pure gold and silver. This allowed King Croesus to stamp out pure coins in either metal. Croesus ultimately was defeated by the Persians, but he and his coinage live on in the phrase "rich as Croesus."

As Lydian coins spread in trade, they were imitated elsewhere, most importantly by Athens, which had the good fortune of access to silver in mines in Attica to the south. The Athenian "owls," named after their imprint, soon traded far and wide. Some economic historians assign Athenian coinage technology a central role in the Greek state's capacity to build the ships that defeated King Xerxes and his invading Persian fleet in the battle of Salamis in 480 BC.[8] Without the financial instrument essential to building the fleet, the flowering of Western civilization might have been stopped in its tracks, or at least so the victor's version of history goes.

Alexander the Great is remembered far more for his military tactics than his economic acumen. Yet his exploitation of new ideas in currency was highly instrumental in creating the largest empire the world had ever known during the fourth century BC. Alexander made great use of the innovation of coinage in paying troops and providing provisions across unprecedentedly long supply chains. He faced the vexing problem, however, of how to deal with the fluctuating values of gold and silver coins in different parts of the empire. Alexander's elegant solution was to simply declare a gold-to-silver value of ten to one, using a mix of stockpiles throughout his empire, and coercion to enforce it.[9] Alexander's approach made Macedonian coinage simple and useful, and a precursor to more modern versions of coinage. Nevertheless, as Sargent and Velde explain in their marvelously titled book *The Big Problem of Small Change*, it wasn't really until the nineteenth century, when pure fiat currency became more widespread, that the problem of co-circulation of coins in different metals was truly solved.[10]

Technology has always played a central role in currency, because of the need to produce monies that are easily seen to be genuine and not counterfeit. Referring once again to William Stanley Jevons's classic (1875) book on money, it is notable how much attention he gives to making life difficult for counterfeiters, warning that governments need to use sophisticated milling machinery to discourage imitators. His discussion is eerily similar in many ways to issues that treasuries discuss today in their constant search for more counterfeit-proof paper currencies, a quest that has resulted in ever more colorful and complicated-looking paper (or now in many countries, polymer plastic) currencies. If anyone doubts the importance of technology in coinage, one only has to note that England turned to Sir Isaac Newton in 1696 to serve as warden of the Royal Mint, and later master of the Mint in 1699. Newton helped Britain recoin its currency after debasement and counterfeiting during the Nine Years' War; he also invented the milled edge, aimed at discouraging counterfeiting and clipping, a version of which still appears on many of today's coins.[11] As we shall see later with paper currency in chapter 6, however, nothing seems to defeat the counterfeiters forever. The UK Royal Mint has now announced that it will produce a new 12-sided pound coin in 2017 to fend off growing counterfeiting problems with the traditional milled version.

Although counterfeiting has been a constant concern everywhere, the biggest threat to the value of the currency is often the government itself. In Rome, coin debasement produced cumulative inflation of 19,900% over the period 151–301 AD, a period that saw major revolts and plague.[12] The problem was a recurrent one, even as European coinage became more developed, as table 2.1 illustrates. The table lists select peak debasement years and the percentage by which the silver content of coinage was

Table 2.1: Selected peak debasement years for European coinage, 1300–1812

Country	Year	Decline in Silver Content (%)
Austria	1812	−55
Belgium	1498	−35
England	1464	−20
England	1551	−50
France	1303	−57
France	1718	−36
Germany Bavaria	1424	−22
Germany Bavaria	1685	−26
Germany Frankfurt	1500	−16
Italy	1320	−21
Netherlands	1496	−35
Portugal	1800	−18
Russia	1810	−41
Spain New Castle	1642	−25
Sweden	1572	−41
Turkey	1586	−44

Source: Reinhart and Rogoff (2009).

reduced; it should dispel any notion that commodity currencies are safe. King Henry VIII of England, with his 50% debasement in 1551, has to settle for third place to France's 57% debasement in 1303 and Austria's 55% debasement during the Napoleonic Wars, and there are several other close contenders.[13] The debasements of the Middle Ages can be understood at a visceral level by visiting almost any currency museum, such as the Bank of Japan's in Tokyo or the German Bundesbank's in Dresden, and seeing the many episodes over which coins tended to become smaller and smaller over time.

The ability of coins to persist despite periodic sharp debasements illustrates an absolutely fundamental property of long-lived successful currencies: they succeed in part because citizens have faith in the government that stands behind the currencies, and they succeed in part because the government can exercise its coercive power to insist that they be accepted, at a minimum in payment of taxes, debts, and government contracts. Balancing the carrot and stick of currency regimes remains a fundamental problem to this day.

THE BIRTH OF PAPER CURRENCY IN CHINA

For all its flaws, including ones that Goethe highlighted in *Faust*, there are very good reasons why, over the years, paper money has mopped the floor with its competitors all over the world. Paper money delivers portability, homogeneity, security, durability, and convenience. It serves perfectly well as a unit of account and a medium of exchange, and during periods of low inflation, it also serves well as a store of value.

The story of how money developed in China holds some interesting lessons, which we draw on later in chapter 7. There I argue that as paper currency is gradually phased out, eventually even the remaining small notes should be replaced with moderately substantial coins, to make it even more difficult to carry large quantities of currency.

The Chinese appear to have developed coinage independently of Western civilization, though there is naturally a debate over who came first. It turns somewhat on how crude a definition of "coin" one uses, and whether early private coins are counted. The economic historian Niall Ferguson gives clear precedence to the West, arguing that it was not until 221 BC that China's Qin Shin emperor (Qin Shihuangdi) introduced the first standardized minted bronze coin, to be used throughout the empire.[14] Early Chinese coins were minted as likenesses of cowrie shells, a commodity currency that had been used previously in China and had to be imported, as the shells were not found locally.

In China, unlike in Europe, such base metals as copper, tin, and lead served as the main raw materials for coins. Iron was also used. Because of the low value-to-weight ratio of these coins, one had to be able to carry heavy loads to pay large amounts. The Chinese did use silver ingots as stores of wealth and as a medium of exchange, as the Middle East and Europe did before the Lydians, but these were not standardized and coined.

Europe's adoption of precious metals gave the European coinage much more versatility. Interestingly, though, China's inferior coinage materials might have provided the impetus for its early introduction of paper money, the main technology we use today.[15] China, of course, had fixed woodblock printing at least as far back as the Tang dynasty in the seventh century AD, and a moveable ceramic-type printing process around the time of the Song Dynasty in the eleventh century, long before Johannes Gutenberg produced his first Bible in 1455.

The history of early paper money in China covers seven dynasties, each with its own monetary rules and institutions. In addition, the important province of Szechuan had its own currency for a time.[16] But paper currency did not develop overnight. The technology evolved, and public acceptance of paper evolved along with it. Chinese merchants and financiers originally came up with the idea of issuing proxy notes that could be redeemed for coin to avoid the difficulty and danger of transporting large amounts, a process that repeated itself much later in Europe. Proxy notes led to another major development—the use of provincial paper promissory notes so that China's far-flung provinces could pay taxes to the center more easily and efficiently. By the early 800s, the central government had prohibited private operators and taken control itself of the provincial note issuance system. "Flying money" (nicknamed for its tendency to blow away in the wind) is considered by some Chinese historians to be the first paper money.[17]

The heyday of paper money in China runs from the eleventh century through the fifteenth century. It was under the Mongol regime in China that paper currency reached something closest to its modern form, albeit absent any kind of institutional device to control inflation—like an independent central bank—that we now recognize as essential. When Genghis Khan's grandson, Kublai Khan, ascended the throne of China in 1260, the paper currencies of previous regimes and local currencies had become nearly worthless. They were called in and replaced with a national currency of silver notes that had the unusual feature of being worth only half their face value in silver, if ever tendered for exchange at the Khan's treasury.[18] (In chapter 10, we will see Kublai Khan's idea of creating a wedge between paper currency and the official unit of account echoed in the ingenious Eisler-Buiter-Kimball scheme for paying negative interest rates.) Unlike many previous note issues, Kublai Khan's notes had no expiration date.

By 1262, Kublai Khan's government had prohibited the use of gold and silver as a medium of exchange, with the highly credible threat of death for those who dared disobey. By the late 1270s, convertibility into species became increasingly difficult, effectively transforming the Mongol currency into a pure fiat money.[19] As mentioned in chapter 1, a pure fiat monetary regime is one in which the currency cannot be taken to the central bank or treasury in exchange for gold or silver, or any other commodity for that matter.

When Venetian merchant and adventurer Marco Polo arrived at the Khan's court in the mid-1270s, few wonders of the East amazed him as much as China's paper currency system. Polo ultimately devoted an entire chapter of his travelogue to the Chinese currency: "How the Great Khan Causeth the Bark of Trees, Made into Something Like Paper, to Pass for Money All Over His Country." A few key quotes capture the main themes:

> In this city of Kanbulu [Cambulac-Peking] is the mint of the Great Khan who may truly be said to possess the secret of alchemists, since he has the art of making money.
>
> He causes the bark to be stripped away from mulberry trees (the leaves of which are used for feeding silkworms), and takes from it the thin layer that lies between the coarser bark and the wood of the tree. This being steeped, and afterwards being pounded in a mortar until reduced to pulp, is made into paper. When ready for use, he has it cut into pieces of different sizes, nearly square, but longer than they are wide. . . . The coinage of this paper money is authorized with as much form and ceremony as it were actually pure gold or silver. . . . [I]t receives full authority as current money, and the act of counterfeiting . . . is punished as a capital offense.
>
> When thus coined in large quantities, this paper currency is circulated in every part of the Great Khan's dominions; nor dares any person, at the peril of his life, refuse to accept it. . . . Upon these grounds, it may certainly be affirmed that the Great Khan has a greater command of treasure than any sovereign in the universe.[20]

Although Polo was an extremely astute economic observer, neither he nor the Khan's ministers seemed to fully understand the limits to which the printing press could be used to finance government spending on a sustained basis.[21]

By the time of Kublai Khan's death in 1294, inflation had sharply eroded the paper currency.[22] In his 1906 book *Currency in China*,

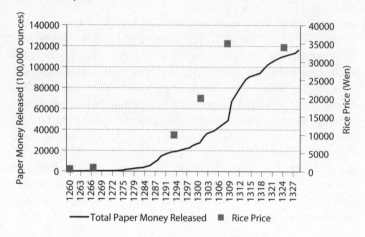

Figure 2.1: Paper money printing and rice price in the Yuan dynasty. Source: Tullock (1957) and Huang (2008).

historian H. B. Morse estimates that the Mongol issuance of silver notes rose from 12 million in 1265 to almost 120 billion in 1330, an increase vastly disproportionate to any territorial gains. By 1356, if not before, virtually all Mongol paper currency was considered worthless. Figure 2.1, which plots total paper money issued (solid line) and the yuan price of rice (boxes) from 1260 to 1329, shows all the traits of classic high inflation driven by money-financed deficit spending.

After the Mongols were overthrown and the Ming Dynasty came into place, things did not get much better. Again the government issued new paper currency notes in 1375, and again by 1400, they had become worth only 3% of their face value.[23]

The story of China's early paper currency is a rather sensational one. Perhaps it would have saved other regions of the world a good deal of grief had they understood it better. At some point after each successive dynasty established its monetary regime, its leaders could not resist the temptation to rely excessively on printing to pay for finances, eventually debasing the currency and causing rampant inflation, as in Goethe's satire. The Chinese full well understood the importance of imposing a government monopoly and limiting the use of alternative transaction media, if necessary by pain of death, to ensure as large a demand as possible for their "product." For example, in 1294, the Mongol dynasty issued an imperial decree forbidding the use of bamboo money, presumably a budding competitor to the junk paper that the Mongols were forcing people to use. They also at times resorted to heavy-handed price controls. Yet, no matter how powerful the emperor, the system would ultimately self-destruct as the gain from defiance became too great. In time, even the emperor's envoys fell prey to the same incentives to cheat as everyone else. (Think of the severe risks run by many Chinese entrepreneurs, officials, and ordinary citizens even today to evade the country's still strict currency exchange controls.) By 1500, after successive waves of inflation, China abandoned government-issued paper currency, not to take it up again until the country was reopened in the nineteenth century.

BEN FRANKLIN AND PAPER CURRENCY IN THE COLONIAL UNITED STATES

If paper notes came slowly to Europe, it was probably more out of post–Dark Ages ignorance than informed caution. Unlike China, where the state moved in relatively quickly, paper notes were long a vehicle of private banks that issued notes redeemable for specie (usually gold or silver). After awhile, issuers realized that they could get away with floating more notes than they had reserves, risking trouble but making a huge profit in the interim. That is exactly what happened in Europe's first note issuance. Johan Palmstruch was a Dutch merchant who in 1656 founded Stockholms Banco, a quasi-state bank in the sense that half its profits had to be turned over to the state. Five years later, in 1661, Palmstruch persuaded the government to let him issue notes, redeemable at his bank for gold and silver deposited there. To make a long story short, Stockholms Banco issued more notes than it had specie and eventually ran aground. Palmstruch was sentenced to death, though he escaped with a commuted sentence. Palmstruch's experience is a caricature of the history of private banking and provides the kind of rationale governments always use to eventually usurp private monies; governments can have debt crises, but they are far less vulnerable to runs than are private banks.[24]

A few decades later, in 1694, the Bank of England also issued notes convertible to specie, though it was not yet a true central bank. It was only with the Bank Act of 1844 that the Bank of England's notes gained the right of legal tender and could thus be used to settle any debt.[25]

Bragging rights for the first full-fledged modern fiat currency in the West belongs to the enterprising colonists of the young United States. As poor immigrants, the colonial Americans did not possess a significant quantity of British sterling, nor did the early colonies yield discoveries of the precious metals needed to mint their own coins. In early years, the colonists often relied on wampum, fur, tobacco, and other commodities. They also used foreign coins, especially Spanish pieces of eight (*peso de ocho*), the 8-real silver coin that was the de facto international currency before eventually losing out to British sterling. But with growing pressures from rising commerce, the colonies struck on the idea of issuing paper currency, with Massachusetts leading the way in 1690. (As a Massachusetts resident today, this somehow does not surprise me.) It was a wild ride. Eventually, all the colonies joined in, with Rhode Island and South Carolina issuing so many notes that their purchasing power quickly evaporated. Other states, most notably Virginia, were more careful.[26]

In 1729, the 23-year-old Ben Franklin made an indelible mark on the history of paper currency with his self-published book *A Modest Enquiry into the Nature and Necessity of a Paper Currency*. Although Franklin did not have access to modern monetary theory (and confused wealth and money in some places), overall the book is brilliantly intuitive. For example, Franklin had an innate grasp of what later came to be called the quantity theory of money: "There is a certain proportionate Quantity of Money requisite to carry on the trade of a Country freely and currently." Franklin eloquently explained the conundrum the colonies faced with the shortage of British coin for transactions. He also understood such subtleties as the different price behavior of traded and nontraded goods, a point that resonates with international economists today. Even in those places where Franklin's economic logic is more dubious, his wry wit still shows through: "Lawyers and others concerned in Court Business, will probably many of them be against a plentiful Currency; because People in that Case will have less Occasion to run in Debt, and consequently less Occasion to go to Law and Sue one another for their Debts."[27]

Franklin's passion for currency led to his being commissioned with designing and printing currencies for various colonies, including Pennsylvania, New Jersey, and Delaware. A man who commanded huge scientific respect as well as being a stickler for small improprieties (as evidenced by his famous treatise on "The Morals of Chess"),[28] Franklin in many ways was the prototype of a modern central banker. Franklin later became an advocate of a national currency both during colonial times and after the revolution.

Paper currency also played a major role in the American War of Independence from 1775 to 1783, financing the vast majority of the colonists' military expenditures. The public's familiarity with paper currency, and willingness to accept it on faith for goods and services, provided invaluable assistance to the success of the revolution. The public's faith was indeed tested, as the inflation that took place during the war was epic—192% in 1779 alone.[29] Eventually, the continental currency became famously worthless (hence the phrase "not worth a continental"). Although the United States made it through the war, confidence in any kind of national currency was a casualty. The first epoch of American currency effectively ended in 1787 when, at the Constitutional Convention, the founding fathers took away the power to issue money from the states, and the national government confined itself to coining money for the next three-quarters of a century.

Although the inflationary experience of the young United States might have been somewhat at the extreme end,[30] even more mature countries often resort to high inflation to help with finances mired in large-scale wars. The United States itself certainly has. US inflation reached 24% in 1864 during the American Civil War, after the Union reintroduced unbacked paper currency in 1862 to support the war effort. This, of course, was nothing compared to the more than 1,000% inflation that the losing Confederacy suffered with its paper currency. During World War I, US inflation again soared to 19% in 1918.[31] And then of course came the double-digit peacetime inflation of the 1970s. Indeed, there have been enough such episodes since the founding of the Federal Reserve Bank in 1913 that prices in the United States have increased thirtyfold.[32] So much for the Fed's mandate to achieve price stability. Still, the United States has had less cumulative inflation than most advanced economies over the same period. We return to the risks of high inflation in chapter 12.

FROM GOLD-BACKED TO PURE FIAT PAPER CURRENCY

Since its early days in China and the colonial United States, the evolution of paper money has taken other important turns, eventually spreading across the world. This chapter closes with a short summary of key events relevant to later discussion.

The period 1870–1914 is often referred to as the halcyon days of the gold standard, because governments around the world—at least in the advanced nations—basically kept the gold backing of their currencies quite stable, which resulted in very stable international exchange rates among currencies as well. But with the outbreak of the Great War in 1914, the overwhelming financial priority for every government was to fund the war effort. One after another, they abandoned currency convertibility so that the printing press could be used to finance massive increases in military expenditures. And print they did, leading to rampant inflation.

After the war, governments across the world aimed to reestablish the gold standard, both because of a deep belief in its desirability as a currency system and because of romantic associations with the era of strong growth that had preceded the war. Unfortunately, the return to gold was immensely complicated by two factors. First, because governments had printed piles of money to finance the war and its aftermath, there were massive inflationary pressures across the world, and it was unclear exactly how to reset the system. Most governments accepted the necessity of rebooting their currencies at devalued gold parities commensurate with the inflation that had taken place, but figuring out the exact new starting point was hardly a straightforward calculation. Setting too low a value for currency in terms of gold was considered a national humiliation. Setting too high a value implied a wrenching deflation, since that would induce people to unload currency for gold until prices fell enough to bring the goods-buying power of paper currency into line with its value in terms of gold.

This is exactly the fate that befell the United Kingdom when it famously chose to return to its old prewar exchange rate, even at the cost of a massive recession. Winston Churchill, who later became the hero of World War II for the United Kingdom, was Britain's chancellor of the exchequer at the time. Churchill was ultimately responsible for the decision, which he later regarded as the greatest mistake of his career. The episode is beautifully retold in Liaquat Ahamed's book *Lords of Finance* about "the central bankers who broke the world," though it might be more accurate to say the finance ministers did, because the central bankers' power was limited in a world where their main job was to fix their currencies to gold.[33]

A second problem with attempts to restore the prewar gold standard was that it was hard to restore trust in convertibility once it had been so thoroughly broken in World War I.[34] That, together with deflationary pressures from the Great Depression, led one country after another to either abandon, or greatly adjust, their peg to gold in the 1930s. The United States, for example, changed from offering 1 ounce of gold for $20.67 before the Depression to valuing 1 ounce of gold at $35 in 1934, at the same time forbidding private citizens from hoarding gold coin, bullion, or certificates. Naturally, this devaluation of the dollar massively drove up the general level of prices. In the event, this was actually a very effective policy, helping reduce unsustainable debt burdens, drive down real wages, and increase employment. Many economic historians regard the abandonment of the gold standard as the most powerful tool implemented during the Great Depression, even more than the famed public works projects, although those were also helpful.

Instead of trying again to establish the gold standard after World War II, the international community set up the Bretton Woods system of fixed exchange rates with the dollar at the center. In principle, the dollar was linked to gold but only for official purchasers. Other countries, in turn, were obliged to fix their currencies to the dollar. Eventually, the system fell prey to inconsistencies of its own, particularly when inflation in the United States started making the dollar less and less attractive relative to gold, creating an unsustainable dynamic. The Bretton Woods regime finally shattered in 1973, breaking any last vestige of a link between paper currencies and commodities. The world had come full circle to the pure fiat money of the late Mongol rule in China. That is where things still stand today.

CHAPTER 3

Size and Composition of Global Currency Supplies, and the Share Held Abroad

If Marco Polo were able to return to China today, one of the few familiar items he would recognize is paper money, albeit a technologically advanced variant. To be precise, he would find lots and lots and lots of paper money, worth more than $1 trillion (6.7 trillion yuan, to be precise) at current dollar/yuan exchange rates. That is more than $800 per person in what is still a low middle-income country.

THE MASSIVE QUANTITIES OF CASH CIRCULATING

Indeed, the most remarkable fact about paper currency is just how much of it is floating around worldwide, on a scale it is hard to get one's head around. Even more stunning is that the vast bulk of the world currency supply is in large-denomination notes that ordinary citizens seldom see or use, including the United States' $100 bill, Japan's 10,000-yen note (about $93 at present), the Eurozone's 500-euro note (about $570), Switzerland's 1,000-franc note (about $1,035), and a host of cousins from other countries. (Exchange rates among currencies are famously volatile, so conversions to dollars give only rough magnitudes.[1]) For the United States, as highlighted in the introduction, there is roughly $4,200 in cash per capita, 80% in $100 bills, 84% if we throw in $50s. Yes, some of it is abroad, and some of it is in cash registers and vaults. A very small amount has likely been lost, destroyed, or even buried in graves as gifts to the deceased in the afterlife (a practice that has been documented in some Asian countries).[2] Still, as we shall see, all the evidence suggests that a great deal of it, probably at least half, is held in the domestic (legal and underground) economy.

The situation for the single-currency Eurozone bloc is broadly similar, with about 3,200 euros per capita outstanding (about $3,600), over 90% of which is in notes of 50 euros and above, with 30% in 500-euro notes alone. It is true that cash is quite popular in Germany (less so in France), but few German families report anything like 12,800 euros per family, and again, a great deal of the holdings are unexplained. In general, governments have a very good idea how much cash they put out there, and one can find detailed information in most (but not all) countries' central bank reports. It is far more difficult to find information on who the major classes of currency holders are. As we shall see, this is in no small part because treasuries and central banks simply do not know.

What is remarkable about the huge demand for cash is that it persists and grows despite the proliferation of alternative payment mechanisms. Credit cards have been around since the 1950s, debit cards from the 1960s, electronic payments since the 1990s, and, more recently, mobile payments. And printed bank checks, of course, have been around for more than two centuries. It is not surprising that cash is still competitive as a transaction medium for small daily payments, but such payments do not begin to explain $4,200 per person.

Figure 3.1 charts the US currency in circulation from 1948 to 2015 as a share of gross domestic product (GDP).[3] The solid line represents the overall currency supply, the dashed line represents $100 bills. Dollar demand peaked during World War II at 11% of GDP, but then dropped steadily to less than 5%, where it stayed during the 1970s and 1980s. One impetus for falling demand was surely the advent of credit cards, but in addition, the high inflation and interest rates of the 1970s and early 1980s made holding cash very costly. Starting in the 1990s, the demand for cash has been steadily rising, reaching more than 7% of GDP today.

Notable is the steady rise in the share of $100 bills. Part of the explanation, of course, is that $100 is not worth nearly as much today as it was many decades ago. Notorious Depression-era gangster John Dillinger reportedly liked to carry a few thousand dollars in carefully rolled-up packs of $5s, $10s, and $20s. Back then,

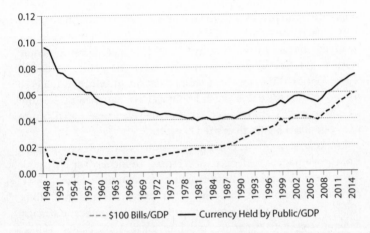

Figure 3.1: US currency/GDP, 1948–2015. Source: St. Louis Fed, Federal Reserve Economic Data; US Treasury; IMF, International Financial Statistics.

$100 was about $1,800 in today's dollars, more than any actively circulating bill in the world today except the 10,000–Singapore dollar note (worth more than $7,000).[4]

Many other factors contribute to the rise in demand for $100 bills from the 1990s, including the generalized fall in interest rates and growing demand from emerging markets. And it is also true that prices have cumulatively risen significantly over the past 25 years. If we go by the consumer price index, a $100 bill in 1990 had the purchasing power of $180–190 in 2016, although for technical reasons having mainly to do with accounting for new products, this is probably a considerable overstatement of how much more $100 was worth in 1990 than it is today. Regardless, such explanations have to be weighed against the explosion in alternative transaction technologies over the past six decades. And don't forget the small detail that most of the cash outstanding is unaccounted for.

The trajectory for the Eurozone (the single-currency zone in Europe)[5] is broadly similar, though with some interesting and informative differences. Cash was already broadly popular prior to the circulation of the first euro banknotes in January 2002, albeit per capita holdings in Germany and Austria were almost double those of France, a situation that persists to this day. Figure 3.2

shows the ratio of currency to GDP in the Eurozone dating back to 1995, when it was just over 5% of GDP. The demand for currency dropped sharply in the run-up to 2002, in part because people were afraid they would have trouble converting large hordes of legacy national currencies, a small fraction of which was never turned in. But since then, cash holdings have marched up steadily to where they are now over 10% of the Eurozone's GDP, more than one-third higher than the US ratio.

Lest one write off the popularity of dollars and euros to demand from governance-challenged developing countries, note that all the advanced countries have issued huge quantities of their own currency. Yet none of the others, except Switzerland and Hong Kong (and perhaps Singapore), can claim a significant foreign demand for their paper (or polymer plastic) currencies. Unless somehow Eurozone and US internal demand are radically different from other countries with similar financial systems and levels of development, it is safe to say that a lot of dollars and euros must be held domestically (in tax evaders' attics, drug dealers' closets, construction contractors' basement safes, etc.).

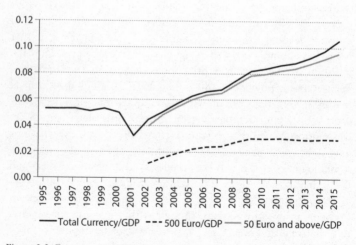

Figure 3.2: Euro currency/GDP. * Before 2002, legacy national paper currencies over GDP. Source: European Central Bank.

Yen notes are hardly common outside Japan, though there are certainly some floating around popular Japanese tourist destinations, such as the casinos of Macao or the golf clubs of Hawaii. Japan has a much higher ratio of outstanding currency to GDP (almost 19%) than either the United States or the Eurozone. Japanese holdings of currency per capita amount to more than $6,600 per person, or roughly $27,000 per four-person family. True, one can point to a number of factors that might explain high Japanese cash balances, including low rates of physical crime, two decades of ultra-low inflation, and conservative behavior by an aging population.[6] Still, Japan has its Yakuza (mafia) and its tax evasion, and a substantial fraction of the cash is almost certainly explained by underground holdings. Indeed, many estimates of the underground economy suggest that it is larger in Japan than in the United States, as we shall see in chapter 5. One reason might be a certain ambivalence in Japan about how rigorously tax laws should be enforced; some Japanese scholars trace the problem to the tension between the governing Diet, which writes tax laws, and the tax administrators who try to interpret them.[7] This tension is discussed in the academic literature but also illustrated in popular Japanese films, such as *A Taxing Woman*.[8] Figure 3.3 shows

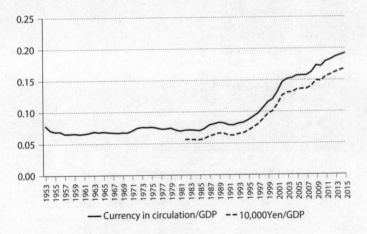

Figure 3.3: Japanese currency/GDP. Source: International Monetary Fund, International Financial Statistics; Bank of Japan.

the evolution of Japanese currency since the early 1950s. As with the United States, there is a sharp upward trend in currency demand beginning in the 1990s, and the share of cash holdings in the 10,000-yen note is more than 90%.

And it is not just Japan. Figure 3.4 shows currency issuance relative to GDP across a broad range of countries. Among the countries toward the top of the list, it is not surprising to find the Swiss franc and the Hong Kong dollar, as these are the two most important paper currencies besides the dollar and euro in international usage. The countries with very low currency to GDP

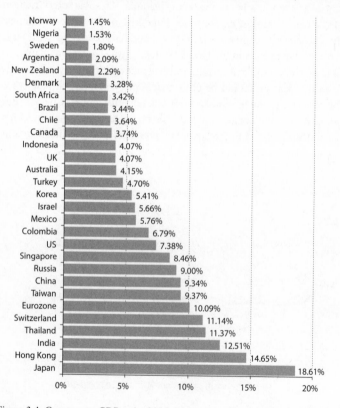

Figure 3.4: Currency-to-GDP ratio, 2015. Source: Central bank sources, National statistical bulletins.

ratio include a mix of countries that have taken action to phase out cash (Norway, Sweden, and Denmark) and high-inflation countries, where holding cash is expensive, because it quickly depreciates in real value. The currency ratios for Canada and the UK are both roughly half that of the United States, a point we shall return to later in this chapter.[9]

The phenomenon that large notes account for nearly all currency is also fairly universal, although one has to account for widely differing practices across countries in what denominations are issued (figure 3.5). I have already mentioned the 500-euro and 1,000–Swiss franc mega-notes, and of course the legacy 10,000–Singapore dollar note. The largest active note in Canada is worth 100 Canadian dollars, but until 2000, there was a $1,000 note, which still accounts for a little more than 1% of Canada's currency supply.

One might expect that the largest UK note, worth 50 pounds (about $75) would attract a large share of total sterling demand, but its share is under 20%.

Figure 3.5 counts only shares of the single largest note still in active circulation (except as noted for Singapore and Canada). Table 3.1 extends the definition of large notes to include (approximately) $50 and above. By this definition, the share of large notes expands sharply and accounts for more than 80% of the currency supply in most advanced countries. In many, the share is more than 90%.

Finally, just to give the reader the full gestalt of the size of global currency holdings, figure 3.6 shows currency per capita across a range of advanced and middle-income countries. This comparison can be somewhat misleading, because it can be very sensitive to exchange rate fluctuations (necessary to convert foreign currency units into dollars) and because we are comparing countries with very different per capita incomes. Nevertheless, being able to compare the magnitudes of the different currency supplies in a common unit is revealing.

Switzerland is by far the king, with per capita currency outstanding more than twice that of the United States. But Hong Kong and Japan are also very high, about 50% above the United

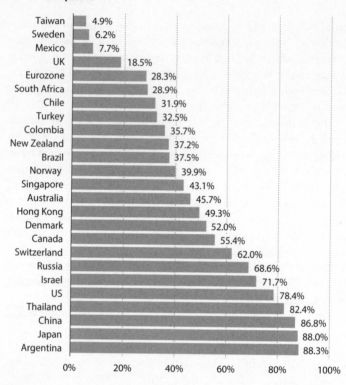

Figure 3.5: Share of largest banknote in total currency supply. Notes: Data is for 2015, except 2014 for Chile, China, Colombia, Hong Kong, Russia, Singapore, South Africa, and Taiwan. Singapore includes the legacy 10,000–Singapore dollar note (not printed since 2014 but remains in circulation and equals 5.3% of total currency). Canada includes the legacy 1,000–Canadian dollar note (stopped printing in 2000, and is now 1.2% of total currency). Sweden is 1000-krona note. Source: Central bank bulletins; Singapore data courtesy Monetary Authority of Singapore.

States, while the per capita Eurozone currency holdings are only slightly smaller than those of the United States.

If the Great Khan saw the figures in this chapter, what might surprise him most is not that so many governments have pumped out so much paper currency, but rather that they have done so without creating massive inflation. Where is all the demand coming from? An obvious question is: how much of it is being held abroad? We turn to the latter question next; the short answer is

Table 3.1: Proportion of large notes in circulation, by country

Country	Year of Data[a]	Proportion of Large Notes in Total Currency in Circulation[b] (%)	Local Currency Threshold Used to Define Large Notes[c]
Switzerland	2015	96.6	50
Israel	2015	94.8	100
Norway	2015	94.1	200
Russia	2014	93.5	1,000
Australia	2015	92.2	50
Japan	2015	91.1	5,000
Eurozone	2015	90.7	50
Singapore	2014	90.6	50
Taiwan	2014	89.6	1,000
Argentina	2015	88.3	100
China	2014	86.8	100
Brazil	2015	85.5	50
South Africa	2014	85.1	100
Mexico	2015	84.7	500
United States	2015	84.2	50
Hong Kong	2014	83.4	500
Thailand	2015	82.4	1,000
Sweden	2015	79.2	500
Denmark	2015	75.4	500
Canada	2015	71.3	50
New Zealand	2015	70.7	50
United Kingdom	2015	68.6	20
Turkey	2015	58.4	50
Colombia	2014	35.7	50,000
Chile	2014	31.9	20,000

[a]Most recent year of data available from central bank bulletins. Data for Colombia, Denmark, Hong Kong, Norway, Switzerland, Taiwan, the United Kingdom, Sweden, Singapore, Mexico, Israel, and China are currency in circulation, not necessarily outside bank vaults. Singapore data are from the Monetary Authority of Singapore.

[b]Large notes are defined to be those with value approximately US $50 or larger. For the United Kingdom, the 20-pound notes are listed for illustrative purposes, even though this amount (roughly US $30) is clearly below the threshold. For China, the table lists the 100-yuan note, the country's largest note.

[c]Entries for Australia, Brazil, Canada, Russia, South Africa, and Turkey list currency issued instead of currency in circulation outside banks.

that foreign holdings seem to be significant only for a few select currencies and might explain as much as 50% of US dollar holdings. But even for the United States, the sums that appear to be held domestically are still enormous.[10]

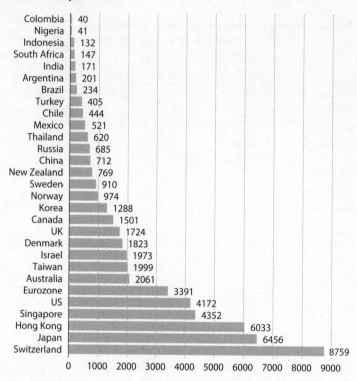

Figure 3.6: Local currency per capita in US dollars. Notes: All currency data are for end 2015, except Norway data are for 2014. Converted at end 2015 exchange rates. Population data are from the World Economic Outlook database. Currency data are as in Figure 3.4.

FOREIGN HOLDINGS

It is not hard to imagine reasons for a nearly universally accepted currency like the US dollar to be used extensively abroad.[11] In countries with a history of macroeconomic instability, dollars are an attractive alternative to an unstable local currency, albeit possibly carrying some risk of detection and seizure. Of course, a great deal of illegal trade involves the exchange of dollar notes, but legal trade can as well. In some developing countries, for example, the banking system is so weak that it is difficult to procure the kind of short-term credits that are the lifeblood of global trade, so instead deals often take place in cash.[12] In countries with a large underground economy (tax evading or otherwise criminal), the dollar is used both as medium of exchange and as a store of value. Measurement of these phenomena, however, is fraught with difficulty. It is extremely hard to say with any great precision how much paper currency leaks out of the United States unofficially, or conversely, what percentage of currency the Federal Reserve ships abroad subsequently crosses back into the United States undetected.

True, most countries require international travelers to report large amounts of currency entering or leaving the country. For the United States, the amount is $10,000; for the European Union, it is 10,000 euros. For drug cartels, exporting cash from the United States is a risky business that can at times cost as much as importing product. Nevertheless, mountains of cash seep across the borders, and it is difficult to know for sure how much goes unrecorded in government accounts, especially as amounts just under $10,000 do not require any reporting.

Fortunately, as noted earlier, extensive foreign holdings (as a share of total currency issued) are a significant factor only for a few countries' notes, including the US dollar, the euro, the Hong Kong dollar,[13] and the Swiss franc. For Switzerland, it is worth observing that in addition to holding Swiss francs outside Switzerland, foreign residents also hold large quantities of francs inside Swiss bank vaults. Other countries' domestic-currency-to-GDP ratios give us some scope to benchmark US currency holdings, ideally trying to control for a variety of variables, such as tax rates and crime rates (which appear positively correlated with demand for paper currency) and credit and debit card penetration (which is negatively correlated).[14]

Canada, for example, is a country with many similarities to the United States, including a broadly similar financial system and the same denominations of notes. Thus the fact that the ratio of currency to GDP in Canada is about half that of the United States, 3.7% versus 7.4% (see figure 3.4), is informative and consistent with a first rough guess that about half of all US currency is held abroad. There are, of course, several important variables to control for. For example, Canada has higher general government taxes than the United States. But the United States has higher crime rates. Overall, given that currency outstanding in Canada appears to be on the low side in cross-country comparisons, using it as a benchmark probably tends to give conservative estimates of the share of cash held domestically in the United States.

Estimating Foreign Holdings Using Proprietary Official Data and Other Methods

With the stakes so high, it is small wonder that the Federal Reserve Board and the US Treasury have devoted considerable effort and ingenuity to better understanding the scale of foreign demand for US currency.[15] To give the reader a flavor of the challenges and uncertainties, it is helpful to discuss the main methods that have been tried, all very crude approximations requiring heroic assumptions. The simplest approach is to make use of official data on currency shipments coming in and out of the country. The individual Federal Reserve Districts have data on net currency shipments to foreign institutions (most outgoing shipments come from the New York office, but the Reserve Districts serving Miami and Los Angeles also have some demand). The government also has access to customs data, because anyone carrying more than $10,000 in or out of the country is supposed to fill out a customs form. By cumulating these flows over time, one can get an approximate measure of the stock of currency abroad. Needless to say, this approach has holes one can drive a truck through, literally. The customs reporting requirement is likely widely ignored, with cash being smuggled in and out in all sorts of ways. Smugglers use some of the same techniques for transporting drugs to transport currency; for example, having "mules" swallow tightly wound packets of currency to take them across the border.[16] Inspection of travelers leaving the United States is much lighter than inspection of travelers entering.

One can also use the ratio of currency to coins for Canada versus the United States. The key assumption is that coins are basically only used domestically, and that virtually all currency outside the country is held in paper notes. Assuming that Canadians hold roughly the same ratio of notes to coins as US residents do, and that Canadian dollar notes are essentially used only in Canada, one can infer how many notes US residents must be using. Put differently, to the extent that the ratio of US dollar notes to coins is higher than Canadian dollar notes to coins, it is assumed that the difference is entirely accounted for by foreign demand.

Another method again uses Canada as a benchmark and exploits the significant seasonal demand for currency. One might expect that foreign demand would exhibit much smaller seasonal fluctuations, especially around Christmas. The seasonal approach basically assumes that to the extent the US seasonals are proportionally smaller than seasonals in Canada, the difference must be due to foreign demand. As a simple illustration, suppose that currency demand in Canada averages 20% higher around the Christmas season, but in the United States, it is only 10% higher. The inference then would be that half of US currency demand must come from abroad. This inference could also be cross-checked against other data; for example, if the Christmas seasonal in retail sales is the same in both Canada and the United States, but the seasonal in currency demand is twice as large in Canada, this would be corroborating evidence. Implementing the seasonal approach is considerably trickier than it sounds. For one thing, foreign demand might also rise at Christmas (oligarchs shop, too), and domestic hoarding of notes might be higher in the United States than in Canada. In addition, there are other key dates when currency demand might spike (e.g., around April tax refunds), and one also has to sort out trend growth and business cycle fluctuations.[17]

Perhaps the most ingenious approach is what Federal Reserve economists Richard Porter and Ruth Judson have termed "the biometric method."[18] Their clever idea is to take advantage of changes that have occurred over time to dollar notes, such as when a security thread was embedded into the US $100 bill in 1990 and the US $50 bill in 1992. The Federal Reserve knows the quantity of all bills in each generation of issuance, say, before and after the embedded security stripe. If the Federal Reserve districts find that a very large share of bills returning to their offices are of the latest generation, then the inference is that a lot of the earlier bills must have emigrated (the calculation is a bit more involved, but that is the gist of it). It is termed the biometric method after the work of Danish biologist Carl Pederson, who invented the idea in the late nineteenth century of tagging a small number of fish or birds and seeing what percentage of subsequently captured fish or birds was tagged. Then, assuming tagging has no effect on survival or capture, the overall size of the population can be extrapolated from the ratio. For example, if 100 birds are tagged in a population, and 10% of all birds subsequently captured are tagged, the inference is that the total population must be 1,000. The application to currency is very clever, by treating changes in currency design as akin to tagging. However, many assumptions are involved. One must assume, for instance, that the population of bills is not affected by domestic hoarding of bills, which might be confused with foreign holdings. Back in 1996, using these approaches, Porter and Judson originally argued that between 55% and 70% of all US currency is held abroad, though in more recent work, Judson's estimates center more closely on 50%.[19]

In principle, the biometric approach can be further refined in the future by taking advantage of the fact that new cash-sorting machines can extract serial numbers from bills; this is even easier with new polymer plastic bills that are more durable and easier to read. Information on serial numbers will allow central banks to someday map out the life of individual bills as they enter and exit the financial system. With details on serial numbers, much more elaborate and nuanced versions of the biometric method ought to be possible.

How can one integrate all these approaches? In the early 2000s, a joint task force comprised of representatives from the US Treasury, the Federal Reserve, and the Secret Service tackled this question. The task force also exploited on-the-ground reports by special teams sent to 40 countries known to be major dollar users (e.g., Russia and Argentina). In the field, the task force teams interviewed authorities and bank officials, and they conducted their own surveys. Their official report concluded that about 60% of US cash was held abroad at that time, although they cautiously attached a large

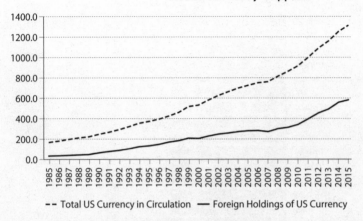

Figure 3.7: Foreign holdings of US currency (in billions of dollars). Source: Board of Governors of the Federal Reserve System.

standard error band around that estimate.[20] There remains considerable debate about the exact number, though increasingly, most estimates are coalescing around 50%.[21]

The Federal Reserve does publish an official guestimate for foreign holdings of US currency; the series is plotted in figure 3.7.[22] Unlike the three-agency task force estimates mentioned above, this is a series that is updated regularly, albeit based on much more limited information. The central piece of data is the cumulative net flows of $100 bills from select regional Federal Reserve Districts known to have heavy demand from foreign institutions (mainly the New York Federal Reserve). For 2015, the estimate is $582 billion, which amounts to 44% of the total currency supply.

Foreign Demand for Euros

There has also been some parallel work on the Eurozone, though it is not as extensive. For example, Seitz (1995), working at the German Bundesbank before the advent of the euro, used Austria as a control for deutsche mark (DM) currency demand, much the same way we have discussed using Canada as a comparator for the United States. Seitz came to the conclusion that perhaps 40% of

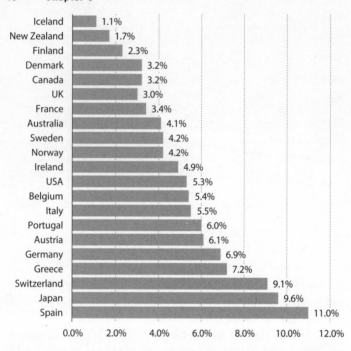

Figure 3.8: Currency to GDP in 1995, advanced economies. Source: Rogoff (1998a); IMF, International Financial Statistics; Central bank bulletins.

DMs were held outside Germany. Interestingly, more recent studies find similar estimates of the share of euros held outside the Euro-zone.[23] Presumably, much of the demand for euros comes from European Union members that are not yet part of the single currency, including central Europe and the United Kingdom.

Supporting the view that a significant percentage of all euros are held domestically is the fact that currency holdings across the periphery of the Eurozone were high before the creation of the euro, and habits change slowly (habits like hiding income from the government). Before the euro, the DM was the foreign currency of choice in Eastern and central Europe. Yet, as figure 3.8 shows, the ratio of national currency to GDP was higher in Spain and Greece than it was in Germany, and also high in Italy,

Belgium, and Portugal, among others. There is no evidence that paper notes for the Spanish peseta, Greek drachma, or Italian lira were in widespread foreign use in the mid-1990s. The implication is that domestic demand for relatively soft local currency was already large in all the periphery European countries, even before their populations had access to the much more attractive euro. Given that currency habits die slowly, it seems plausible to assume that easily half of all euros, and probably a considerably larger share, are circulating within the Eurozone.

That the Eurozone has a higher domestic demand for cash than the United States should hardly come as a surprise, given that tax rates are higher and, in many areas, regulation is tougher. There is also a long tradition of higher tax evasion and corruption in southern countries, such as Italy. Yes, Germans and Austrians like to use cash, but as we shall see, that is not likely to be the main story.

We will have more to say about domestic legal and illegal cash usage in chapters 4 and 5.

CHAPTER 4

Holdings of Currency in the Domestic, Legal, Tax-Paying Economy

Although the share of cash in the total value of expenditures is in steady decline in the legal economy, it is still used in a big way for small transactions. Cash is convenient, and unlike credit cards, you don't have to worry about account numbers being stolen. Transactions clear instantaneously, and cash is almost universally accepted. Almost everyone uses cash to some degree, and in some countries like the United States, many poor and low-income individuals rely on it heavily. When we come to my specific proposal for phasing out cash, there are good reasons for the pace to be slow, for small bills to be left in circulation for a long time (if not indefinitely), and for some of the higher net tax revenues from phasing out cash to be used to achieve universal financial inclusion (e.g., providing free basic debit cards or even smartphones to low-income individuals).

That said, when one looks closely at the evidence on the use of cash in legal transactions, it is extremely hard to see who is holding all the (say) $50 and $100 bills; it is certainly not the poor. People might use cash regularly, but how much of the world's massive cash supply is really circulating in the domestic legal economy?

HOW MUCH CURRENCY DO BUSINESSES AND BANKS HOLD?

Businesses are, by and large, very efficient in their cash management and thus can account for only a small share of total currency in circulation. A couple studies back in the 1990s estimated that seed cash in retail establishments (e.g., in cash registers) is less than

2% of all outstanding cash, with perhaps another few percent in transit to banks at any one time.[1] Given the huge trend of decline in cash used for medium and large retail transactions over the past 20 years, this share can only have declined.

Bank vault cash, even including cash in ATMs, does not explain much of the surprisingly large currency holdings, either.[2] First of all, the amount of vault cash just isn't that big compared to the overall money supply. As of mid-February 2016, US currency in bank vaults and ATMs combined was $75 billion,[3] which equals about 5% of reported currency in circulation. However, out of this $75 billion, $61 billion is treated as required reserves, and doesn't even count in the currency-in-circulation figures used in chapter 3.[4]

HOW MUCH CURRENCY DO CONSUMERS HOLD?

So if a significant share of reported currency in circulation is being used in the legal economy, it is not in cash registers or bank vaults. One has to look to consumers' pockets and cookie jars.

Most of what is known about consumer cash holdings in the legal economy comes from surveys that have been conducted by central banks in recent years, using sophisticated techniques but fairly small samples. The basic takeaway from these studies is that the cash consumers admit to holding can account for perhaps 5–10% of the total currency supply.[5] We begin with the United States and then look at Europe and Canada.

The United States

The two important sources of data on US consumer cash holdings are the "Survey of Consumer Payment Choice" and the "Diary of Consumer Payment Choice."[6] The first is an annual survey conducted by the Federal Reserve that makes use of the RAND Corporation's "American Life Panel" survey respondents. The second is a consumer diary project (where consumers are asked to keep diaries, something akin to the Nielsen diaries for rating TV shows). It gives a more detailed snapshot of consumer holdings of cash, but so far only for the month of October 2012.[7] Nevertheless, the diary snapshot is especially valuable, because, in addition to answering questions on total currency held on person (e.g., wallet, pocket, and purse) and on property (e.g., home and car), respondents were also asked the denominations of the notes they held. Of course, there are well-known problems with both survey and diary methods, but in any event, these are the best sources available.

Both approaches—the annual survey and the more detailed one-time diary snapshot—find that consumers admit to holding only a modest fraction of total cash outstanding, certainly neither the $4,200 per individual counting all denominations nor the $3,400 per individual counting only $100 bills. In the 2012 annual survey, for example, respondents reported holding an average of $46 on person (outliers omitted) with a median of $25. The one-time October 2012 diary respondents reported a slightly higher average amount on person ($56, median $22).[8] Total cash holdings reported, including on property, were $250.

The annual surveys, which attempt to follow a relatively constant and uniform group, have the advantage of allowing one to look at trends. The results show that in parallel to total currency in circulation, there is an upward trend to reported cash holdings and a strong increase since the financial crisis of 2008. Average reported total holdings (on person and around the house) rose by $100 from 2008 to 2012, but then fell by $20 in 2013, the most recent year available.

Thus the order of magnitude for consumer cash holdings is roughly 6–7% of total currency in circulation, or 12–14% of currency *estimated* to be held domestically, presumably mostly for legal, tax-compliant, regulation-compliant activities. These numbers become somewhat higher if one includes outliers from the survey, albeit there is no way to tell how the high rollers actually use their cash. Are the high rollers using cash to pay household help to get a lower rate, to avoid regulation and social security taxes, or to hire migrants without work permits? In any event, counting the high rollers, the share then rises to perhaps 10% of total currency in circulation.[9] Either way, the bulk of US cash in circulation cannot be accounted for by consumer surveys.

Obviously, if consumers are holding only a small fraction of all cash outstanding, they cannot possibly be holding more than a small fraction of the $100 bills in circulation, since $100 bills account for nearly 80% of the value of US currency. Nevertheless, it is interesting to ask to what extent ordinary consumers use them at all. The answer seems to be a "little bit," just enough so that a retailer cannot be 100% sure that the $100 bill a customer wants to pay with was obtained through illegal activity or tax evasion.

According to the October 2012 diary survey, 5.2% of US consumers reported at least one $100 bill in their possession. Among the consumers carrying between $400 and $699, two-thirds had at least one $100 bill. Federal Reserve economists have interpreted this data as underscoring that Americans still value the $100 bill,[10] perhaps to avoid carrying many $20s. Maybe, but showing that 1 in 20 adults carries around a $100 bill is not quite the same as explaining why everyone isn't carrying around at least 34 of them, in addition to smaller notes.[11]

Europe and Canada

What about other countries? The basic logic for businesses and banks is the same: they account for only a relatively modest share of total currency in circulation. If a large share of currency is to be explained by holdings for legal transaction purposes, it can only be by consumers. The European Central Bank (ECB) has undertaken a couple of surveys that we will come to shortly, but first we turn to an interesting project where seven central banks aimed to harmonize the results of one-time consumer surveys so as to achieve broadly comparable cross-country data.[12] The main message is similar to what we learned from the United States: consumer demand for cash does not begin to account for the extant currency supply. Table 4.1 gives estimates of "cash on person," with figures adjusted to US dollars by purchasing power parity exchange rates.[13]

The table confirms that Austria and Germany are cash-intensive countries, whereas France is more similar to the United States. The figure includes only cash on person and not cash on property. Assuming similar ratios of the two for Austria and Germany as for

Table 4.1: Average cash balances in wallet

	Australia	Austria	Canada	France	Germany	Netherlands	United States
Mean	59	148	64	70	123	51	74
Median	32	114	38	30	94	28	37

Note: Values are converted to US dollars by purchasing power parity–adjusted exchange rates.

Source: Bagnall et al. (2014) compendium of harmonized international consumer diary surveys.

the United States, then total cash balances would be, say, $500–600 worth of euros in Germany, and $285–340 in France, hardly enough to explain per capita currency holdings (and remember the survey is only counting adults).

We next turn to more conventional surveys, which, as in the case of the United States, seem to give similar results to the diary surveys. For example, in a 2008 survey of consumer cash usage and holdings, the ECB found fairly small cash holdings, with 57% of respondents reporting they hold only enough cash for near-term transactions. Less than 3% of respondents reported holding currency of between 1,000 and 5,000 euros, and 0.5% reported holding more than 10,000 euros. As for explaining all the high-denomination euro notes in circulation, the survey comes up dry. Only a quarter of respondents overall reported having a 200- or 500-euro note in their possession at least once a year; in France and the Netherlands, under 10% did.[14]

In addition to its household survey, the ECB also conducted a corporate survey. Combining the two, the ECB concluded that individuals and companies together held about 100 billion euros out of the 750 billon total euro currency outstanding at the end of 2008.[15] Thus, as with the United States, most of the demand for euro paper currency cannot be accounted for by legal domestic holdings.

One important takeaway from the surveys is that the large-denomination notes must be almost entirely floating around outside the legal, fully tax-compliant economy. With advances in alternative transaction technologies, mega-notes are at best vestigial and probably much worse.

CASH USAGE IN THE LEGAL DOMESTIC ECONOMY

Usage is a very different concept from holdings. Suppose a consumer spends $50 in cash each day and then replenishes the amount at an ATM. Then she would be spending $1,500 per month in cash transactions, even though she is only holding $50 at a time. The fact that cash holdings are small in the legal economy does not necessarily imply that cash's role is unimportant.

In contrast to the limited data on who holds cash, data on cash usage is rich. Indeed, a broad range of detailed information is available on what transaction technologies consumers use, particularly for retail purchases. Once again, the much-studied United States is a good place to start, even though there are many areas of modern transaction technology where the United States is far from the cutting edge.

The US consumer diary and survey studies contain considerable detail on the breakdown of consumer transactions across different kinds of vehicles, including cash, checks, debit cards, credit cards, electronic payments, and mobile payments. As illustrated by figure 4.1, the basic finding is that cash transactions account for 40% of the number of transactions, but only 14% by value. Correspondingly, checks and electronic payment accounts are used relatively infrequently, yet account for 19% and 27%, respectively, of all transactions by value, since the average payment by these media (in parentheses in the figure) is much larger. Payment cards (debit and credit) account for 42% of all transactions by number, and 34% by value.

Correspondingly, figure 4.2 shows that cash is used two-thirds of the time for transactions of $10 or less, but it is used less than 15% of the time for transactions of $100 or more.

The seven-country consumer diary harmonized study discussed earlier in the chapter[16] finds broadly similar results for Europe and Canada. Cash is by far the most common payment vehicle for transactions in the smallest quartile of size, but for larger payments, it becomes increasingly unimportant.

These results also conform to those found for Eurozone countries reported in the 2008 ECB survey on cash usage, shown in table 4.2. For small transactions (less than 20 euros), cash is the preferred vehicle in every country, ranging from 91% of

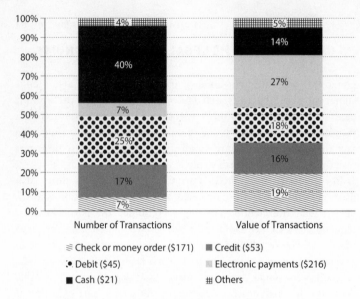

Figure 4.1: Payments by instrument type. Source: Bennett et al. (2014); Federal Reserve Bank of Boston, 2012 Diary of Consumer Payment Choice.

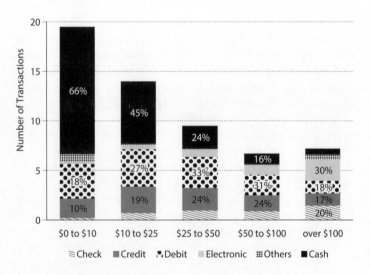

Figure 4.2: Payments per dollar amount per consumer. Source: Bennett et al. (2014); Federal Reserve Bank of Boston, 2012 Diary of Consumer Payment Choice.

Table 4.2: Percentage of respondents always (or often) using cash for different kinds of purchases, by country

Average purchases	Belgium	Germany	Spain	France	Italy	Luxembourg	Netherlands	Austria	Average
Less than 20 euros (e.g. newspapers, bread)	84	91	90	80	91	77	65	82	87
Between 30 and 100 euros (e.g., fuel, groceries)	48	69	64	15	77	27	20	60	55
Between 200 and 1,000 euros (e.g., clothing, furniture)	18	21	30	3	31	10	8	29	20
More than 10,000 euros (e.g., new car)	5	4	6	0	4	3	4	10	4

Source: European Central Bank household survey on use of cash (taken in 2008).

transactions in Germany and Italy, to 65% in the Netherlands. For very large transactions (more than 10,000 euros), cash is still used in only 4% of transactions on average, though Austria was an outlier at 10%. For purchases of 200–1,000 euros, respondents report using cash 20% of the time, though for Austria, Italy, and Spain, cash is used about 30% of the time (note that Italy and Spain are two countries not known for tax compliance). In any event, the shares of large cash purchases have almost surely dropped since the 2008 survey as debit card penetration has deepened, and as some countries have begun to put greater restrictions on cash payments (as we shall see in table 5.1).

The ECB argues that despite all the payment alternatives, some Eurozone citizens still prefer cash for very large payments, for example, to buy a car. The ECB suggests that this may be due to limitations on the maximum size of card payments. This seems like a thin and doubtful argument for why people would prefer cash to electronic transfer or old-fashioned cashier's checks for such large one-off purchases. More likely, there is a substantial gap between reported and actual payments, for example, where cash is used to facilitate underpayment of Europe's extremely high value-added taxes (VAT).

SCANNER DATA FROM RETAIL TRANSACTIONS

A newer approach to understanding consumer preferences for cash comes from using scanner data from retail stores. Scanner data has its own limitations, because it is capturing only one aspect of cash use. However, it has the advantage of allowing researchers to extract data from massive numbers of transactions without having to depend on the reliability of survey responses. Federal Reserve Bank of Richmond economists Zhu Wang and Alexander Wolman explored scanner data from a large retailer covering several states, with most stores located in low-income areas.[17] They found that the average transaction is very small ($7), and that cash is overwhelmingly the vehicle of choice, accounting for roughly 80% of transactions. Their data do not specify denomination of the notes used; presumably only a small share of these cash transactions are in large denominations, such as $50 or $100 bills. However, although cash is dominant in these low-income retail outlets, its share has been declining, and the Fed researchers estimate that it will continue to decline by another 2.5% per year in the foreseeable future.

The scanner data underscore the bifurcated nature of the demand for currency, with low-income households still heavily relying on small bills for cash purchases. Many customers at these stores are unbanked or do not have credit or debit cards (8.7% of all US consumers lack bank accounts).[18] This bifurcation is something we will want to take into account when designing any phaseout of cash. Yet again, it points to the fact that demand for large-denomination notes is qualitatively different from that for small-denomination notes.

Finally, it is often argued that cash transactions are faster on average, though this is by no means obvious. In this regard, another Federal Reserve economist, Elizabeth Klee, also using grocery store scanner data, finds that debit cards and cash transactions take virtually the same amount of time; credit cards take longer and checks significantly longer.[19] Over time, however, one presumes that any speed or convenience advantages of paper currency will dissipate or turn negative. The Klee study, published in 2008, does not include mobile phone technologies, which are quite possibly now faster than cash.[20] Also, what many people take to be the apparent convenience of cash does not take into account the time taken preparing one's wallet or purse each day, much less the time retail stores take counting and handling cash, and so forth.[21]

Overall, the research results suggest that (1) the legal economy accounts for only a modest fraction of all cash holdings and (2) there is still a high demand for small bills for use in retail transactions, even if this demand appears to be diminishing gently over time, especially with increased debit card usage.[22]

CHAPTER 5

Currency Demand in the Underground Economy

So we have concluded that a great deal of the world's cash supply has to be floating around in the underground economy, but what exactly does that mean? The underground economy includes a huge range of blatantly illegal activities, for example, the drug trade, extortion, bribes, human trafficking, and money laundering, just to name a few. But it also includes ordinary people—a great many of them—who use cash on occasion, say, when hiring babysitters or painters, to get a lower rate and to sidestep onerous reporting requirements. And it definitely includes small cash-intensive businesses that prefer to get paid in cash so they can underreport revenues to tax authorities. In some countries, like the United States, the underground economy very importantly includes firms that save on costs by hiring illegal immigrants at low wages, enabling them to undercut firms that hire workers legally.

One can argue in all these examples that if there were no cash, criminals and tax evaders would simply find a different way of doing things. But that is easier said than done, especially for large-scale criminal enterprises or businesses that routinely underreport revenues. Many other methods exist, but compared to cash, they are not as safe for routine use on a large scale and generally not as liquid. There are only so many places you can cash in your uncut diamonds or your gold coins, and licensed dealers are subject to reporting requirements. Yes, crime will continue with or without cash, but for very good reasons, cash is a medium of exchange highly favored by the underground economy, and the underground economy accounts for a significant share of the demand for cash.

THE USE OF CASH TO FACILITATE TAX EVASION

The largest holdings and use of cash in the domestic underground economy likely derive from residents of all types (e.g., citizens, green card holders, employers of illegal immigrants) who are broadly engaged in legal activities but who are avoiding taxes, regulations, or employment restrictions. These are mostly otherwise law-abiding citizens who engage in tax evasion opportunistically, because they know that by using cash, they can hugely reduce their chances of ever getting caught. Survey evidence supports the view that these individuals regard their tax transgressions as morally wrong but take the position that if the laws cannot be easily enforced, they are meant to be pliable.[1] The moral questions are indeed complex; no one wants to live in a society where every minor rule and regulation is rigidly enforced. Such a regime is incompatible with most people's perception of what it means to be a truly democratic society.

However, some transgressions are not so minor or so innocent. Tax evasion, which—as we shall see shortly—is truly massive, creates what public finance economists call a "horizontal equity" problem. When some people don't pay the taxes owed on their true incomes, it means that other people—for example, law-abiding citizens with identical pre-tax incomes—have to pay more. By the same token, if some firms use cash payments to get around anti-pollution regulations while others don't, it gives the former an unfair competitive advantage and of course degrades the environment. When construction contractors use cash to employ illegal immigrant workers at low wages, they disadvantage both domestic workers and other construction firms that hire only legal workers and keep all payments out in the open. In addition to its distributional implications, tax evasion also hampers the efficiency of the tax system.[2] What does that mean? If taxes can be avoided more easily in cash-intensive businesses, then too much investment will go to them, compared to other businesses that have higher pre-tax returns but lower post-tax returns. This kind of inefficient distortion arises when any sector succeeds in getting unwarranted extra tax breaks for itself.

Again we begin with the United States, because more data are available than for most other countries. The key source of data comes from a program of intensive random tax audits, in which the Internal Revenue Service (IRS) effectively picks someone's name out of a hat and then goes all out to check every aspect and detail of their tax return.[3] This is not a pleasant situation for the auditee. Anyone who has studied public finance, however, knows that there is really no other effective alternative to random evaluation trials for gaining meaningful statistics that are not plagued by biases in sample selection. The IRS has used these intensive audits, combined with an array of other information (e.g., investigations into high-income-earner tax shelters), to arrive at an overall estimate of unpaid taxes. For 2006, the most recent year reported, the IRS found that the "tax gap"—the difference between taxes voluntarily paid and taxes due—was $450 billion. This comprises tax evasion in many different sectors, including underreporting of business income, wage income, and rental income.[4] Of the $450 billion, the IRS expected to recover $65 billion, leaving a net tax gap of $385 billion. Put differently, roughly 14% of estimated 2006 federal taxes, or 2.7% of 2006 GDP, will never be paid.[5]

By far the most important area of tax noncompliance comes from underreporting of business income by individuals who conduct a significant share of their transactions in cash. The problem extends to individuals operating as partnerships or small corporations. Overall, small business owners report less than half their income and account for 52% of the tax gap. Since nominal GDP has grown by roughly 30% since the last IRS benchmark year (2006), and assuming tax evasion has grown proportionately with GDP (which seems quite conservative, given that marginal tax rates have significantly increased and the size of the underground economy generally increases when growth tails off), this would translate to a 2015 net tax gap of $500 billion for federal taxes alone. True, some component of this gap is due to tax havens (e.g., in the Caribbean or Panama), perhaps 10–20%.[6] But a large fraction of the remaining tax evasion derives from areas where there is no third-party information available,[7] which of course rules out checks, credit card payments, and the like. That is, of the remaining tax gap, a large fraction (say, at least 50% and probably more) derives from cash-intensive areas.[8]

In the United States, state taxation is roughly 36% of the amount of federal taxation, and local taxation adds another 27% (so combined state and local tax collection is about two-thirds of federal tax revenue).[9] Thus, accounting for evasion of state and local taxes would presumably raise total tax evasion estimates significantly, though not necessarily proportionately, because the tax mix is different. Most states have income taxes (where noncompliance is presumably similar to that for the federal income tax), as well as sales taxes, where the scope for noncompliance in cash transactions is enormous.

To reiterate an important point: the tax gap is sufficiently huge that if eliminating cash can close it by as little as, say, 10%, the revenue gains would be quite substantial. By the crude back-of-the-envelope estimates done here, the gains would be on the order of $50 billion from federal taxes alone and perhaps another $20 billion for state and local taxes.[10] And this calculation does not take into account the efficiency costs of tax evasion. Nor does it include illegal activity, on which taxes are still owed in principle. (Famously, the Federal Bureau of Investigation finally caught up with Depression-era gangster Al Capone by charging him with income tax evasion.)

Tax Evasion in Europe

Because the United States is a relatively low-tax country, and because it relies so heavily on income taxation as opposed to VATs (value-added sales taxes), compliance is likely higher than in most advanced countries.[11] Unfortunately, indirect methods and partial data are all that exist to estimate tax evasion for Europe, as most European countries do not report overall results for the kind of detailed randomized audits that the United States has released.[12] Michigan economist and public finance expert Joel Slemrod cites internal Organisation for Economic Co-operation and Development (OECD) estimates of noncompliance for VATs, which are very important in Europe, of 4–17%.[13]

We do know that tax levels are higher in Europe than in the United States and regulations are (arguably) more burdensome. Most research suggests that the underground economy is correspondingly higher in Europe as well.[14] Estimates vary widely, and there is a huge amount of uncertainty; governments put vast resources into measuring conventional aboveground income, and yet government statisticians acknowledge a broad error band around their estimates. Information on the underground economy is limited, and estimates necessarily involve indirect approaches. Definitions also differ across studies of the underground economy, for example, whether or not it includes all criminal activity or just tax and regulatory evasion.

One influential methododology[15] has been developed by Austrian professor Friedrich Schneider, a pioneer in efforts to measure the underground economy. Schneider's empirical approach forms estimates based on a variety of monetary and labor market indicators, including the labor force participation rate, tax rates, the quality of public service delivery, and other indicators. Figure 5.1 shows the results. It is important to note that the particular definition of underground economy underlying these estimates is a narrow one that does not include illegal or nonmarket activities. Rather, the measure aims to capture all (otherwise) legal market-based production of goods and services that are deliberately concealed from authorities to avoid income, sales, or value-added taxes; social security contributions; certain labor standards like minimum wage or maximum working hours; certain administrative inconveniences; or any combination of these.[16]

Under this narrower definition of underground economy that does not include many types of illegal activities, the United States and Switzerland are estimated to have among the smallest underground economies, at 7.1% and 7.9% of GDP, respectively. Toward the other extreme are Spain at 19.6%, Italy at 22.3%, and Greece at 25.0%. Intermediate are France at 12.0%, Germany 13.4%, and the United Kingdom 10.6%. These figures are averages of annual estimates for 2003–2016; Schneider's approach does show some downward trend for most (but not all) countries. Indeed, it is likely that during the depths of the post–financial crisis

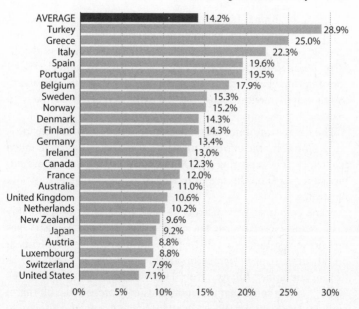

Figure 5.1: Underground economy as percentage of official GDP. Source: Schneider (2016), updated from Schneider, Buehn, and Montenegro (2010).

recession, with large numbers of people losing their jobs in the formal economy, a larger fraction was moonlighting off the books.

Taking the long-term average estimated size of the underground economy in the United States as a share of GDP, which again includes only the shadow economy and excludes most illegal activities, it would come to $1.3 trillion today in dollar terms (7.1% of the 2016 GDP of $18 trillion). Europe's underground economy is much larger in magnitude. Overall GDP is similar to that of the United States, but the share of Europe's shadow economy is more than double; a rough estimate for the absolute size of the Eurozone underground economy would be $3 trillion. Obviously, including illegal activities (e.g., the drug trade) would increase these measures considerably.

The measures of the size of the underground economy in figure 5.1 are broadly consistent with those in other recent studies, including by Rafael La Porta and Andrei Shleifer.[17] They look at a variety of indicators, finding, for example, that for the upper quartile of countries by income, electricity consumption in the informal (underground) economy averages 17.6% of total electricity consumption. La Porta and Shleifer also look at such measures as self-employment, because the self-employed are more likely to underreport income.

The likely size of noncompliance rates in continental Europe is underscored by the extreme measures some countries have taken to close the tax-reporting gap. Many European countries have implemented caps on the size of retail cash transactions, as table 5.1 illustrates.

Some countries have fiercely resisted this trend, most notably cash-loving Germany. So far, the German Finance Ministry has met fierce resistance to a 2016 proposal to cap cash payments at 5,000 euros. (Curiously, the opposition's rallying cry seems to be "Money is coined liberty," from Dostoyevsky's *The House of the Dead*.[18] Never mind that the quote is usually presented a bit out of context: Dostoyevsky is describing his life in prison and goes on to add that usually money was quickly spent on vodka before it was seized in a night search. Indeed, money is a surrogate for all the liberties the prisoners have been robbed of and is itself forbidden. To draw an analogy between life in a Tsarist prison and life in the modern liberal state as a defense of large-denomination notes borders on the absurd.)

Table 5.1: Restrictions on the use of cash in the Eurozone

Country	Maximum cash payment	Date enacted
Belgium	3,000 euros	January 1, 2014
Denmark	10,000 kronor (≈1,340 euros)	July 1, 2012
France	1,000 euros (residents) 15,000 euros (nonresidents)	September 1, 2015
Greece	1,500 euros	January 1, 2011
Italy	<1,000 euros	December 6, 2012
Spain	2,500 euros (residents), 15,000 euros (nonresidents)	November 2012

Source: Beretta (2014); Reuters (http://www.reuters.com/article/us-france-security-financing -idUSKBN0ME14720150318%20Reuters%20March%2018).

Bans on large cash purchases are by no means the most dramatic measure Europe has tried to deal with rampant VAT evasion. An even more extreme measure is to enlist the help of consumers. Starting in April 2014, Portugal followed Greece in offering lottery prizes, which consumers could become eligible for by sending in sales tax receipts.[19] The Portuguese government also offered income tax discounts to consumers who sent in large numbers of sales tax receipts. Within a year, the government had awarded 40 new Audi cars, but tax receipts from the VAT had risen more than 4% during a period when private consumption had risen only 2%. The potential effectiveness of consumer reward programs for verifying retail receipts is underscored by the work of London School of Economics professor Joana Naritomi.[20] Naritomi studied a receipt-reporting reward program in São Paolo, Brazil. Naritomi was able to exploit a unique data set with monthly tax returns from more than a million retail establishments and participation by more than 40 million consumers. She estimated that reported retail revenue rose by 22% over 4 years due to the consumer-reporting and whistle-blowing program.

In sum, even though the evidence for Europe is less reliable than for the United States, the strong presumption is that tax evasion is likely an even larger issue for the former.

Tax Evasion in Canada

Recent estimates of tax evasion for Canada suggest a broadly similar order of magnitude for tax evasion as in the United States. For example, one recent study compares data on consumption by individual households with reported income, the classic approach to detecting tax evasion used by law enforcement authorities, albeit on a very small scale. The study finds that underreported income is between 14% and 19% of GDP in Canada.[21] Interestingly, underreporting of income appears to be a widespread phenomenon that reaches far beyond just the self-employed. Between 30% and 40% of families with salaried income appear to be underreporting some other component of income. This is a potentially important observation, which presumably applies to many other countries as well. It is important not only for fair distribution of the tax burden but also because political support for redistribution policies (e.g., a negative income tax) would presumably be stronger if there were greater confidence in truthful reporting of incomes. If some low-income families underreport income while others report truthfully, this could lead to inequitable distribution of support payments and other resources. This is yet another argument for reducing the role of cash in the economy.

———

In sum, the size of underground economies is vast, creating huge tax gaps of about $500 billion annually in the United States, even if one counts only federal tax. In Europe, given an underground economy perhaps twice the size of that in the United States and higher tax rates, the tax gap is likely far larger, more on the order of $1 trillion or higher.

To get a better sense of orders of magnitude, it is interesting to compare these overall tax evasion figures to estimates of tax evasion stemming from wealth hidden in tax havens like Luxembourg, the Virgin Islands, Bahamas, Cypress, Panama, and, of course, Switzerland. In his 2015 book, *The Hidden Wealth of Nations*, University of California professor Gabriel Zucman has estimated that total foreign financial wealth held in tax havens (including stocks, bonds, and bank accounts) amounts to about $7.6 trillion, or 8% of the world's financial wealth of $95 trillion. Zucman estimates that the combined annual tax losses to the world's governments due to tax havens are at least $200 billion per year, consisting of tax evasion on offshore income (dividends, interest payments, etc.) of about $125 billion, with the rest mainly being avoidance of wealth and inheritance taxes. Of the total $200 billion, the tax revenue loss to Europe is $78 billion and to the United States is $35 billion. These are large figures, but in comparison to overall tax evasion in the United States and Europe, they are only a modest fraction of the total. In any event, even in the case of offshore tax havens, a considerable quantity of wealth still goes in and out in the form of paper currency packed in bags.

OUTRIGHT CRIMINAL ACTIVITIES

We next turn to the use of cash in outright criminal activities, both domestic and foreign. Criminal financing involves many modalities besides cash. As someone who has studied the history of under-invoicing and over-invoicing in international trade, I am keenly aware that there are many vehicles for moving money around, for example, by misreporting amounts on otherwise legal transactions. In the years after World War II, when all of Europe was locked down by intense capital controls, people would routinely get money out of the continent by, for example, striking deals that underreported the payments received for exports and overreported payments made for imports, with capital flight through this channel amounting to roughly 10% of reported trade for many countries and significantly more for a few of them.[22] Even today, money moves in and out of countries like China and India through misreporting of trade.

Indeed, there are plenty of clever ways an illegal transaction can be structured to cover up the true flow of funds, without involving cash, particularly for a one-off transaction. In the United States, for example, it is illegal to pay for organ donations, and therefore it certainly is not possible to pay with a credit card. However, the restriction can be circumvented by using a credit card to grossly overpay a close blood relative for, say, a dress, and then have the relative "donate" the kidney.[23] But there is little question that cash is still king, offering anonymity and real-time clearing of transactions at every level of a criminal operation. The typical low-rent hitman[24] is not looking to get paid in uncut diamonds or by credit card, though a few might naively take bitcoins, thinking the cryptocurrency can never be traced, as discussed in chapter 14.

It would be difficult to list all the areas where cash has pernicious effects without turning this book into an encyclopedia of criminal activity. Discussion of a few major areas is, one hopes, enough to make the point emphatically. I will consider in turn money laundering of criminal earnings, as well as cash in facilitating the drug trade, political corruption, human trafficking, and exploitation of migrant workers.[25]

The business of laundering dirty money by passing it through legal businesses as fake profits is as old as the hills. It is central to organized crime operations all over the world.[26] Earnings from illegal activities often take the form of cash, and finding ways to make the illicit cash earnings seem legitimate is a key component of any large-scale criminal enterprise. The standard device involves taking legitimate cash-intensive businesses (e.g., restaurants, dry cleaners, and construction firms), injecting them with cash, and then cooking the books to make it appear that the money was earned legitimately. I realize that many readers are already well aware of how money laundering works (certainly addicts of the acclaimed television series *Breaking Bad*),[27] but for completeness, a short discussion is essential.

The basics of using double bookkeeping to launder ill-gotten gains are simple. For example, a restaurant can launder cash by claiming that it serves more diners than it actually does. The restaurant simply makes up fake receipts, and reports this "income" on an extra set of books that it keeps for tax authorities. The authorities are not entirely stupid, and if they are suspicious, they might check whether the restaurant seems to be ordering enough ingredients to serve as many diners as it is claiming. The seasoned money launderer (please forgive the pun) prepares for this eventuality by creating fake receipts for those "purchases" also. If this is not feasible, the restaurant will buy extra ingredients and either dispose of them or sell them off at a discount to another restaurant (for payment in cash, naturally). If a criminal enterprise owns the restaurant, then the whole business is in-house. Otherwise, there might be a payment or coercion.[28]

Of course, I have not begun to do justice to the ingenuity of money launderers or the different devices they may use. For example, the informal Hawala transfer system, widely prevalent in the Middle East and North Africa, effectively matches someone who has (say) rupees in India and needs dollars in the United States, with someone in the opposite situation, so money never moves across borders.[29] And this practice is hardly restricted to informal third-world bankers; there are prominent cases of advanced-country bankers being caught up in such matching schemes.[30] I am hardly claiming that all money laundering involves cash, but cash does play an important role in many operations.[31]

The drug trade is a famously cash-intensive business at every level. Major drug busts invariably unveil massive stashes of cash. Not all busts are as large as the $206 million Mexican authorities found in the house of suspected drug trafficker Zhenli Ye Gon as reported in the *New York Times* article "Cocaine Incorporated" (June 2012), but interdictions of mules hauling $5 to $10 million is positively routine. Although there do not seem to be any aggregate statistics on cash seizures for the United States, I invite the reader to try online searching on the words "bust," "cash," "drugs," or the like, to get an idea of the extent of the activity. Admittedly, the oft-quoted fact that some 90% of all US currency has traces of cocaine overstates the connection. The contamination occurs in modern high-speed counting machines, including ATMs, where one bill can pollute a batch.[32]

The RAND Corporation has estimated the combined size of the market for four major illegal drugs in the United States to be more than $100 billion in 2010, with cocaine (including crack) $28 billion, heroin $27 billion, marijuana $41 billion, and methamphetamine (meth) $13 billion. This is only the footprint in the United States.[33] The last attempt to do a comprehensive measure of the global drug market, by the United Nations Office on Drugs and Crime for the year 2003, came up with an estimate of $322 billion. As world nominal GDP has roughly doubled since then, the drug trade has presumably expanded proportionately to more than $600 billion.[34]

Beyond their impact on the major consumer countries, drug cartels wreak havoc in countries like Mexico and Colombia, challenging and undermining their governments. Eliminating cash would hardly eliminate drug cartels. Nevertheless, it would be a significant blow to their business model at many levels. Given the violence and crime that the drug business spins off, the potential benefits to even a small reduction in drug trade crime arguably can have an extremely beneficial effect. Obviously there are other ways of reducing drug-related crime. A simple one would be to legalize marijuana, as Canada recently has been contemplating. In any event, hard drugs would still remain highly problematic.

Corruption

Another area where society incurs massive social costs is the use of cash to corrupt and bribe public officials. The social costs of corruption presumably are orders of magnitude greater than the scale of the bribes themselves, but even estimates of the payments are staggering. The World Bank attempted to create a comprehensive worldwide measure of bribes at the beginning of the 2000s, when it conducted an international survey of enterprises, asking firms how much they had to pay in bribes annually to get licenses, to help deal with regulations, and to obtain favorable decisions on public procurement. The Bank also drew on surveys of households that asked how much they typically had to pay in bribes to procure public services. The World Bank came up with a round number for bribes globally of $1 trillion for the years 2001 and 2002. Assuming the figure has roughly doubled in line with global GDP—which seems very conservative, given that developing countries have accounted for the lion's share of global growth over the past 15 years—the worldwide scale of bribes would now be closer to $2 trillion.[35]

Few dispute that corruption is one of the biggest obstacles to development. A classic paper by economist Paolo Mauro found substantial evidence that corruption has a significant negative impact on economic growth. The same theme arises in the work of many economic historians, including the seminal work of David Landes and later work by Daron Acemoglu and James Robinson.[36]

One doesn't have to go to developing countries to find spectacular cases of bribery. Louisiana Congressman William Jefferson was sentenced in 2010 for taking tens of thousands of dollars in bribes, including $90,000 that the FBI found wrapped in foil buried inside pie crusts in his refrigerator. The mayor of Charlotte, North Carolina, resigned in 2012 when he was accused by the FBI of taking $48,000 in a sting operation. Perhaps the granddaddy of all sting operations is ABSCAM, the code name for a covert FBI operation that ensnared one senator and six members of the House of Representatives in the late 1970s. In this case, the payoffs were to assist in obtaining casino licenses and granting a phony sheik US residency. The incident is famously memorialized in director David O. Russell's widely acclaimed film *American Hustle*.

And sometimes the cash flows the other way. Former US Speaker of the House J. Dennis Hastert was accused of lying to the FBI and structuring cash withdrawals as a way to hide $3.5 million in payoffs to cover up past misconduct.[37]

Canada, where the construction industry is notoriously corrupt, formed its Commission of Inquiry on the Awarding and Management of Public Contracts in the Construction Industry in 2011. A former organizer for the Union Montreal, the governing party in the city of Montreal from 2001 to 2012, testified to the commission that the party's chief fundraiser had a safe in his office so stuffed with cash—including old 1,000–Canadian dollar bills—that he needed help closing it.[38] Even ultra-honest Finland found itself transfixed by the case of a senior police officer involved in the narcotics trade, with cash found buried in his backyard and hidden inside his house.[39]

Although corruption persists in advanced economies, the scale of the problem is far worse in developing countries. The politically popular anticorruption campaign, launched by Chinese President Xi Jinping after he came to power in November 2012, showed how pervasive the problem had become in the world's largest economy. Cash is hardly the only way bribes are done in the emerging world; before the anticorruption campaign, Chinese tourists abroad were voracious consumers of luxury goods, especially items like leather belts and purses that could be used as gifts to bribe officials back home. But cash likely pays an even bigger role. In November 2014, Chinese anticorruption officials arrested General Xu Caihou, who was accused of accepting bribes for promotion within military ranks. The government needed 12 trucks to haul off all the cash at his residence, apparently all in renminbi, equal in value to several million dollars.[40]

China may have a corruption problem, but it is not nearly as paralyzing as in some other emerging markets. Transparency International estimates that former Nigerian president Sani Abacha embezzled from $2 billion to $5 billion, though this was less than Suharto did in Indonesia (between $15 billion and $35 billion) or Ferdinand Marcos in the Philippines (between $5 billion and $10 billion, not counting wife Imelda's legendary shoe collection). And even these figures pale next to unofficial estimates of Russian President Vladimir Putin's wealth, which range from $70 billion to $200 billion.[41]

True, the United States' 2010 Kleptocracy Asset Recovery Initiative makes a small dent in the corruption problem.[42] But as the April 2016 leak of the detailed records of the Panamanian law firm Mossack Fonseca recently demonstrated, far greater efforts are needed. The "Panama Papers" revealed the hidden offshore accounts of 140 public servants and politicians, including 12 current and former presidents, prime ministers, and monarchs, as well as friends and relatives of politicians.[43]

A culture of corruption can be extremely difficult to change, even when a country's leaders are determined to do so. Mexican drug lord El Chapo Guzmán has been able to use bribes to pave the way for his escape twice now from maximum security prisons in Mexico, the second time reportedly by offering a $50 million bounty, presumably paid in cash stored in one of Guzmán's many hideaways. As of this writing—and it is hard to stay current on Guzmán's arrests and escapes—he is back in custody and apparently on his way to a US prison, where escape is more difficult, though it still happens.

Obviously, corruption predates paper currency and will live long after it is gone. Nevertheless, there is little question that the ability to make anonymous, real-time, untraceable payments in cash facilitates it. Yes, especially as large notes are phased out, those engaged in corruption and other criminal activities will find other ways to do business, and there will be an even greater incentive for innovation. But other ways of making payments (gold, uncut diamonds, bitcoins) each have their problems, ranging from illiquidity and high transactions costs (uncut diamonds) to risks of ultimate tracing (bitcoins). As this book stresses repeatedly (because the point is so essential), of course criminals can use transaction technologies that circulate completely outside the legal economy. However, as long as the government blocks the doors into the legal economy, it can seriously undermine the liquidity of black market transaction media and dramatically increase the cost of using them compared to cash.

To end our discussion of corruption on a brighter note, the early efforts of the Modi government in India are interesting as an attempt to use the Internet to bypass corrupt officials. India is famous for its "license Raj," the euphemism for its deliberately heavy-handed regulatory system, designed to give officials enormous scope to ask for bribes. The license Raj has long been a huge yoke on India's progress in economic development. After Narendra Modi was elected prime minister in May 2014, one of the first plans he rolled out was to allow Indians to apply for a variety of licenses online, making the payments electronically and therefore eliminating the usual cash bribes at the city hall license bureau. The idea of prohibiting cash payments as a way to contain corruption has also been used in Hong Kong, where, for example, you will probably be out of luck if you even try to pay your monthly gym membership fee in cash. As we discuss in chapter 13 on international issues, phasing out cash is not a practical option in the foreseeable future in most developing economies, which simply don't have the payment infrastructure to sustain a mostly electronic payment system. Nevertheless, for some developing countries, simply taking advanced-country currency out of the equation would be highly beneficial.

Human Trafficking, Human Smuggling, and Exploitation of Migrants

Human trafficking is another major international crime area where cash plays a dubious role. The United States Department of State describes the intensive global effort aimed at discouraging human trafficking both in the United States and internationally. Though no one really challenges that this problem is pervasive, efforts to quantify it and to create a worldwide measure are fraught with methodological, statistical, and conceptual problems. These problems partly stem from differing definitions and institutional capacities across different countries.[44]

The International Labour Organization has nevertheless offered some widely quoted statistics that are perhaps suggestive of the scale and scope of the problem, even if they have to be regarded as exceedingly imprecise.[45] According to the International Labor

Organization, roughly 21 million people are victims of forced labor, of which 11.4 million are women and girls. Of these victims, 19 million are exploited by private individuals or enterprises, the rest by state or rebel groups; 4.5 million are victims of forced sexual exploitation.

Broad evidence from national law enforcement agencies indicates significant trafficking of sex victims into Western Europe, particularly from Eastern Europe and the former Soviet Union, often using false advertisements of work. The government of France, for example, estimates that the majority of the 20,000 people in France's commercial sex trade, 90% of whom are foreigners, are likely victims of human trafficking, with trafficking networks expanding outside Paris to also include Lille and Nice.[46] This is hardly just a European problem; it is also a rampant problem in the Middle East, for example. Even in the United States, the press periodically has exposés of how young girls are lured from places like the Midwest into lives of prostitution in New York and elsewhere on the East Coast. Efforts to stop forced prostitution run up against the problem that it is extremely profitable: the International Labor Organization estimates that worldwide, the annual profit per victim of sexual exploitation is $21,800, though the figure is much higher in advanced countries, perhaps on the order of $100,000.[47]

Illegal Immigration and Border Control

Exploitation of migrant workers is another major area that feeds on cash all along the chain, from cross-border smuggling of workers (human smuggling), to businesses that pay migrants off the books, a common enough practice in both agriculture and construction around the world. (A classic film reference is Jerzy Skolimowski's 1982 film *Moonlighting*, starring Jeremy Irons, which sympathetically portrays the harsh life of a Polish carpenter working illegally and off the books in the United Kingdom.)

Estimates of the total number of migrant workers are on the order of 230 million worldwide.[48] According to the United Nations Office on Drugs and Crime, the International Labour Organization, and the United States Department of State, migrant workers are extremely vulnerable to exploitation. Of course, back in the 1960s and 1970s, Mexican-American activist César Chávez famously devoted his life to improving the treatment of itinerant farm workers, had important successes in California and Florida, and influenced legislation throughout the United States. Nevertheless, with the huge continuing influx of illegal workers in the United States and other advanced economies, exploitation of migrant workers remains a pressing issue.

Illegal immigration is a cash-intensive process, and the existence of cash makes it far harder for countries to control their borders. First, migrants typically pay smugglers in cash to bring them across the border: $1,000–$3,500 per individual to cross from Mexico to the United States, and $3,000–$10,000 to go from Central Asia to Western Europe, according to a 2011 Financial Action Task Force Report.[49] Second and far more important, businesses that choose to rely on illegal immigrant workers can pay them in cash to reduce the risk of detection. It is this final demand from employers that ultimately fuels a large part of illegal immigration.[50]

The extent of illegal immigration varies tremendously across countries; for one thing, it is much more difficult for immigrants to blend into some countries than into others. In a melting pot like the United States, unauthorized immigrants (residents without legal status) constitute more than 11 million people, or 3.5% of the population.[51] The range of estimates for Europe are lower, between 0.25% and 0.60% of the total population in France and Germany, 0.02% and 0.09% for Denmark, and 1.5% and 1.9% in Greece.[52] Nevertheless, the issue is almost as contentious across Europe as it is in the United States.

Whatever one's position on legal immigration, few would argue with the proposition that under normal circumstances, countries have a sovereign right to control their borders and to determine their immigration policy. The issue is becoming increasingly prominent across advanced economies. Some US politicians are proposing extreme measures, such as building a giant razor wire fence across the US-Mexican border, much as Hungary has done and other European countries are considering. Yet there seems to be precious little awareness of how much more difficult and risky it would be for employers to routinely hire illegal workers if they could not pay in cash, and how phasing out paper currency might prove a far more effective remedy than the alternatives being considered. Yes, again, anonymous payments can be made in ways other than cash, from prepaid cards to Amazon credits to virtual currencies. These all carry their risks and costs, however, and government policy can be directed toward magnifying these risks and costs. Controlling borders is likely to become an ever-increasing problem in the future, and improved control has to be listed as a major potential benefit of phasing out cash or restricting its use. That said, any plan to fully phase out cash will need to address the problem of providing amnesty to the existing illegal immigrants. Allowing time to deal with illegal immigration is one of many reasons the proposal in chapter 7 leaves smaller notes in circulation for an indefinite period.

To be clear, I strongly favor allowing increased legal migration into advanced economies. Any economist who takes income and wealth inequality seriously realizes that, despite the enormous progress of the past three decades, differences across countries simply swamp the within-country inequality that Thomas Piketty and others worry about. The 2015 Nobel Prize winner Angus Deaton, author of the 2013 book *The Great Escape*, has forcefully made this point. International migration from poor countries to advanced ones creates massive welfare gains for the immigrants. The issue is likely to become an even more important humanitarian concern if, as likely seems the case, climate change makes some parts of the world that are now densely populated uninhabitable. One can hope that enabling countries to better control their borders might lead to a more rational debate on immigration policy, though I admit that might be optimistic.

Terrorism

Terrorism has been perhaps the single biggest driver of global anti-money-laundering initiatives and restrictions on anonymous transactions, including cash. The terrorist attacks of September 11, 2001, in New York, Virginia, and Pennsylvania led to a dramatic

US effort to tighten enforcement of global money-laundering regulations, especially on bank reporting of large cash deposits and withdrawals. Responding to the November 2015 terrorist attacks in Paris, the European Commission is now proposing stricter rules on cryptocurrencies and prepaid cards.[53] As this book goes to press, the European Central Bank (ECB) has finally decided to stop printing new 500-euro notes, with one important reason being to reduce its use in terrorist financing.[54] The urgency of combating terrorism has, more than anything, tilted the balance toward compromising privacy to strengthen security, particularly in the United States.

The scale of cash used in terrorist financing is likely nowhere near the same magnitude as that for other crimes and tax evasion. Even ISIS (Islamic State of Iraq and Syria), which by all accounts is by far the best-funded terrorist organization/state in recent history, has expenditures of perhaps $1–2 billion per year, modest compared to a major drug cartel. Certainly, ISIS has made extensive use of cash, not least by looting the vaults of cash in territories it has occupied.[55] The antiterrorism aspect of restricting cash as well as other means of anonymous and pseudonymous payments is certainly an important one, and perhaps it will ultimately prove the catalyst for faster action. However, in the scale of global cash holdings, terrorism is a relatively minor factor.

Counterfeiting

Some mention must be made of counterfeiting. When the US Secret Service was founded in 1865, its main job was to fight counterfeiting. At the time, between one-third to one-half of the US money supply was counterfeit. By 2001, according to the US Treasury, less than 0.01% of all US currency was counterfeit;[56] a 2012 Federal Reserve study supports this claim.[57] That said, the vigilance one observes at many retail establishments in dealing with large-denomination notes, even in the United States, suggests that some wariness is reasonable. Although the counterfeit rate is no doubt low, it is hard to imagine any government admitting there is a big problem with its currency until it had a convincing plan for solving it.

We have already mentioned how the US Treasury has introduced several rounds of modified $100 bills to reduce the threat of counterfeiting, most recently the multicolor bill issued in October 2013 that contains a plethora of security features. The new notes are possibly intended as a counter to such threats as the legendary North Korean counterfeit $100 "supernote." When discovered in 2004 in a seizure at the Port of Newark, federal agents found that these supernotes contained the same composition of fibers as genuine notes, featured the same high-tech color-shifting ink, and were otherwise nearly flawless.[58]

But as the new genuine $100 notes become increasingly sophisticated, how long will it take the public to be able to appreciate their subtleties sufficiently to be able to discriminate genuine from counterfeits bills? Will they need to eventually scan the bills and run them through a sophisticated program, basically eliminating one of the few remaining advantages of cash?

The counterfeiting issue is quite serious in some countries. For example, in recent years, the problems in China have become such that even ATMs were being polluted by counterfeit bills. The risk of counterfeit currency became such that many retail stores felt it necessary to run bills through verification scanning machines before accepting them. To address the problem, the Chinese government began introducing new, more counterfeit-resistant bills at the end of 2015. The face of Mao still adorns the new 100-yuan notes, but they now contain features like ink that changes color when viewed at different angles. Counterfeiting has not proven insurmountable for most countries, but it does require constant innovation to stay ahead of it.

PUBLIC HEALTH

In addition to facilitating criminal activities, used paper currency can be a vehicle for spreading disease.[59] Researchers at New York University analyzed $1 bills and found evidence of thousands of microbes, including a wide range of bacteria, even some antibiotic-resistant ones.[60] Though most people are aware of the hygiene problems associated with handling cash, one can imagine paper currency being an agent of transmission in some future pandemic. In some tropical countries, such transmission is already a serious threat to public health.[61]

Then again, one might argue that shared touch screens at retail checkout counters, ATMs, and the like have problems of their own, and some new technologies could turn out to have bigger health concerns than cash causes. All in all, the public health issue concerns do not seem to be a first-order argument against cash at present.

———

In this chapter and the preceding one, we have seen just how huge the costs of cash are in terms of tax evasion and crime. Next we turn to examining just how much central banks and treasuries receive directly from the business of printing paper currency.

CHAPTER 6

Seigniorage

Governments enjoy considerable profits from their monopoly on paper currency, which costs next to nothing to print and yet can be spent at face value. As we shall see, the revenues from paper currency are substantial, and for central banks constitute the biggest counterargument to phasing out cash. On top of giving up the annual profits central banks earn from supplying currency to both the legal and underground economies (we have termed the latter reverse money laundering), any assessment of the costs to phasing out cash must take into account the need to issue interest-bearing government debt to buy back zero-interest currency. Right now that is not much of an issue, because short-term rates on debt are basically zero, but there is certainly no guarantee they will remain this low in the long run. But we begin with an examination of the revenues governments are earning now.

Most people are aware of the "inflation tax" that the government collects when it debases existing currency by printing more new currency than the economy needs, thereby causing inflation. The holders of currency pay the tax as the value of the real spending power of their cash goes down; the government effectively collects the revenue when it spends the currency it prints. But governments can also earn profits on printing money even without causing inflation simply by accommodating growing transactions demand, usually linked to underlying growth in the economy. Demand can also rise when a generalized fall in interest rates takes place, reducing what economists refer to as "the opportunity cost" of holding currency. The trend fall in interest rates and inflation rates over the past three decades has certainly been a factor in the rise in demand for paper money, despite the proliferation of alternative transaction media. And, importantly, demand can also rise because of growth in the underground economy, for example, if higher tax rates spur greater tax evasion or if crime rates increase.

The noninflationary portion of the government's profit from printing money is really a "rent" that the government gets through exercising its monopoly on paper currency.

The government's total profit from printing money—including
both the inflation tax and the monopoly rents accrued by accommodating greater real demand—is sometimes referred to as "seigniorage," a term that derives from the old French word *seigneur*.
The word's origins trace to the days when coins were made of
gold, silver, and bronze. The word refers to the difference between
the face value of coins minted by the government and the cost of
inputs, including both materials and production costs. Unbacked
paper fiat currency just takes the practice to a higher level. According to the Federal Reserve, it costs 12.3 cents to make a $100 bill
and 4.9 cents to make a $1 bill.[1]

As seigniorage goes, Marco Polo's description of paper money
creation as alchemy was not far off. Between 2006 and 2015, the
US government earned 0.40% of GDP per year by printing new
notes and spending them. For 2015, it earned just under $70 bil-
lion, right on the 10-year average as a percentage of GDP. The European Central Bank earned 0.55% per year, which, benchmarked
by 2015 GDP, would be roughly 60 billion euros ($66 billion).
True, these profits are likely flattered by the extremely low level of
interest rates that have prevailed after the crisis,[2] but even before
policy interest rates collapsed to zero, the US take was still averaging 0.25% of GDP. (This calculation does not include seigniorage from electronic bank reserves, which of course should increase
after paper currency is phased out. The government's profit will
depend on a variety of regulatory factors, such as the minimum
level of reserves that banks will be forced to hold against deposits
and what kind of interest rate the central bank pays on these.)

MEASURES OF SEIGNIORAGE

Importantly, there are two ways to think of seigniorage in a modern context, and both matter if one is contemplating scaling back
the paper currency business. The calculations above for the euro
and the dollar were based on using the simple and intuitive concept

of "monetary seigniorage."[3] This concept asks to what extent the government is able to spend beyond its means each year by printing money and spending it. This is certainly how the monarchs of the Middle Ages thought about seigniorage, and for many purposes it is the main thing to focus on here. Going back to the case of the United States, if inflation is 2%, then the inflation tax on the $1.4-trillion paper money supply held by the public (including vault cash) is $28 billion, or more than one-third of the total profit.

The exercise of seigniorage in modern times is not quite so crude as it was in the Middle Ages, even if it amounts to much the same thing. Instead of having the government print money and buy things directly, modern-day seigniorage is a three-stage process. In stage one, the government spends beyond its means (its tax revenues) and issues interest-bearing debt to cover the difference. In stage two, the central bank—a fully owned subsidiary of the government—issues electronic bank reserves (which are the electronic equivalent of cash) and uses the proceeds to buy up government debt. Over time, the central bank usually earns a profit, because the longer-term debt it typically buys usually pays a higher interest rate than the bank reserves it issues. In stage three, the central bank turns over any revenues in excess of its expenses to the government. It is all very civilized, and if the central bank has significant independence, the system is far more than window dressing, as we shall discuss at length in chapter 12. From an accounting point of view, however, the three-stage process boils down to the same thing as if the government just purchased goods directly with its money creation. (One can occasionally find autocratic and populist governments today that still sometimes do things the medieval way, dispensing with the niceties of open market operations and having the central bank ship truckloads of cash directly to the government to spend. The Kirchner era in Argentina (2003–2015) famously had little regard for central bank independence.)

Although monetary seigniorage is perhaps the most natural way, there is also a second way to calculate seigniorage revenues, sometimes referred to as "opportunity cost seigniorage." This second approach asks: what if the government relinquished its monopoly over currency entirely, pulled out of the business, and had to rely solely on debt to finance any shortfall in income over expenditure (just like the rest of us poor slobs)? At present, interest rates are very low; the average interest rate that the US Treasury paid on its marketable debt in March 2016 was just 2.03%, so an extra $1.4 trillion in debt would cost only just over $28 billion a year.[4] However, if the average interest rate on marketable government debt was a more "normal" 4% (corresponding to a 2% inflation rate and 2% growth rate in real income), then opportunity cost seigniorage would be $56 billion in nominal terms (though in real terms, adjusting for inflation, the cost of the interest-bearing debt would be only 2% annually, or $28 billion).

Figure 6.1 shows average revenues from printing paper currency as a percentage of GDP for a range of countries, using the monetary seigniorage approach. Switzerland and Singapore, at 0.60% and 0.62%, respectively, have average revenues similar to the Eurozone's 0.55%. Canada and the United Kingdom are much smaller at 0.18%. China is not listed on the table, because the available dataset does not go back far enough, but in recent years, its monetary seigniorage on paper currency has averaged 0.5% of GDP a year, in the middle between the United States and Eurozone rates.[5] Most countries' seigniorage profits in recent years have almost certainly been exaggerated by the extremely low level of interest rates. The US number will likely drop to a steady-state number closer to 0.3% of GDP when interest rates normalize, and then only after an adjustment period when seigniorage will be low or even negative as people adjust their portfolios out of cash and into interest-bearing assets. The reasons for high seigniorage revenues in Russia are different: the government collects a high tax rate due to high inflation, on a large monetary base, thanks to a strong tradition of using cash in a very corrupt system.

Even at today's elevated levels, the seigniorage-to-GDP ratios in Figure 6.1 are far below the corresponding estimates reported for tax evasion in chapter 5. For the United States, estimated tax evasion is 2.7% for federal taxes alone, and perhaps another percentage point higher if state and local taxes are included. As noted in chapter 5, tax evasion is likely even more significant in Europe.

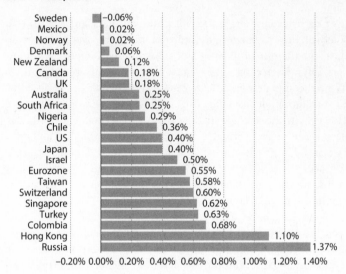

Figure 6.1: Seigniorage revenue/GDP, 2006–2015 average. Source: IMF, International Financial Statistics; and Central bank sources. Norway data are for 2006–2014.

Of particular note is Sweden, where the public's use of notes and coins has declined since 2007, not only relative to GDP but also in absolute terms. Hence the profit from currency printing, measured in this way, is negative.[6] Indeed, the Riksbank has already rightly started to discuss why in the long run a central bank should be focused on the health of the overall economy and not on its profit-and-loss statement.[7] Sweden was relatively unique in this experience in the aftermath of the financial crisis of 2008, but as mentioned above, it is easy to imagine demand temporarily shrinking elsewhere when interest rate normalization begins, in which case other central banks may experience the same phenomenon. Note that the Swedish central bank would still be making money over most of this period using the opportunity cost definition of seigniorage. We return to the Swedish experience in Box 7.1 of chapter 7.

Seigniorage revenues have been relatively modest as a share of GDP for many decades. It is true that in the high-inflation 1970s, seigniorage revenues from paper currency were notably higher for some European countries. For example, between 1974 and 1978, seigniorage revenues from currency (outside banks) ranged from 2.2% to 2.7% annually for Greece, and from 1.1% to 1.4% annually for Italy.[8] But given the advent of alternative payment media, including credit and debit cards, levels this high are unlikely to be seen again in most advanced countries absent a brief spike from a large burst of unanticipated inflation.

HOW MUCH WOULD SEIGNIORAGE REVENUES SHRINK?

If currency were substantially phased out, the extent to which seigniorage revenues would shrink would depend in part on how much residual currency the public ends up holding after the transition. Suppose, for example, the only change is to eliminate large-denomination notes, $50 and $100 bills in the case of the United States. My conjecture is that this would actually lead to a substantial initial shrinkage in the currency supply, mainly because smaller bills will be much less popular than large bills in the underground economy. As of the end of 2015, only 3% of the US paper currency supply was in bills of $10 or smaller and only 16% if one includes $20 bills.[9]

Let's suppose that the total outstanding share of dollars fell by 50%. After buying these bills up, if necessary supplemented by a special Treasury bond issue, the currency supply would still be $700 billion. If the demand for the remaining notes grew at the same pace as it has over the past 10 years, the Federal Reserve would still be earning $35 billion a year, enough to cover the Federal Reserve's 2015 operating budget of $4.3 billion many times over.

Even if paper money revenue disappeared completely, the central bank would still earn money from electronic bank reserves, with the exact profits depending on the interest rate paid to banks relative to the interest rate the central bank earns on its assets. One imagines that in a fully electronic world (with all low-income individuals receiving heavily subsidized debit accounts), demand for reserves at the central bank would rise, potentially quite sharply. And this process is hardly exogenous. The government has numerous regulatory levers it can pull, for example, taking more forceful steps than it has in the past to pull the plug on money market funds, which in the current environment remain a regulatory end-around.

In the extreme case, the government could adopt a version of the 1930s "Chicago plan," which would essentially allow banks to issue money-like instruments only if they were 100% backed by government debt, which presumably can include central bank reserves.[10] The name relates to Chicago economists Henry Simon, Frank Knight, Milton Friedman, and Irving Fisher (the last actually a Yale professor), who advocated the idea of "narrow banking" to mitigate moral hazard problems and eliminate bank runs (assuming that the government itself is fully solvent). A Chicago-type plan would mark a quantum change in the financial system and would radically reroute the way capital flows in the economy. By expanding the scope of the government's monopoly on all retail transaction media, the government would be able to raise vast amounts of capital, essentially usurping one of the private banking system's main funding mechanisms. Indeed, by some estimates, required bank reserves could reach 180% of GDP, more than substituting for all other placement of government debt.[11] In this case, it is conceivable that the government would have to purchase other kinds of assets to produce the requisite supply of "safe" government debt. The presumption is that alternative markets for lending to small- and medium-sized businesses would develop, for example, funds that bundled loans.[12] The Chicago plan is extreme. But the point is that the government has a plethora of levers it can pull to increase reserve holdings, should it want to effectively increase its tax on electronic balances to substitute for reduced revenues from paper currency. And, by the way, doing so might just increase the stability of the financial system.

THE COST OF SUBSTITUTING INTEREST-BEARING DEBT FOR PAPER CURRENCY

If a government fully phases out paper currency, there is a sense in which it will have to forgo both monetary seigniorage and

opportunity cost seigniorage. Obviously, it forgoes monetary seigniorage, because it won't be printing fresh currency anymore. But
at the same time, it will have to issue ordinary interest-bearing debt
to buy back the currency it is retiring. Given that the ratio of currency to GDP in the United States is 7.4%, its debt-to-GDP ratio
would rise 7.4% as the currency is phased out. As we have already
calculated, the nominal cost is about $28 billion right now at to-
day's ultra-low average interest rate on government debt. If the inflation rate is also 2%, the real burden would be zero, because the
government could just let the debt (used to buy back the currency)
grow at 2% without changing its real (price-adjusted) value. But,
as we have just discussed, there is every chance interest rates will
rise, raising the cost of financing the debt. At a 4% average interest
rate on debt and 2% inflation rate, a real burden of $28 billion per
year would be added to the $70 billion a year that the government
would forgo in monetary seigniorage, for a total of $98 billion per
year. (If the economy is growing in real terms, then the cost of the
debt service component will fall as a share of GDP over time.)

In truth, this calculation is likely an overestimate. If average real
interest rates paid on government debt ever rose to 2% or 3%
(from near zero today), monetary seigniorage would likely drop
considerably, perhaps even back to pre-crisis levels of $30 billion
a year. They could even be negative for an extended period (as in
the case of Sweden) as the world adjusted downward its paper
currency portfolio in light of higher interest rates. A systematic
treatment of the trade-offs, uncertainties, and expected net cost of
a currency phaseout would need to be undertaken to properly assess the costs. But the general point is that the government would
have to issue debt to mop up any shrinkage in the currency supply,
assuming it wants to keep inflation under control.

There is an important nuance, however, which I will take up
now rather than wait until chapter 7, where I detail a blueprint
for phasing out most currency. Even with a complete phaseout of
paper currency, it is not necessarily the case that all currency will
be traded in. A lot depends on how difficult the government makes
it for denizens of the global underground economy to tender their
cash hoardings. Current anti-money-laundering rules already im-
pose significant reporting requirements on banks when large cash

deposits are made. It is not as if a drug dealer can just waltz in and deposit $10 million without drawing attention.

In a standard currency conversion, the government has a strong incentive to reassure everyone that the status quo will remain, so as not to undermine future demand for its product. Suppose Japan decided to modernize its currency, creating a "new yen" worth 100 times the old yen; right now the yen is worth roughly 1/100 of a dollar, so a new yen would then trade at something closer to one for one with the dollar. To execute the currency reform, the government would trade 100–new yen notes for legacy 10,000-yen notes, 50–new yen notes for legacy 5,000-yen notes, and so forth. Governments often reconstitute their currency like this after a long period of inflation, say, after a war. Of course the government would like to take the opportunity to penalize crooks for their past misdeeds by making it hard for them to turn in cash, but then the underground might become far leerier about holding local cash, driving future seigniorage profits down. So, in normal currency conversions, governments often make it relatively easy to turn in cash.

If a country is really phasing out its paper currency, however, it does not need to worry quite so much about undermining future demand. It is therefore well positioned to take a more aggressive stance on dirty money. My conjecture is that with even modest reporting requirements, a measurable share of all currency would never be turned in, perhaps 10% or more. If the government insisted on keeping much stricter reporting requirements, similar to those in place today for large cash deposits, it is entirely possible that 20% or more of all cash would never be tendered. This figure, of course, is sensitive to the time frame given for money to be turned in, the exact conditions, and so forth. Obviously if, say, the Eurozone institutes strong reporting requirements to try to trap dirty money in the phaseout of 500-euro notes, criminals will be more hesitant to switch to hoarding 200-euro notes, knowing that these might also be hard to convert when it comes time to phase them out.

Even ignoring this nuance, adding in the real (inflation-adjusted) financing costs of the debt required to buy back currency still does not overturn the fact that the potential gains from reducing tax evasion should at least offset the forgone costs of seigniorage, even in the extreme case where all currency is phased out and the government buys back all dirty money at par. For the United States, a plausible range for the medium-term real income revenue loss to the government is between 0.3% of GDP (assuming zero real interest rates on debt and a return to more modest seigniorage revenues) and 0.6% of GDP (assuming seigniorage revenues remain 0.4% of GDP and a rise in the real interest rate to 3%). One subtle but important point: although we have not yet come to assessing the potential benefits to decisively breaking the zero bound on negative interest rates, the benefits are likely to be particularly important if nominal interest rates would otherwise remain very low for an extended period. Yet this is exactly the scenario where cash demand and monetary seigniorage are most likely to be at the high end of our estimates. We are also abstracting from potentially higher revenues on electronic reserves, which should rise in a less-cash world.

For Europe, thanks to its large underground economies, particularly in the periphery countries, recent monetary seigniorage rates are higher (roughly 0.55% of GDP versus 0.4% in the United States), and the currency supply is larger as a share of GDP (10.1% versus 7.4%). Thus the real cost of phasing out currency is larger as a percentage of GDP and might range from, say, 0.4% to 0.8% of GDP. However, the benefits of phasing out paper currency, particularly in terms of higher tax revenues, are likely significantly higher as well. Indeed, the net gains for Europe to phasing out paper currency might well be much larger than for the United States.

The United States and the Eurozone are somewhat exceptional, because of big foreign demand for their notes. The calculus of phasing out paper currency is even more compelling for other advanced economies whose currencies are mainly used domestically. Seigniorage rates for Canada and the United Kingdom are less than half those of the United States, and roughly a third those of the Eurozone. Hence the opportunity cost of retreating from the paper currency business is correspondingly less. For Japan, recent monetary seigniorage is only 0.4% of GDP, but the money supply is a far larger share of GDP, close to 19% (see figure 3.4). This makes the annual real cost for Japan extremely sensitive to the real interest rate on debt issued to buy back currency, with a low-end estimate being 0.3% of GDP and a high-end estimate being 0.9% of GDP. The low number is likely far more meaningful. The exceptionally high level of cash holding in Japan almost certainly reflects in part the fact that the country has had near-zero nominal interest rates for two decades. If real interest rates on Japan's debt remain anywhere near current levels, the costs of carrying debt issued to buy back the currency would be negligible. Anyway, if the average real interest rate Japan had to pay on its massive government debt (more than 130% of GDP, even in net terms) rose to 3% from current levels, the country would have much bigger problems than its currency supply. And even if it managed to avert default, a sharp rise in real interest rates would almost certainly lead in the long term to a massive shrinkage in currency demand.

THE POLITICAL ECONOMY IMPORTANCE OF SEIGNIORAGE

The development of much greater central bank independence in many countries over the past three decades has been perhaps the single most transformative change in global macroeconomic policy since the breakup of the Bretton Woods system of fixed exchange rates in the early 1970s. Therefore it is important that the central bank not be turned into a political punching bag in a currency phaseout, as its profits will sharply decrease. Aside from being a modest but nice source of income for the government, seigniorage revenue has an important political economy function in supporting central bank independence. It turns the central bank into a huge profit center that earns far beyond what it needs to operate, enabling it to remit the rest back to the national treasury. This immense profitability provides central banks with a considerable amount of discretion on where to draw the line between expenditures that are necessary and those that are not. This freedom, in turn, enables central banks to retain expert staffs of macroeconomists that help give the central bank unusual expertise and heft in the government. This same expertise also helps them be better prepared to address crises. It is fair to ask, then: just how can this independence be preserved if revenues from paper currency creation are allowed to shrink?

Central bank independence is a very important issue, but as long as we live in a world where electronic reserves at the central bank are the de facto unit of account and medium for settling interbank financial transactions, it seems likely that central banks will have more than enough revenues from electronic money to cover their operating costs in most circumstances. One way to protect central banks in their transition to a less-cash economy is to have a special Treasury issue to soak up a significant fraction of the currency, so the burden does not all fall on the central bank. Despite the challenges to central bank independence, the status quo, where central banks make vast extra profits by providing a key financing instrument for the underground and criminal activity worldwide, is hard to defend.

CHAPTER 7

A Plan for Phasing Out Most Paper Currency

Having laid out the serious drawbacks to paper currency, we are now ready to turn to the practical question of how it might be (mostly) phased out. This might seem premature, given that, except for seigniorage revenues, we have only cursorily discussed paper currency's many virtues: preserving privacy, dealing with blackouts and other emergencies, security from cybercrime, providing a medium of exchange for unbanked low-income individuals, and achieving what specialists call real-time clearing of transactions. On top of all that, there is inertia and custom; plenty of people would just rather not have to deal with any kind of change. The reason for deferring these issues until now is that they are much easier to put in perspective in the context of a concrete proposal.

The proposal here is driven by three guiding principles. First, the ultimate goal is to make it more difficult to engage in anonymous untraceable transactions repeatedly and on a large scale. Relatedly, it is intended to make it more difficult to secretly transport and store large quantities of cash. The idea is to reduce wholesale use of cash in tax evasion or illegal activities. For the most part, the use of cash in large legal transactions is becoming increasingly vestigial and unnecessary, at least in advanced economies.

Second, the speed of transition needs to be slow, stretching changes out over at least 10–15 years. Gradualism helps avoid excessive disruption and gives institutions and individuals time to adapt. It puts authorities in a position to make adjustments as issues arise and as new options become available. This is an important point; obviously, over any long course of transition, new technologies and new issues will arise, and any realistic plan has to acknowledge this possibility.

Third, it is essential that poor and unbanked individuals have access to free basic debit accounts (or the future equivalent), and possibly also basic smartphones, as several countries have already done or are contemplating. The cost is ideally borne directly by the government, though it can also be imposed on banks that will eventually pass the costs on to paying customers. Under the current system, financial exclusion imposes high costs on the poor (e.g., high fees for cashing checks or wiring money), and a strong case can be made for providing better access to financial services even under the current system. The costs are small compared to providing universal health care, and the potential benefits are large.

As for privacy, it is important to separate out protection from government snooping and protection from relatives, friends, employers, or other private entities. Of course, people will always want to keep some expenditures or income secret from spouses, parents, and friends. The government can perfectly well allow such transactions as long as they do not entail recurrent large expenditures and income to be completely hidden from the government. And there need to be ways to allow relatively small expenditures to be secret, even from the government, say, up to a few hundred dollars or equivalent, perhaps a bit more.

In principle, the ultimate objective is to find a balance between allowing for small completely anonymous transactions while forcing large completely anonymous payments through relatively illiquid and high-cost transaction vehicles other than cash. The current system fails miserably to strike that balance. Again, the proposal here illustrates general principles in a concrete fashion, but of course there is room for significant refinements and improvements. The goal here is not a quixotic attempt to stamp out all illegal activity and tax evasion but to make it more difficult and expensive to conduct these activities anonymously.

Later in this chapter, we consider myriad practical issues, such as "how do we survive blackouts?" or "wouldn't phasing out paper currency make us more vulnerable to cybercrime?" One can think of endless objections to change, but most are quite superficial and can be easily dealt with, especially given a long transition period.

We will also defer discussion of the issues surrounding the policy of negative interest rates until part II of the book. For one thing, it is perfectly possible to phase out paper currency and at the same time prohibit the central bank from setting negative interest rates (though this would be a mistake). And although phasing out paper currency is certainly an elegant way of making negative rates feasible, there are other ideas for how this might be done, and we will take up these alternatives in due time. Importantly, a mix of approaches is possible, particularly along the transition path to phasing out paper currency. To the extent negative interest rates are a central goal, further transitions and adjustments need to be put in place to make negative interest rate policy fully effective.

Let's start with where countries might want to be in the long run. Again, the plan here is intended to illustrate ideas and can be adapted and tweaked in many directions.

A Long Run without Paper Currency

1. PHASING OUT PAPER CURRENCY: All paper currency is gradually phased out, beginning with all notes of $50 and above (or foreign equivalent), then next the $20 bill, leaving only $1, $5, and (perhaps) $10 bills. These small bills would be left in circulation for an indefinite period. In the final phase, small bills would be replaced by equivalent-denomination coins of substantial weight.

2. UNIVERSAL FINANCIAL INCLUSION: The government provides all individuals the option of access to free basic-function debit card/smartphone accounts, either through banks or through a government option. This can be substantially implemented by making government transfer payments into the debit account after it is created.

3. PRIVACY: Regulatory and legal framework aims to discourage other means of making large-scale payments that can be completely hidden from the government.

4. REAL-TIME CLEARING: This is a technical point, but an important one. Government helps facilitate development of the "rails" of the payment infrastructure to achieve (near) real-time clearing for most transactions.

We discuss each item in turn.

PHASING OUT PAPER CURRENCY

The largest-denomination notes, which are by far the most problematic, should be phased out first. In the case of the United States, the largest bills are the $50s and $100s. The absolute simplest approach is to follow the blueprint of Canada, which began to phase out the 1,000–Canadian dollar note in 2000, or Singapore, which began to phase out the 10,000–Singapore dollar note in 2014. Sweden did the same in 2013 with its 1,000-krona note, as will be examined in more detail in Box 7.1. The United States could simply stop printing new $100 and $50 bills and instruct financial institutions to send any bills that come into the system back to the central bank for exchange and destruction. Over time, the large notes would gradually be reduced to a minor share of total currency. By the way, some clever reader might ask whether, during the transition period, large notes might actually sell at a premium, since they are now in scarce supply, and the central bank no longer stands ready to print more as needed to keep the prices of all notes in alignment with face value. In this case, the El Chapo Guzmáns of the criminal world might get a big capital gain on their cash holdings. Fortunately, this is pretty much a nonissue, because holders of existing large-denomination bills will also have to worry about the possibility that the government might start requiring a lot of information from anyone trying to turn them in at banks, or worse, simply declaring them null and void. Indeed, it is highly probable that large-denomination notes would trade at a discount rather than a premium.

A gradual phaseout of large notes could take a couple decades, but there are faster approaches. For example, the government could set a date after which large notes expire. Large note holders could tender their bills for exchange either at private banks or at regional government offices. Exchange at federal offices would be done for free up to a certain amount, then with a modest handling and processing charge thereafter. Private banks would be allowed to charge a fee to cover the costs of paperwork, ferreting out counterfeits, and security; maximum fees could be set by regulation.

Arrangements would be made with foreign central banks to cover individuals who wish to exchange money abroad. Foreigners could also bring currency to the United States for exchange, subject to the usual customs reporting requirements for amounts over $10,000.

The time period of the exchange would need to be determined, but for the sake of concreteness, one idea would be for the process to give people 2 years to use private banks, and longer (say, 7 years) to use regional central bank offices. This approach follows the standard blueprint for currency reforms, which is to make things relatively easy early on, but then to force late adopters to travel farther, fill out more forms, and as time goes on, to reveal more information, particularly about large sums.

The process by which the Eurozone countries exchanged legacy national currencies (e.g., the deutsche mark, the French franc, the Italian lira) for euro notes and coins provides helpful elements of a blueprint. However, as already observed in chapter 6, the government in our case can afford to be somewhat more aggressive in requiring information and details from anyone bringing substantial sums of large-denomination notes either to trade for smaller ones or for electronic currency. Because the government is on a path to exiting the paper currency business, it is in a position to enforce laws more vigorously than in a typical currency exchange, where the government might be worried about reputational concerns and maintaining future demand.

Smaller notes would be allowed to circulate indefinitely, say, for at least the first two decades of the overall transition. A final stage, optional but recommended, is to eventually require that even the small bills be turned in, either for electronic money or for the newly minted $5 and $10 coins. These would be sufficiently substantial that it would be burdensome to carry around and conceal large amounts, say, $10,000 or more.[1]

The idea of shifting from small bills to coins is to discourage substitution. Eliminating the large bills is already helpful. A million dollars in $100 bills weighs approximately 22 pounds (10 kilos), and, if stacked, rises to 43 inches (or 109 centimeters). It can fit comfortably into a large shopping bag. Obviously, with $20 bills, all measures would be five times as much; with $10 notes, $1 million is suddenly 220 pounds (100 kilos) and 430 inches (1,090 centimeters). It is also proportionately costlier to count, verify, handle, and store. Of course, significant substitution is possible, but the weight, bulk, and storage space are costly. Ultimately, with coins, the weight and bulk can be made an order of magnitude greater than for paper bills. Properly designed, the weight of coins, though quite modest for ordinary day-to-day transactions, would make them awkward for transporting large amounts or conducting large anonymous transactions.

The inspiration for going back to the future on coinage comes from ancient China, where coins were made of iron and other heavier base metals, rather than gold and silver, arguably accelerating the transition to paper. In the case of a deep recession, where the central bank is forced to institute substantial negative interest rates for a presumably short period, the costs of counting and storage of large amounts would also be proportionately much larger than today and should be sufficient to allow central banks to institute negative interest rates to any degree realistically likely to be necessary without triggering a run to cash. My guess is that making the largest note $10 would already be sufficient to allow significantly negative interest rates (say, −3%) for fairly long periods without a wholesale run from Treasury bills to cash, and even more negative rates would be possible for brief periods. If necessary, other measures can be taken to raise the cost of hoarding on a mass scale, for example, charging a fee to redeposit cash into the financial system, or (in the extreme) one of the more sophisticated mechanisms considered in chapter 10. Once paper currency has been sufficiently marginalized, more complex plans to marginalize it further would become easier for the public to digest.

It should be noted that mainstream private payment media already provide a mechanism for small-scale quasi-anonymous transactions, for example, prepaid cards. Indeed, as cash is phased out, it will be important to redouble efforts to discourage these as an alternative for moving large sums anonymously; the issue is already on the radar screen of major governments.

Finally, some might ask: what is to stop criminals from using $100 bills for transactions among one another, long after the bills are no longer accepted in the formal (legal) economy? Such a convention could arise, of course, but as noted in several places in this book, the value and liquidity of any candidate currency would be sharply diminished if there were no way to convert it into payments for ordinary goods and services, so this concern should be regarded as a minor issue. To be completely clear, $100 bills would not simply trade at deep discount but otherwise be as useful in transactions for criminals as they were before. In fact, legacy $100 bills would also be inconvenient and difficult to dispose of in perpetuity. If a market for $100 bills did develop, in all likelihood, it would reasonably quickly become marginalized.

UNIVERSAL FINANCIAL INCLUSION

In principle, no new instruments are required to shift to a less-cash world; in particular, cryptocurrencies are not required. Transactions would likely continue shifting to debit cards, as is already happening now. Over time, transactions are likely to shift increasingly to smartphones.[2] The main issue is how to serve low-income individuals who are unbanked. Low-income households and individuals go without banks for various reasons, including the inability to meet minimum deposit requirements, monthly service fees, and lack of convenient access in lower-income neighborhoods.

In the United States, more than 8% of households were unbanked in 2013, according to an FDIC survey.[3] Another 20% were underbanked, meaning they also used alternative financial services outside the banking system, including prepaid cards, payday loans, pawn shops, and check-cashing services. More than 25% of adult Americans do not have a credit card.

Unfortunately, the cost of not having bank access is high. Check-cashing services charge exorbitant fees; for immigrants and others who need to wire funds abroad and transfer money to relatives, the transaction costs can amount to 10–15% or more. Storing cash at home and carrying cash greatly increases the chance of theft.[4] The risks of being subject to fraud are much higher outside the regulated financial sector. The poor may benefit from being able to use paper currency, but overall, financial exclusion implies large costs for basic services. In sum, the status quo is extremely regressive.

A long-run solution is to provide government-subsidized access to financial services for the poor, giving them equal access to electronic currency and, at the same time, helping reduce some of the costs associated with financial exclusion. In principle, providing access can be done through a regulated banking sector, but there could also be a government provider of basic services. A basic account could, for example, allow up to a certain maximum number of transactions per month with no minimum balance requirements and only modest charges for transactions over the limit. The cost of providing subsidized electronic currency accounts for low-income individuals should be relatively modest, say, on the order of $32 billion per year (for example, 80 million free basic accounts at $400 per year).[5] Again, it is possible to shift this cost to banks, forcing them to provide virtually free basic debit accounts, as some countries have done. Of course this is an implicit tax that is ultimately passed on to other depositors and borrowers.

If providing such basic services sounds spendthrift, remember, programs will be built in the context of a transition to electronic payment vehicles that would likely bring net revenue to the government overall, given higher tax receipts. Shifting away from cash will also help reduce crime-related expenditures. Increased financial inclusion will have numerous collateral benefits in fighting domestic inequality. A simple way to introduce universal debit cards is to pay benefits electronically in basic debit accounts, as some countries, including Denmark, are already doing.

In anticipation of the possibility of negative interest rates, the government might guarantee that deposits at the universal accounts up to a certain amount (say, $1,000–$2,000) would always receive a nonnegative interest rate, for example, through rebates to banks. This should not interfere in any significant way with the basic functioning of monetary policy in a negative rate environment.

Now it must be acknowledged that some percentage of the unbanked want to be off the radar screen and out of the system for reasons having nothing to do with tax evasion or illegal activity. In the proposal here, such individuals could still employ a range of other assets from small bills and coins, to jewelry and precious metals, to regulated cryptocurrencies. The need for a safety valve for citizens at the edge of society is a valid one, but it is a weak argument for maintaining a paper currency system that causes so much collateral damage.

With or without a shift to electronic currencies, mobile telephony and the Internet are already revolutionizing financial services in ways that help the poor. Mobile banking has made significant inroads in Africa, and Internet lending is challenging the standard banking model. One is almost tempted to make an analogy to ancient China, where inferior coinage precipitated the invention of a much better transaction technology—paper money. A thorough discussion of banking services goes far beyond the ambitions of this book. What should be understood is that the poor do not benefit from the status quo, often being hugely disadvantaged by obstacles that prevent them from enjoying the benefits of modern banking. Relatively modest subsidies can overcome this inequity. In addition, poor neighborhoods would experience many other advantages, particularly in terms of decreased crime, that would likely accompany a shift away from cash.

Naturally, the devil is in the details. Remember that the illustrative plan allows smaller bills to circulate for an extended period, so there would be plenty of time to iron out specifics. I tend to think there should be a government provider of subsidized debit cards, designed to catch those people that the private sector will not service, even with subsidies. There are also basic questions about how to design family accounts that need sorting out with appropriate government regulation, but the residual small bills or coinage system should be more than sufficient so that junior can go to the store to buy an apple.

PRIVACY

When phasing out paper currency, the most fundamental and difficult issue is how to balance an individual's privacy rights with the government's need to enforce laws, collect taxes, and combat terrorism. This is an important and subtle question that requires considerable attention, and it goes far beyond the narrow confines of any debate on the role of paper currency.[6] Whatever one thinks of American privacy activist and former National Security Agency contractor Edward Snowden, the revelations that have come out from the material he released show that the government already has eavesdropping capabilities once thought to be purely in the realm of science fiction. And it is only going to get worse. Extensive government monitoring of cell phones and emails has already exploded as an issue. GPS systems in telephones and autos allow tracking of these devices. In major cities like London, New York, and Beijing, security cameras are everywhere. Combined with high-powered computing and vast databases, governments already have the capacity to intrude on privacy that would have been unthinkable 20 years ago.

And it is not only government surveillance that is changing the privacy landscape. Taking advantage of the rapidly decreasing cost of information storage and sorting, behemoth tech and retail companies catalog your every click, cell phone companies trace your movement from cell tower to cell tower, and social networking sites record intimate details of your online person. In many cases, information is bought, sold, and exchanged. Late twentieth-century notions of privacy already seem quaint.[7] There is a huge and ongoing battle over privacy across the technology spectrum about conditions under which private companies can be forced to share their proprietary databases with the government, and also over the sale of encrypted devices without a backdoor that would allow the government to unlock information for purposes of national security or criminal investigations. How this balance ultimately evolves will profoundly affect the landscape for alternative anonymous transaction technologies. It will certainly influence the future course of cryptocurrencies, which we take up in chapter 14; governments everywhere are facing the question of how to balance regulation with fostering innovation in this space. Nevertheless, one should have little doubt that governments have all the tools necessary to prevent any alternative transaction media from deeply infiltrating the legal economy on a sustained basis, thereby greatly undermining their value relative to the present-day status of cash.

In theory, a government could itself offer debit accounts that were guaranteed to be private. Unfortunately, that promise would not be worth the paper it was written on, so to speak. Given governments' past behavior, who could take such a promise seriously? A government is not going to create an encryption system itself without making sure it has the key. And if it has a key, it will eventually be used as the government sees fit. Governments already intensely monitor bank transactions for crime and terrorist activities; one can expect the same with any new type of debit account, and ultimately any transaction technology that interfaces with the financial system.

That said, one can imagine a government creating a system where transactions are anonymous for private citizens, and one that contains significant restrictions on government access as well. Tax information, for example, is already accorded heavily protected status in most countries. One could, in principle, extend that privilege much more broadly, perhaps on small individual accounts with strict limits on how much money can be in them. Such a system would have to be stress tested to see whether it is truly credible. For example, could the government be forced to reveal any private transactions information it knows in a child custody battle?

REAL-TIME CLEARING AND PERSON-TO-PERSON TRANSACTIONS

Paper currency is still superior in many person-to-person (P2P) transactions, allowing for real-time clearing in a way that, at present, electronic payment mechanisms cannot duplicate. Ordinary credit cards and debit cards take a day to clear, creating credit risk that can be mitigated but not eliminated through monitoring, since some merchants only process charges with delay. PIN-protected debit card charges do clear nearly instantaneously, though for the moment not all merchants in the United States have the resources to process these. If neither buyer nor seller has access to the growing number of credit and debit card readers (for example Square Cash, a plug-in for tablets that allows street vendors to process credit cards), there is still no fully satisfactory substitute for cash. But unfolding electronic technologies are peeling away these limitations of digital payments. For example, apps like Venmo, Google Wallet, and Square Cash offer the possibility of allowing one individual to write a check to another individual with reasonably fast clearing. This is not to mention large players like WeChat and Facebook as they enter the game. P2P options are likely to proliferate and improve. Indeed, the range of transactions for which cash is still dominant is slowly dwindling. (Denmark is among several countries that have already developed widely used systems; see Box 7.1.)

Many of the changes that need to take place to promote real-time clearing can be sped up considerably through government action. The Automated Clearing House system in the United States, for example, is an anachronism by global standards, and so far the Federal Reserve has not invested the relatively modest sums necessary to replace it.[8] Some of the resistance comes from incumbent banks, which realize that an upgraded electronic check clearing system could serve multiple purposes, potentially allowing new entrants to issue entirely new payment systems that compete with and even supplant existing technologies. Eventually all of this investment and change will take place. The issue of real-time clearing will take longer to resolve for small retail transactions, simply because it is harder to amortize the fixed costs, but this is another area where allowing the continued circulation of small bills (and later coins) should significantly mitigate transition problems.

FURTHER ISSUES

What about Foreign Currencies?

Would a shift to an electronic currency have to be coordinated internationally? Coordination would have significant advantages from a global social welfare point of view, as discussed in chapter 13, but it is not essential. From a domestic macroeconomic perspective, existing restrictions on cross-border movements of international currencies, combined with reporting requirements for large currency deposits at financial institutions, already make laundering foreign currency difficult, as it is not easily spent domestically. Chapter 13 discusses in some detail why foreign currency cannot fill the void left by domestic currency, provided authorities exercise a modicum of vigilance.

Would Monetary Policy Be Affected?

Would eliminating paper currency make the conduct of monetary policy more difficult, even ignoring the possibility of negative rates? There is absolutely no reason to believe so. Indeed, most modern macroeconomic models either ignore paper currency or assign it an extremely minor role—it is almost superfluous.[9] In such a world, money remains a unit of account but loses its status as a means for transactions. In fact, monetary policy could be conducted in much the same way as today, with the government setting the overnight interest rate on nominal debt with the aim of stabilizing output and inflation. Electronic money (at present, bank reserves held at the central bank) can perfectly well serve as the unit of account; there would not be a problem.

This is because in the limit of a cashless economy, the government—through its control of the size of bank reserves—would still be able to control the price level via the overnight nominal interest rate. The essence of the argument is that the government is a very large player and can use its size and massive taxation potential to credibly set the short-term rate. Assuming some level of price stickiness—so that some component of the price level cannot jump—then command of the short-term rate is enough to give the government enormous influence over the current and expected path of inflation, and complete power to achieve any desired average inflation rate over the long run. There are some qualifications to the preceding optimistic discussion, probably slight and easily dealt with, but worth mentioning. First, monetary economists have long suspected that the uniqueness of cash, as opposed to other forms of government IOUs (i.e., bonds), is more fragile than most people realize. Back in the 1980s, Neil Wallace, a monetary theorist who was then at the University of Minnesota, made an extremely interesting and provocative conjecture. He argued that the only thing that makes cash special today is that the government chooses not to issue bonds in small denominations; otherwise, these bonds would compete with cash for transactions, and stabilizing prices would become extremely difficult. This might sound a bit far-fetched, but it is a bigger challenge than you think, and we explore the issue in a section of the appendix. Although Wallace did not necessarily envision electronic currency, his analysis raises real questions about what would happen if cash became electronic, with none of the other distinguishing features from bonds that we have today, which are already almost entirely electronic. The short answer is that the Wallace conjecture is probably not such a problem, given the success central banks have had in stabilizing the value of money even as transactions substitutes like debit cards have flourished. Besides, we are keeping small notes around. But the conjecture still merits consideration. An even more abstract but still potentially important issue is that "multiple equilibria" are endemic to modern monetary models. The use of money in transactions and as a unit of account is ultimately a social convention. Any large-scale change risks disturbing the status quo, potentially leading to unstable and unpredictable consequences. Again, in practice, this concern has not proved such a problem, as long as the government moves in slow measured steps, but theory suggests it cannot be entirely dismissed either.[10]

Effect on the Optimal Choice of Inflation Target

Central banks could retain their current inflation target (typically around 2%). In the very long run, this level is not necessary in a cashless world, because there is no reason to worry about retaining room for interest rate cuts in the event of a recession. The central bank could target a lower or higher inflation rate, though (as I stress in chapter 9) the transition costs of changing targets too quickly could be huge, and not having to ever worry about this is a major advantage of being able to use negative rates. In theory, a lower inflation rate would help reduce relative price distortions that arise in a world of staggered price- and wage-setting, and it also would reduce the distortions created by the tax system.

Seigniorage and Central Bank Independence

This topic has been covered in chapter 6. After the transition, steps would need to be taken to ensure that central bank independence was not significantly compromised once the central bank was no longer viewed as a major profit center. This problem is handled easily enough. Indeed, if the global real interest rate rose sufficiently, the central bank might even pay interest on reserves that would be passed through to depositors, so that on average over time depositors earned a positive rate of return, even if rates were on occasion negative.

VARIANTS

The proposal of this chapter should be viewed as illustrative only and can clearly be tweaked and changed in many dimensions, depending on the objective. For example, restricting the maximum size of purchases in retail transactions and putting expiry dates on paper notes to force them to be traded in periodically are both steps that could make cash less attractive. Once only small bills or coins are in circulation, it should be possible to institute fairly large negative rates without causing a wholesale run into cash but, as noted earlier, further steps can be taken in the unlikely event that still proves a problem. Again, as the private sector innovates on methods for conducting undetectable transactions, the government will continue to need to take measures to raise the costs of these alternatives, as it already does today. And I do not claim here that phasing out cash would eliminate tax evasion and illegal activities, only that it would help reduce them at the margin from what they would have been otherwise. And finally, recall that these ideas are for the present directed only at advanced economies. As discussed in chapter 13, most developing countries are not yet in a position to provide the universal transaction alternatives required. Moreover, in countries with weak institutions, the informal (tax- and regulation-evading) sector remains essential to a large segment of the population, given structural weaknesses in the formal sector (the legal economy).

As for whether phasing out cash is fantasy even for advanced countries, Box 7.1 looks at the cases of Sweden and Denmark, which have already taken some substantial steps toward reducing the use of cash.

Box 7.1. The Scandinavian Precedent

In the move to a cashless (or, to be precise, less-cash) society, the Scandinavian countries are attempting to lead the way. Through a mix of anti-crime and anti-terrorism measures, as well as a strong social predilection toward adopting new IT, Norway, Denmark, and Sweden have witnessed a dramatic drop in cash usage while not seeing the same sharp rise in cash holdings as in most other advanced countries. Sweden is particularly far along in the process.

Several factors have played a part. Like many governments in Europe, Sweden has cracked down on evasion of value-added taxes. Rather than hold a lottery as Portugal did, the Swedish government has required certified cash registers with a special control unit (black box) attached to the register. The black box downloads all sales, and the data can be read directly (only) by the Swedish tax agency.[11] At the same time, many Swedish bank branches no longer have cash or ATMs. This development was partly in response to strong demands for safety from the bank tellers' union, after a series of violent bank robberies. At the same time, payments technologies have advanced, for example, P2P real-time payments systems.

One important step the government has taken was phasing out the largest note in circulation;[12] the 1,000-krona note (about $115) became invalid at the end of 2013. The combined effect of this broad range of changes has been remarkable, and the demand for notes and coins has fallen from 106 billion kronor in 2009 (yearly average) to 77 billion in 2015, as figure 7.1 illustrates.

(Continued)

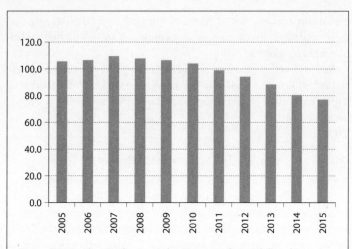

Figure 7.1: Sweden: Banknotes and coins in circulation (billion kronor). Source: Swedish Riksbank (data are averages for year).

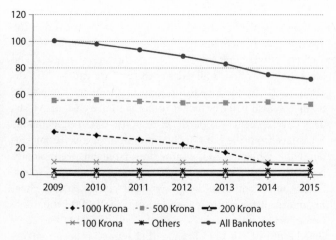

Figure 7.2: Declining total demand for large notes in Sweden (value in billion kronor). Source: Swedish Riksbank.

Interestingly, nearly all the drop in Swedish currency demand so far has come from the phaseout of the 1,000-krona note, as can be seen in figure 7.2. Demand for 500-krona notes has also fallen slightly over the same period.

The Swedes have been forced to address many issues along the way. For example, many churches have installed card-reading machines, so donations can be made by card instead of by cash. The government has given homeless people devices for accepting cash payments from cards also. Although the Riksbank is still printing paper currency, there are some who predict that Sweden will be effectively cashless by 2030. Cash use is still significant, accounting for about 20% of the number of transactions, though by value the number is far lower, perhaps 5–7%.[13]

It will certainly be ironic if Sweden, the first country in Europe to issue a paper currency connected to the government (see the discussion of Johan Palmstruch in chapter 2), became the first country to get rid it.

Denmark has also made major progress toward moving away from cash. Of the country's 5 million citizens, 2.8 million have Mobile Pay, an app that allows one to make payments at a store or to another person. In contrast to earlier implementations of a similar idea, the Danish mobile payments system does not require participants to have accounts at the same financial institution, making it far more universally acceptable. Indeed, the Danish government has spoken about eliminating the need for cash registers. The Danish government has long made transfer payments electronically through free basic debit card accounts, effectively solving the problem of how to achieve financial inclusion for the unbanked.

The Swedish and Danish experiences cannot necessarily be generalized to a large heterogeneous country like the United States. Nevertheless, they show that, at a practical level, a transition of the sort discussed in this chapter is a very real possibility.

EMERGENCIES AND SECURITY

Emergencies

Certainly, a lot of the angst over electronic currency comes from deeply rooted fears of digital theft and paralysis after a major power outage. Although these fears are understandable, let's try to analyze them rationally. First, most people don't hold enough cash to provide a significant level of diversification against cybercrime. Per chapter 4, the average person in the United States is carrying around only $50 or $60, possibly with another couple hundred in the house or car. Even for the beleaguered middle class, cash holdings are only a small fraction of total wealth. Most people have far more in their bank accounts, pension funds, or other digital assets; if they are really worried about cybercrime, these should be the big concern. And, of course, physical cash itself is vulnerable to theft.

Power outages are a serious issue, and one of the more compelling reasons for allowing small notes and change to continue to circulate long after large notes have been withdrawn. Nevertheless, the average person does not carry large cash balances, and ATMs may not work during a power outage. The fact that you *could* have cash doesn't mean you *will* have cash. Indeed, arguably, the most important disaster preparedness today is a smartphone, and it will only become more so as payment systems migrate to mobile telephony. As already noted, smartphone apps for P2P payments continue to proliferate. One of the major lessons from Hurricane Katrina in 2005 was to push cell phone towers to have backup generators or batteries. As a result, when Hurricane Sandy hit the East Coast in 2012, most people retained at least spotty cell phone access. Supermarkets and pharmacies also typically have backup power and should be able to process payments. As cell phone apps grow, they will surely replace cash as the major transaction medium in power outages. Cell phones run out of power, of course, but it is far more cost effective for most people to have a couple inexpensive battery chargers around, or to charge their cell phone in their car, than to hide $500 around the house.

Disaster relief planning websites also note that checks can be used in a disaster, assuming checks are still around in 20 years. In a sufficiently prolonged emergency when there is no longer any way to recharge cell phones and supplies of small bills are depleted, the government can air-drop currency for temporary use, redeemable for electronic currency after the crisis. Paper currency adds little to the mix if there are large-denomination coins and smartphones, and even today, cash arguably ranks much lower than many other emergency preparedness items.

Security

Many people pay cash for small purchases not so much because of convenience but to try to control their exposure to credit card theft. The odds of having your data ripped off on a small purchase are arguably pretty much the same as on a large purchase. This is, however, an especially American phenomenon, because the United States has been slow to adopt more secure payment systems, though this is at last changing. For example, the embedded chip-and-PIN technology that is common in Europe is a superior technology that makes the most common thefts today much more difficult. The United States has been slow to adopt the superior chip-and-PIN technology in part because retailers have lobbied not to be forced to upgrade their systems, but fortunately, it is gradually happening anyway.

Some might wonder about people who simply cannot remember their PINs, but these kinds of problems have already been addressed in Europe. One low-tech approach that has been applied, for example in Denmark, is to give people the option of getting an additional prepaid card that does not require a PIN and can be reloaded periodically at the bank. If lost, the money on the prepaid card will be lost (just like cash being stolen), but nothing more. A similar approach should work for people who like to put a fixed amount of cash in their wallet as a means of keeping track of their expenditures for the week.

Biometric identification methods, including fingerprint, voice, and retina are possible, and have already become prominent in digital banking and government transfers in India, where over a billion people are now registered. Credit card companies already make use of neural networks to detect payment fraud. (A purchase coming from Russia for a designer handbag being shipped to the French Riviera might be regarded as suspect for a cardholder who lives in Boston.) Security is constantly evolving. Some Federal Reserve officials have talked about using a variant of the blockchain methodology pioneered by the cryptocurrency Bitcoin to create payment platforms that have built-in security due to its distributed public ledger verification process. We consider this technology in chapter 14.

There are certainly going to be other special cases where cash is still needed. An interesting example is the recent experience of marijuana shops in Colorado after the state legalized the drug in 2014. Two years on, some shops are still finding themselves with only limited access to the local banking system, because even though marijuana has become legal at the state level, it remains illegal at the federal level. And any bank under federal supervision is proscribed from doing business with an entity that is breaking federal law; Visa and MasterCard would not process payments for pot dispensaries for similar reasons. Hence the Federal Reserve has found itself having to send large cash shipments to help the shops operate.[14]

The list of possible problems that might arise in an electronic currency world is certainly daunting. Most of us have washed cash in the laundry; it generally comes out little worse for wear. (Given the germs that cash carries, who knows, maybe it is even good to literally launder it sometimes.) A smartphone or high-tech credit card might not survive so well. Again, though, this is a silly objection. Over the time frame of implementation, the technology will become cheaper and more durable. Probably you will be able to use any one of several vehicles to access your debit account. And fortunately— just as for such questions as "what if I drop my smartphone in the bathtub?" or "what if I accidentally put my smartphone in the washing machine?"—we can be reasonably sure that over the next 20 years, as people's dependence on smartphones and similar devices continues to grow, more robust technologies will be developed.

A simple but important point is that, ironically, the end objective of many cybertheft schemes often involves cash, typically withdrawn from an ATM.[15] This is sometimes how criminals ultimately remove the funds they have transferred to bank accounts they control, possibly withdrawing currency via a network of people to avoid being conspicuous.

Because the technology is evolving so rapidly, I am hesitant to go into much more detail, beyond saying that phasing out paper currency does not really move the needle much on society's vulnerability to cybercrime. Some of the present-day obstacles to improving security are really more political than economic. Some innovations in security, such as the potentially disruptive distributed-ledger technology embodied in cryptocurrencies like Bitcoin or Ethereum, may eventually lead to major improvements in financial security, at least at the core of the payment system, as discussed further in chapter 14.

It is particularly hard to see in any of these arguments why large-denomination notes are important. Probably they would be looked on askance after a power outage, earthquake, or other kind of catastrophe. I won't deny there are going to be residual issues that simply take time to sort out. Again, all these problems are good reasons to go slow and to leave some rump part of the paper currency system around for an extended period.

In any case, in a severe enough catastrophe, even cash might be difficult to use, leaving only barter. When I worked as a young economist at the Board of Governors of the Federal Reserve in the early 1980s, I remember being bemused one day when a few select top officials and governors participated in a mock nuclear attack evacuation. I believe the helicopters were whisking away the Fed's officials to deep caves in West Virginia, where, in principle, they could continue to keep the nation's currency system operating. Honestly, it was straight out of *Dr. Strangelove*. We lowly peons were supposed to follow the instructions in the back of our phone books, which, as I recall, said something along the lines of "hide under your desk and avert your eyes from flashes of bright light." With all due respect, in such a catastrophe, I sincerely doubt knowing that the head of the Federal Reserve is safe in a cave in

West Virginia will make me feel better about having the $60 in my pocket, even if my desk protected me. This example may sound absurd, but certainly the possibility of having to deal with calamities and disasters is absolutely an important consideration, and another reason why cash needs to be phased out gradually.

Adjusting Regulations

Before cash is fully phased out, it will be important to reduce regulations in many areas that are not intended to be enforced strictly and that stay on the books only because cash allows them to be obeyed in the breach. For example, paying babysitters legally in Paris is much simpler and easier than in New York City, where reporting requirements are considerably more onerous. And while certainly part of the idea is to be able to tax individuals and businesses more equitably and fairly, making it more difficult to use cash might require lightening tax rates on small businesses, which are likely to bear the major brunt of a shift in regime.

CONCLUSION TO PART I

Paper currency has always facilitated tax evasion and crime; this phenomenon is hardly new. Over the years, however, the constant evolution of new transaction technologies has whittled down the role of cash in the legal economy until it remains important for small transactions but has become increasingly vestigial in medium-sized and large transactions. This point is brought into sharp relief by the ever rising and ever more dominant share of large-denomination notes in the currency supply of advanced countries. The $100 bill and the 500-euro note, for example, are relatively unimportant in everyday retail transactions. Yet they dwarf small bills in their share of currency supplies in the United States and Europe. The evidence was already overwhelming two decades ago, when I first began to argue that retaining large-denomination notes was penny-wise and pound-foolish; the likely benefits from marginally increased tax receipts and marginal reductions in crime almost certainly outweigh the lost seigniorage revenues from printing paper currency. This case appears to be even stronger today.

New technologies have now made even small-denomination notes increasingly less essential than they once were, a fact that is underscored by the progress that some countries (notably Sweden and Denmark) have already made toward reducing the use of cash. The change does not necessarily have to be wholesale; it seems likely that most of the benefits from phasing out paper currency can be achieved by slowly eliminating all but the smallest notes (say, up to $5 or possibly $10), and possibly in the end replacing even these with coins that while practical at a small scale, would be quite burdensome to store and transport in large numbers. This transition would address both the crime and tax evasion issues and would significantly raise the costs of hoarding that might otherwise undermine a shift to negative interest rates, as discussed in the next part of the book. If mass-scale hoarding of small notes or coins still proves to be a problem, it can easily be dealt with by putting restrictions on the maximum size of cash payments (as is already the case in much of Europe), and by introducing charges for very large deposits (or groups of deposits) of small bills, something banks would likely need to do anyway to offset costs. This kind of prohibition would discourage large-scale use of cash in crime as well as in hoarding. Of course, once the full transition to substantial-sized coins is made, large-scale cash transactions and hoarding should be expensive enough to make both nonissues.

By making the transition at a slow and deliberate pace, it should be possible to address various issues as they come up, much as the Swedes and Danes appear to be doing successfully. Technological limitations, such as how to make P2P payments electronically and how to achieve real-time clearing, are melting away with advances in telephony.

All in all, the case for going to a less-cash society if not quite yet a cashless society seems pretty compelling, with most of the various and sundry objections being easily handled, given enough lead time. Facilitating negative interest rate policy is not the main reason for phasing out paper currency, especially large-denomination notes. But it is an important collateral benefit that we turn to in part II.

Negative Interest Rates

CHAPTER 8

The Cost of the Zero Bound Constraint

Central bankers trapped in today's zero bound environment must feel like they are living in an alternative reality, an episode from the *Twilight Zone*. Back in the 1970s and 1980s, when many of today's top financial policymakers were cutting their teeth, inflation had soared into double digits, peaking at over 13% in the United States, and over 20% in Japan and the United Kingdom. Nothing policymakers tried seemed to defeat the scourge of inflation. Finally, Paul Volcker arrived as chair at the Federal Reserve determined to wring inflation out of the system, ultimately taking the federal funds rate (the central bank's policy rate) to 20% in mid-1981. Volcker's tightening policies ultimately worked wonders in taming inflation expectations. But it took a few years, and in the short run, severe monetary tightening hit the economy like a ton of bricks, leading to a recession and tremendous political pushback. Carpenters and builders mailed in two-by-fours to protest they had nothing else to do with their lumber. Car dealers sent coffins to the Fed filled with the keys of unsold vehicles. Farmers blockaded the Fed's front entrance with tractors. Having just arrived from graduate school as a young economist at the Fed, I watched the Volcker disinflation unfold with amazement.

The same dynamic played out over time throughout the world. British Prime Minister Margaret Thatcher confronted inflation in much the same way as did Volcker (the Bank of England did not gain operational independence until 1997). Inflation fell from 20% in 1980 to 5% in 1983. The high inflation of this era, more than anything else, provided the impetus for the single currency in Europe, the euro. The Latin countries, including France, Spain, Portugal, and Italy, were having great trouble conquering inflation on their own, and eventually decided that anchoring to the super-solid German deutsche mark was the only way out. Yes, there were other reasons to create the euro, but stabilizing prices was by far the most persuasive argument for ordinary people. Controlling inflation went from a secondary consideration in many countries to the overarching target of monetary policy. Indeed, the European Central Bank (ECB) has inflation control emblazoned in its mandate; output stabilization does not formally appear.

Be careful what you wish for, you just might get it. Here we are today at ultra-low inflation and near-zero interest rates, where the challenge for central bankers has morphed from convincing people that they will never inflate to convincing them that they are not "inflation nutters" (former Bank of England head Mervyn King's phrase). Truly, if you had told anyone 35 years ago that central banks would be facing this problem, they would have thought you were crazy. And even if you managed to convince them it was true, they probably would have viewed the situation as an unqualified success. In central banking parlance, the equivalent of "You can never be too rich or too thin" (attributed to the Duchess of Windsor) has long been "You can never have trend growth too high or inflation too low."

So what happened? How did policy interest rates collapse to zero? Certainly a part of the problem is that inflation-targeting evangelism—and there is really no other word for it—created institutions that were simply too inflexible to deal with the dramatic changes the world has experienced over the past 20 years. Inflation *can* be too low, and inflexible inflation-targeting regimes are not too good at dealing with it, especially as interest rates drift toward the zero lower bound, also known as the "liquidity trap."

The zero bound has become a stubbornly persistent problem for essentially three reasons. First and foremost, inflation has collapsed and inflation expectations along with it. Starting with New Zealand in 1989, most advanced-country central banks have gradually coalesced around an inflation target of about 2%, which in itself implies dramatically lower interest rates than when inflation averages 10%. To help make this part of the book self-contained, let us review a bit of terminology that will be used recurrently. The *nominal* interest rate is the actual interest rate, for example, the one-month Treasury bill rate that the government pays to borrow from private markets. Another important nominal rate is the over-night interest rate on interbank loans that most central banks treat as their core policy interest rate. (This is the one you read about in a news story that says "The Federal Reserve raised/lowered rates today.") The *real* interest rate is a theoretical construct that is formed by taking the nominal interest rate and subtracting off the expected (future) rate of inflation over the time period of the loan, something economists can approximate but cannot observe or measure exactly.[1]

In the normal course of things, most economic theory and prac-tice suggests that when inflation expectations fall by 1%, then, after an adjustment period, all interest rates across the spectrum also fall by 1%. The logic is that what everyone cares about is what you can buy with money, not its face value, and to the ex-tent higher inflation is perfectly anticipated, everyone will adjust (nominal) interest rates, wages, and prices accordingly. So when inflation is only 2% instead of, say, 6%, there is much less padding when central banks are looking to cut interest rates. This, by the way, is the basic idea behind proposals to raise central bank infla-tion targets from 2% to 4%, which we shall take up in chapter 9.

The second reason the zero bound has reemerged is that eco-nomic volatility has turned out to be much greater than most econ-omists had imagined, with the aftermath of the financial crisis of 2008 producing the deepest and most protracted recession since the Great Depression of the 1930s. The greater economic volatility, the more likely it is that economies will be facing severe downturns requiring drastic central bank interest rate cuts, and therefore the more likely it is that the zero bound limit will bite.

The third reason the zero bound has been so problematic is that real interest rates have trended down dramatically, falling below zero at very short horizons, and roughly 1.5% at very long horizons, both well below more "normal" levels. The reasons real interest rates have fallen are many, but some of the main factors in-clude high savings from fast-growing emerging markets and aging populations in advanced economies, factors that in 2005 Ben

Bernanke famously pointed to in describing the "global savings glut."[2] Since 2008, intense post–financial crisis regulation and risk aversion have also pushed real interest rates down.[3] Another important factor is slower growth. Some economists, such as Northwestern University's Robert J. Gordon, argue that the root cause of post–financial crisis slow global growth is a sharp trend drop in the rate at which productivity is increasing, due above all to a declining rate of economically valuable inventions. Others, led by my colleague Lawrence Summers, argue that there has been a secular decline in global aggregate demand. Personally, I think it is hard to reach any definitive conclusion on where long-run growth is headed, especially since slow growth periods almost invariably follow deep systemic financial crises (as documented in my 2009 book with Carmen Reinhart).[4] Even if real interest rates eventually do rise a couple of percentage points to more normal levels, it is now clear that they can sometimes be very low or even negative for sustained periods. Indeed, it is sobering to realize that Japan's financial crisis began back in the early 1990s, and yet the country is still struggling with the zero bound two decades later.

Exactly how bad is it for an economy to have monetary policy constrained by the zero bound on policy interest rates? It is hard to know; the range of experience has been too short and too limited. The issue first came to the forefront of debate during the Great Depression. Allowing for technical differences in money markets at the time, policy rates hit the moral equivalent of zero in the early 1930s and stayed there throughout the Depression and into World War II. The zero bound became an issue again in Japan in the 1990s, and it certainly influenced US policy after the bursting of the late 1990s tech bubble, with the Fed eventually stopping cuts after its policy interest rate hit 1% in 2001. And it has now again become an issue around the world since 2008. How much of the weak post-crisis global growth has been due to the constraint of the zero bound, and how much due to other factors, such as a sclerotic banking sector, the collapse of government spending on infrastructure, post–financial crisis rebalancing, the tapering off of the China growth supercycle, and the like? No one really knows. (This ignorance does not seem to discourage some economic policy commentators from giving unqualified advice.) The empirical debate will take decades to settle, if past economic debates are any guide.

The issue we shall take up in this chapter is to try to assess exactly how serious the zero bound constraint is quantitatively. First and foremost, normal monetary policy becomes ineffective at fighting recessions. A few studies have suggested that at the peak of the financial crisis, given dire inflation and output forecasts, normal central bank reaction functions would have taken interest rates all the way down to –4% or –5% in the United States, had that been feasible. In Europe and the United Kingdom, interest rates would also have gone negative, if perhaps less so. Indeed, by now, some central banks have tiptoed into negative rate territory, including those of Sweden, Switzerland, Denmark, the Eurozone, and Japan. But so far, they have been reluctant to cut rates much below negative 75 basis points (–0.75%) for fear of setting off a run from government debt into paper currency that would both limit the effectiveness of monetary policy and potentially entail huge logistical and security problems. Besides, there has been a lot of pushback from some quarters, with Japanese central bankers getting grief even for setting interest rates at a barely negative level of –0.1%. So far, though, it is pretty tame compared to what Paul Volcker faced.

Some have argued that the zero bound hasn't really turned out to be all that important, because central banks have found pretty good ways to get around it, using unconventional tools such as "forward guidance" and "quantitative easing." The first involves telling investors that the monetary authorities intend to elevate inflation in the future, even if they cannot do it now. When it works, forward guidance succeeds in bringing down the real interest rate, even if the nominal interest rate is stuck at zero, since of course the real interest rate is the nominal interest rate minus the expected rate of inflation. A second idea is quantitative easing (QE). We discuss QE in much greater detail later in this chapter, but essentially it involves using short-term central bank debt to buy long-term assets, such as government debt, thereby bringing long-term government interest rates down. The hope is that other long-term interest rates (e.g., on mortgages and corporate debt) will follow, because interest rates on government debt tend to be a benchmark by which all other rates are set.

A few empirical papers argue that these unorthodox central bank policies have accomplished more than meets the eye.[5] Nevertheless, the stunning challenges that the Bank of Japan and the ECB have faced in lifting inflationary expectations suggest that unconventional policies are vastly less effective than plain vanilla interest rate policy might have been, if unfettered negative rate policy were fully possible—that is, if all the institutional, legal, and other barriers were cleared away, as we discuss in chapters 10 and 11. Even at the Federal Reserve, which has produced many of the chirpier appraisals of unconventional monetary instruments, nobody really wants to have to rely on them again, not least because they involve risks that are difficult to measure or understand.

If the zero bound led only to uncertainty about the effects of monetary policy, it would be bad enough, but it has clouded the entire debate on macroeconomic stabilization policy. Indeed, there is a growth industry based on studying how the zero bound affects other policies, such as government spending, government deficits, structural reform, and the international transmission of macroeconomic policies. Just as the normal laws of physics seem to be upended when an object approaches a black hole (or, to be more precise, the normal laws imply weird consequences), the laws of economics seem to be upended when a recession-stricken economy hits (or at least approaches) the zero bound. For example, some have argued that by running a larger deficit, a government can generate so much growth that a country's ratio of debt to GDP actually comes down.[6]

Another line of thought is that certain kinds of structural reform are potentially counterproductive at the zero bound, lowering growth in the short run.[7] In particular, if higher future productivity translates into expectations of lower future prices, the result is lower inflation expectations and therefore a higher real interest rate, assuming the monetary authority is paralyzed by the liquidity trap and unable to respond. In theory at least, this real interest rate channel can be so intense that it drives down today's demand

and output, even though in the long run higher future productivity growth is beneficial, and even though under ordinary circumstances consumers might feel richer immediately, thereby pushing demand up. By similar logic, structural reforms to increase price flexibility, which is normally associated with increased economic efficiency, can be problematic if the immediate impact is to lower inflation expectations.[8] True, many of these results are far better viewed as cautionary counterexamples rather than central scenarios, but even so, they illustrate the cloud that the zero bound casts over many policy decisions apparently unrelated to monetary policy.

Again, we just don't know how important all of this is empirically, because too many factors are in play and too few cases exist to really sort everything out. For example, after the financial crisis of 2008, there were many dire (and thoroughly unequivocal) warnings that the United Kingdom's gradual fiscal tightening (from an initial position of having the largest deficit among the major advanced economies) would lead to a depression. These proved overly simplistic and naive. Still, given only limited empirical evidence and a strong theoretical presumption that the zero bound can have substantial quantitative effects for output and employment in deep recessions, few economists are prepared to say that it is something no one should worry about. It matters not whether you think government should be bigger or smaller or that structural reforms are good or bad.

Various ideas for mitigating the zero bound are taken up in this chapter and in chapter 9, but there are really only two serious approaches to taking it off the table. First, central banks can significantly raise their target inflation rates, so that the average level of interest rates is higher. This would leave more room to cut rates in a recession. Second, countries can engage in institutional and legal reforms that—in conjunction with phasing out paper currency (or adopting one of the other approaches considered in chapter 10)—simply obliterate the zero bound.

Raising target inflation rates has merit but also problems. First and foremost, the transition problem is formidable. Central banks have been saying for years that they deeply believe in targeting 2% inflation. To suddenly shift to 4% inflation targets would almost certainly roil international financial markets in ways that could potentially be quite destabilizing. If the announcement is ill timed, it could even lead to another global financial crisis. In addition to impinging on tens of trillions of dollars in long-term bonds and other contracts that were written predicated on the central bank's promise of 2% target inflation, a dramatic shift in central bank policy would undermine assumptions about the incentives and behavior of central banks that lie at the core of global financial stability in today's world. The famous "taper tantrum" of May 2014 (when Fed chair Ben Bernanke merely hinted at eventual monetary tightening) could seem like a walk in the park by comparison. It is easy to imagine that the transition from a 2% inflation target to a 4% target could easily take 5–10 years. Moreover, as we shall see, it is not completely obvious that life would be better overall, because higher inflation has drawbacks.

It is fairly clear how having a higher general level of inflation would work; we have been there before all too recently. How exactly might taking short-term policy interest rates well below zero help the economy during a deep recession or bout of disinflation? In theory, negative rate policy works pretty much the same way interest rate cuts work when rates are at positive levels. With a lower cost of borrowing, firms will invest more and consumers will spend more, particularly on consumer durables, such as refrigerators and autos. Lower interest rates also push up the price of assets from housing to stocks to fine art, making people feel wealthier and more inclined to spend. Last but not least, lower interest rates tend to weaken the exchange rate (loosely speaking, because it makes holding bonds in domestic currency less attractive). A weaker exchange rate helps stimulate demand abroad for a country's exports, while simultaneously shifting home demand away from imports toward competing home-produced goods. For example, more tourists come to the United States when the dollar is cheap, and more Americans vacation at home when traveling abroad has become more expensive. In principle, higher demand will eventually drive up wage and price inflation.

Admittedly, the above discussion sweeps a lot of subtle and important issues under the rug. My description of how monetary stimulus affects inflation is consistent with standard New

Keynesian dogma. Lower interest rates raise aggregate demand, thereby bidding up prices. But this discussion is also consistent with a "monetarist" interpretation of the transmission mechanism, in which negative rates on currency induce people to economize on their holdings of cash. As they draw down their cash, higher spending drives up demand and prices. We don't need to get into the subtleties of differences across the channels, and they are not mutually exclusive; through the lens of either interpretation, negative rates will put upward pressure on inflation.

The idea that negative rate policy is just "central banking business as usual" relies on the assumption that cutting interest rates in negative territory (e.g., from −1.0% to −1.5%) works pretty much the same way as interest rate cuts in positive territory does (e.g., from 1.5% to 1.0%). In theory, anyway, the assumption that the two cases are quite similar holds up in most standard macroeconomic models (e.g., a canonical New Keynesian model, where the main frictions derive from slow adjustment of nominal wages, prices, or both). From a practical perspective, the symmetry of the two cases requires that all institutional, tax, and legal changes have been made to clear the way for negative rates. This can be done easily enough, as discussed in chapters 10 and 11.

Another assumption for symmetry is that negative rates do not raise entirely new financial stability concerns. Most concerns that have been voiced about negative rates causing financial instability are much the same as one hears about why a long period of low or zero rates is problematic, and the answers are similar. I shall argue that, in some cases, being able to resort to significantly negative rates can help raise inflationary expectations and lead to a much shorter period of low rates than if negative rates were not feasible.

Let us begin by looking at historical experience with the zero bound and go on to examine ways that central banks have tried to mitigate the problem until now, short of open-ended negative interest rates. Chapter 9 considers ideas that have not really been tried yet, such as raising the inflation target. We explore negative interest rate policy in earnest in chapters 10–12, including ways to achieve negative rates other than phasing out cash as well as how to mitigate various downside risks and concerns people have voiced.

HISTORICAL EXPERIENCES WITH THE ZERO BOUND

Except for Japan in the 1990s, the zero bound had not previously surfaced since the Great Depression. Figure 8.1 shows policy interest rates for the United Kingdom going back to 1930. During the Great Depression, the United Kingdom stopped cutting rates at 2%, partly out of fear that lower rates would wreak havoc in London financial markets with investors fleeing bonds, and partly because banks were already so awash in liquidity that private money market rates had sunk below 1%.[9] The effect of being stuck at 2%, which the Bank of England policy rate reached in 1932 and remained at (except for a brief interlude) for two decades, is in many ways parallel to being stuck at zero; at either value, monetary policy is paralyzed.

In the United States, the discount rate charged by the New York Federal Reserve never dropped below 1%, as illustrated in figure 8.2. (In the 1930s, the different regional Federal Reserve banks set different discount rates, with the New York Fed's generally being the lowest.)

As in the United Kingdom, excess bank reserves were so high and market rates were so far below the discount rate that banks

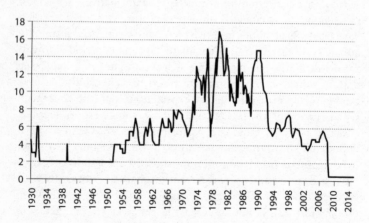

Figure 8.1: UK policy rate, 1930–present. Source: Bank of England, Historic Rates (available at www.bankofengland.co.uk).

rarely turned to the Fed for funds anyway. Figure 8.3 shows short-term market interest rates in both countries.

Thus both UK and US monetary policies were effectively paralyzed by the zero bound during the Great Depression.

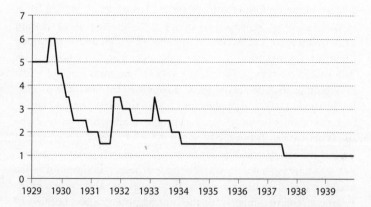

Figure 8.2: New York Federal Reserve discount rate, 1929–1939. Source: St. Louis Federal Reserve, Banking and Monetary Statistics, 1914–1941, pp. 441–442; and Federal Reserve Economic Data.

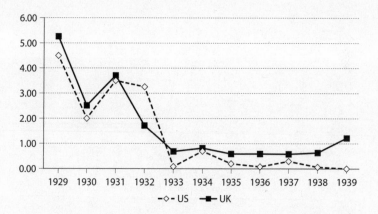

Figure 8.3: US and UK market rates, 1929–1939. Source: Reinhart, Reinhart, and Rogoff (2011).

The zero bound has reared its ugly head globally in full force since the financial crisis of 2008. Figure 8.4 shows the path of nominal policy interest rates for the United States, the Eurozone, and the United Kingdom since 2000. As one can see, the ECB's policy rate (the short-term main refinancing or "refi" rate) reached 1% by May 2009, 0.25% by May 2013, and, as of March 2016, zero. The United States cut its policy rate (the federal funds rate) to between zero and 0.25% by the end of 2008, and it remained there for 7 years until the first slight uptick in December 2015. The UK policy rate (the Bank of England base rate) reached 0.5% in March 2009, and stayed there through 2015; the Bank of England halted at 0.5% instead of zero for technical reasons, including fear that banks were still undercapitalized after the financial crisis. Whether the difference between 0.5 and zero is consequential from a monetary policy point of view is a matter of some debate, but it is not essential to our discussion here.[10] It should also be noted that each country's central bank uses a slightly different instrument (or instruments) for their target policy rate(s) because of institutional differences in their banking systems. For example, the ECB has a separate rate for its deposit facility (for bank overnight deposits at the central bank) and, as of March 2016, this rate was –0.4%, below the refi rate of 0.0%.

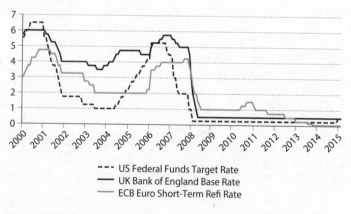

Figure 8.4: 2000–2015 Policy interest rates for the Federal Reserve, European Central Bank, and the Bank of England. Source: Federal Reserve Board, European Central Bank, and Bank of England.

Japan's policy interest rate has been hovering around the zero bound for two decades and was lowered to –0.1% in January 2016. It is not just the large-country central banks: Canada, Norway, and Israel have all been scraping near the zero bound since 2009, as have Sweden, Switzerland, and Denmark, who have all dipped slightly into negative territory (as of February 2016, the Swiss and Danish central banks had set policy rates of –0.75%, while Sweden's repo rate has reached –0.5%).

Academics may be debating the quantitative significance of the zero bound; central bankers are not. The policy world is hugely uneasy about the difficulties central banks have had in lifting rates off the zero bound once it has been reached. Moreover, there are concerns that even once liftoff has been achieved, the risks of recidivism are high. In addition, a big debate rages in the policy community over tentative early efforts at using negative rate policy, though as noted earlier, the fact that the current wave of cuts is sharply circumscribed dulls the effectiveness of this policy. Equally important, as discussed in chapters 10 and 11, other institutional changes may be necessary to make negative rate policy fully effective, and these changes may take time to implement.

Perhaps the most sobering thought is the realization that at some point (perhaps before the ink on this book is dry), another recession will inevitably occur. Then, in the normal course of things, central banks will want to sharply cut rates to stabilize the economy and cushion the rise in unemployment. However, with policy rates in the Eurozone and Japan likely to remain constrained by the zero bound for a considerable period yet, and with US and UK policy rates only barely higher, there just isn't going to be a lot of room for interest rate cuts unless a way is found to make negative rate policy more effective.

Table 8.1 shows the cuts that central banks have made during the recessions that began in 2001 and 2008. Note in particular that the Federal Reserve cut interest rates 5% during the financial crisis of 2008, and 4.75% after the bursting of the tech bubble in 2000. Yet, on current projections, there is no guarantee that the Fed will have interest rates even back to 3% before the next recession. Not every central bank is as aggressive as the Fed, but even so, the ECB cut by 3.25% in the initial year of the 2008 financial

Table 8.1: Central bank discount rate cuts in response to two crises

Central bank	Discount rate cut (peak to trough) (%)	Period of cuts
After the Financial Crisis of 2008		
United Kingdom	−5.25	December 2007–March 2009
United States	−5.0	August 2007–December 2008
Sweden	−4.5	September 2008–July 2009
Norway	−4.5	August 2008–May 2009
Australia	−4.25	August 2008–April 2009
Canada	−4.0	December 2007–April 2009
Eurozone	−3.25	September 2008–May 2009
	−4	Through 2015
Singapore	−3.55	August 2008–January 2009
Switzerland	−2.375[a]	September 2008–March 2009
	−3.375	Through 2015
During the Recession of 2001 after the Tech Bubble Collapse		
United States	−4.75	December 2000–October 2002
Canada	−3.75	December 2000–March 2002
Switzerland	−2.75	February 2001–February 2003
United Kingdom	−2.0	March 2000–January 2003
Australia	−2.0	January 2001–April 2002
Eurozone	−1.5	April 2001–November 2002
Sweden	−0.5	August 2001–February 2002

[a]The rate hit 0.25. Source: Central bank data.

crisis and by 1.5% in 2001. On the current trajectory, it is hard to see where room for interest rate cuts of that magnitude will come from. What then is the plan? This lack of room for maneuver is why central banks are looking so hard for new ideas. Yes, they can go back to some of the same tricks they tried in 2008—quantitative easing and forward guidance, as considered in some detail later in this chapter. But most central bankers are rightly skeptical that these alternative approaches are anywhere near as potent as interest rate cuts.

BRIEF TOUR OF THE LITERATURE ON QUANTITATIVE IMPLICATIONS OF THE ZERO BOUND

Modern work on the zero bound has its genesis in research done at the Federal Reserve Board in the first half the 1990s, work that is often overlooked.[11] Fed economists anticipated many of the issues that would later become central to the debate, including quantitative easing, the role of fiscal policy, and the idea that an inflation target of 4% instead of 2% might substantially alleviate the problem.[12] In 1998, Paul Krugman very elegantly showed a simple way to model the zero bound in a textbook New Keynesian model. More importantly, he advanced the idea that after years of successful inflation fighting, the new credibility problem for central banks was convincing the public they were prepared to occasionally surrender to higher inflation when the situation warranted.[13] The issue of credibility is always important in monetary policy, but it is especially fundamental to tackling the zero bound. The basic point is that even if the monetary authorities cannot lower the *nominal* interest rate below zero, they can still lower the *real* interest rate if they can convince the public that they can and will inflate in the future, perhaps even promising to let inflation rise above target after the economy has normalized. That monetary policy can operate in this way has been well understood since the early 1980s and indeed was the topic of one of my first published papers out of graduate school.[14] Krugman's important insight was that monetary authorities had done such a good job convincing everyone that they would never allow inflation to rise too much above target that they had lost the ability to promise a bit of higher inflation tomorrow even if a credible promise would be enormously helpful today.

As the financial crisis of 2008 unfolded, several widely cited papers by Federal Reserve System economists argued that the costs of the ensuing recession might have been considerably ameliorated if negative interest rates had been possible. John Williams, who later became president of the San Francisco Federal Reserve, found that if the zero bound had not been in the way, then another 400 basis points (4%) of cuts to the federal funds rate would have been extremely helpful.[15] He estimated that this would have bolstered the US economy by $1.8 trillion over 4 years. Another senior Federal Reserve economist, David Reifschneider, found that optimal monetary policy would have involved going to −500 basis points (−5%).[16] Analyses based on standard monetary policy rules suggest that both the United Kingdom and the Eurozone might have chosen interest rates of –2% to –3% had the option been on the table. As already noted, such estimates have to be regarded as rough guesses.

In addressing welfare issues quantitatively, it is essential to think not just about how wonderful it might have been to have had the option of negative policy rates in the financial crisis, but also about how valuable this option is likely to be in the future. Is the zero bound a freak occurrence that only happens after systemic financial crises, which in turn don't seem to happen very often in advanced countries? The financial crisis of 2008 came seven decades after the Great Depression ended with World War II. If the next financial crisis is not going to be for seven more decades, why go to the trouble of making fundamental changes to the financial structure now, when everything will almost certainly have morphed substantially by then anyway?

Back in 2000, Federal Reserve economists tried to tackle exactly this question, admittedly using data from a period when the odds of hitting the zero bound seemed remote. Using model simulations, they came to the conclusion that the risks were pretty small. Zero bound episodes were likely to be infrequent and, even when they did occur, short-lived and relatively mild in the sense that zero would not be too far above the optimal rate, which is negative but not feasible.[17] Therefore, even if the zero bound was going to bite occasionally, it was not a problem worth turning our monetary institutions upside down over. Obviously, with the experience of the financial crisis of 2008 behind us, and most major central banks stuck for years at the moral equivalent of the zero bound, these early sanguine estimates have to be reevaluated.

The results of early Fed research on the likelihood and severity of zero bound episodes have had to be revised for basically five reasons. First, many of the early models were estimated over the Great Moderation period (from the mid-1980s until the financial crisis started unfolding in 2007), when macroeconomic volatility was very low.[18] Second, the equilibrium global short-term real interest rate has dropped dramatically from the 2.0% enshrined in early versions of John Taylor's famous monetary policy rule to anywhere from –1.0% to +1.0% today. A lower real interest rate gives less of a cushion before nominal policy interest rates hit zero; a section in the appendix illustrates the Taylor rule and how the presumed equilibrium real interest rate is an important consideration in determining whether central banks might want to set policy rates at negative levels.[19] A third reason is that the models used in simulating the effects of the zero bound generally do a poor job of capturing the sluggishness that characterizes post–financial crisis growth, typically predicting a much faster snap back. A fourth reason is that the models do not adequately capture large parameter uncertainty, which creates the possibility that big unexpected shocks might be more frequent than the basic calibrations suggest. Last but not least, inflation expectations have continued to drift down, which in turn draws down the overall level of interest rates.

Even so, the rapidly evolving academic literature is far from unanimous in concluding that the zero bound is a big problem for conventional monetary policy. A few key further points in the literature are introduced in an appendix to this chapter (grouped with other appendices at the end of the book), which gives a flavor of some of the issues that need to be taken into account.

QUANTITATIVE EASING

We now turn to alternative approaches that central banks have adopted to deal with the zero bound, short of negative rates. This section deals with the policies that the monetary authorities actually used during the financial crisis, namely, quantitative easing (QE) and forward guidance. Our purpose is to ask to what extent these various alternatives obviate the need for negative interest rate policy, or at least mitigate it to a large extent.

Since the financial crisis of 2008, most advanced-country central banks, including the Federal Reserve, the ECB, the Bank of England, and the Bank of Japan, have engaged in massive and aggressive quantitative easing. The scale of the interventions has been extraordinary. The Federal Reserve's balance sheet rose from around $700 billion at the outset of the financial crisis to a peak of more than $4 trillion and roughly 25% of GDP. Though the timing was different, the ECB[20] and the Bank of England also engaged in massive QE, not quite reaching the peak scale of the Fed as a percentage of GDP, albeit the ECB is still very much in expansion mode as of this writing. And the Bank of Japan's QE program has already reached 70% of GDP, proportionately far greater than in the United States. And if it maintains its current pace, the Bank of Japan's QE program is on track to hit the 100% of GDP mark within 2 years.

Quantitative easing has been the focus of extensive recent empirical research, though subject to the major constraint that experience so far has been limited.[21] We will turn to this research shortly. In a nutshell, much of it basically constitutes event studies that look at the impact of quantitative easing announcements on market interest rates. There is almost certainly a transitory effect (even when the announcements are partly anticipated). But it is hard to know how long lasting the effects have been, basically because of the strong downward trend in long-term real interest rates after the financial crisis, a trend that seems to have its roots in many factors other than just central bank policy. My own reading of the murky evidence is that QE policies did help alleviate the recession, and arguably, central banks should have done even more, despite concerns that arose about financial stability. Many central bankers would agree. Nevertheless, even the most enthusiastic central bank adherents of quantitative easing say they have little intention of using it again once policy interest rates rise above zero and the normal tools of monetary policy are restored.[22] No one should seriously think QE is an all-purpose substitute for conventional interest rate policy.

If you have gotten this far in the book, you probably already understand why this massive "money printing" (short-term bank reserves are part of so-called high-powered money) has not led to correspondingly high inflation. When the short-term policy interest rate is already zero and is expected to remain so for an extended period, electronic bank deposits at the Fed and very short-term government bonds become extremely close substitutes; a bank can either hold a 4-week Treasury bill at zero interest or hold overnight bank deposits at zero interest that it can reliably roll over for a month. Thus, at the zero bound, when the central bank issues overnight debt (bank reserves) to buy long-term government debt, there is not necessarily any great difference from the case where the Treasury Department just issues short-term debt instead of long-term debt. After all, as noted in chapter 6 on seigniorage, the government owns the central bank—lock, stock, and barrel.

Put a different way, when Milton Friedman advanced his famous k-percent rule for growth of the monetary base (currency in circulation plus deposits held by banks and other depository institutions at the central bank), he assumed that any increase in the money base would eventually have a proportional effect on other monetary aggregates. As the banks exploited their higher reserve base to increase loans, the money injection would make its way out into the broader economy, increasing demand and putting pressure on prices that would lead in turn to proportional increases in the various price indices. If an increase in bank reserves just sits at the central bank and never goes out into the economy, there is no increase in *aggregate* demand, and the standard channel by which monetary expansion puts upward pressure on prices is shut down.

Quantitative Easing Explained

A lot of hocus pocus and confusion about the channels through which it has an impact surrounds QE. Superficially, at least, the basic idea behind this balance-sheet game is simple, bearing in mind that the government fully owns the central bank and therefore the bank's profits and losses. When the central bank executes quantitative easing to buy long-term government debt, it is basically shortening the maturity structure of government debt held by the public. That is because overnight reserves are debt of the central bank and therefore indirectly debt of the government, so QE really swaps one kind of debt for another. By reducing the supply of long-term government debt in the hands of the public, the government hopes to drive down long-term interest rates as pension funds, insurance companies, and other natural buyers of long-term debt are forced to compete for a smaller supply of long-dated government bonds.

Conversely, the supply of short-term debt in the hands of the public rises, and normally this would lead to a rise in short-term interest rates in order to induce the private sector to willingly hold the higher supply. Because long-term interest rates have a bigger impact on aggregate demand than do short-term interest rates, the net effect is still to increase aggregate demand. If policy rates are stuck at the zero bound, however, there is no countervailing rise in short-term rates, and the aggregate demand effect is even stronger. As discussed below, this is not quite the free lunch it might sound like, because when the government does too much short-term borrowing, it becomes more vulnerable to a sudden upward pressure in global interest rates.

A broader form of quantitative easing, which virtually every central bank also used during the financial crisis, involves issuing overnight bank reserves (electronic money) to buy *private* assets. Of course, this practice has a greater effect on the economy, because the government is taking private risk on to its balance sheet, an operation that clearly has a significant fiscal policy element and likely has a more significant effect. Much of the policy literature and all of the popular press also label central bank purchases of private assets as QE but it is more accurately called fiscal QE, because it is in fact a composite of two distinct operations. The first is pure QE, a swap of overnight bank reserves for long-term government debt. In the second operation, the Federal Reserve sells long-term government debt on its balance sheet and uses the proceeds to buy private debt or other assets. In financially liberalized advanced economies, the latter operation is normally the province of fiscal authorities, not a central bank acting in its narrow monetary policy capacity. Either by charter or by tradition, most advanced-country central banks are highly reluctant to get involved in operations that seem to favor particular markets. A dramatic and successful exception occurred during the Asian financial crisis of the late 1990s, when the Hong Kong Monetary Authority stunned the world by buying into its country's stock market to fend off a currency attack. Back then, it was considered an unorthodox and highly successful maneuver. For advanced economies, this kind of intervention has been the exception, not the rule, at least before the 2008 crisis. That crisis changed everything. In the political paralysis that followed, central banks were forced to shoulder added burdens.

There are good reasons for well-run modern advanced-country central banks not to routinely engage in purchasing private debt but instead to mainly buy public debt. They do not want to serve as a conduit for the government to direct credit to favored sectors without approval from the legislature. Normal interest rate policy is neutral, in the sense that it affects the entire economy without explicitly picking winners and losers among the different sectors. Certainly at the height of the financial crisis of 2008, it made a lot of sense for the Federal Reserve to intervene in key private markets, given that the entire system was freezing up. In normal times, central banks would vastly prefer that the fiscal authorities be the ones to make essentially political decisions on what sectors, if any, should receive favored credit.[23]

This discussion of QE so far has left out one potentially important nuance that must be mentioned. Just as the government owns the central bank, modern macroeconomics emphasizes that the taxpayer "owns" the government, and therefore its portfolio. That is, even though taxpayers may exert frustratingly little control over the government, it is they who ultimately gain or lose through all its financial operations. Under some admittedly extreme assumptions, basically ignoring many distortions and imperfections, quantitative easing does exactly nothing! The effect on the portfolio the private sector owns directly is offset by the effect on the government portfolio that the private sector also owns, albeit quite indirectly.[24] That is, if the government lost money by purchasing private mortgage-backed securities that went into default, it is the public that would eventually have to pay the higher taxes to cover the losses. A hyper-rational taxpayer in a frictionless world would internalize this risk and adjust her own portfolio accordingly. In the extreme limit, exchanges between public and private portfolios have no effect; when the government issues short-term debt and goes into private markets to buy long-term debt, there is no net effect, because the exchange is "all in the family." I realize that this conceptual exercise of first noting that the government owns the central bank and then that the public owns the government does make a government bond seem a little bit like a Russian nesting doll (a matryoshka).[25]

In the real world, many imperfections make government debt operations consequential, but if the starting point is neutrality, one can get very different answers than if one uses the crude Keynesian assumption of pretending that the government is an entity entirely unto itself. Among serious academic theorists (as opposed to polemicists), the relationship between debt and the risk profile of expected future taxes is an important qualifier in any analysis about the effects of QE.

Given the theoretical and empirical uncertainties surrounding the channels and effects of quantitative easing, it is hard to know whether it is welfare improving, even if it does seem to temporarily impact interest rates. After all, if the post–financial crisis economy is characterized by an acute shortage of safe long-term assets, then is reducing the supply available to the private sector necessarily welfare enhancing?[26] If QE is mainly affecting markets through signaling future central bank interest rate policy, might there be a less extravagant way to achieve this with more predictable effects? Existing theory is also murky on such basic questions as whether it is the cumulated stock of past QE or the flow of new injections of QE that matters most.

I hope this section has cleared up some of the mystery surrounding quantitative easing. If not, then "Quantitative Easing Explained" (the section title) also happens to be the title of a hilarious and truly brilliant 6-minute cartoon video produced in 2010 by real estate manager Omid Malekan that contains a lot of genuine insight, though hopefully readers of this book will also spot a few misconceptions.[27]

Empirics of Quantitative Easing

Even though the empirical evidence on QE is far from decisive, pretty much everyone agrees that the first round of US quantitative easing, at the height of the financial crisis , was very important. The Fed—operating with extraordinary creativity—plugged holes in a wide range of private markets and prevented a much deeper collapse.[28] Other central banks around the world engaged in similarly aggressive policy, albeit their scope for doing so was very much affected by pressures and constraints from governments. However, at least for the United States, there is much more skepticism about whether later rounds of QE, after things had calmed down, were also effective. These later episodes are commonly referred to as QE II and QE III.

As noted earlier, fairly incontrovertible evidence indicates that major announcements of changes to quantitative easing policies have significant short-run effects on the bond market. When on March 18, 2009, the Federal Reserve announced that it would purchase up to $300 billion of additional long-term government bonds, US 10-year bond rates dropped by 40 basis points (0.4%) within the hour. When on May 22, 2013, Federal Reserve chairman Ben Bernanke suggested that the Federal Reserve would begin to taper back its roughly $85 billion a month purchases of bonds and mortgage-backed securities, global financial markets immediately went into a tizzy in what is now known as the Taper Tantrum. In one of the most influential early academic studies, Arvind Krishnamurthy and Annette Vissing-Jorgensen found that the second round of QE conducted by the United States, which involved only purchases of government bonds, brought down long-term interest rates by roughly 50 basis points.[29] But as already noted, this kind of evidence is fundamentally an event study that is most useful for understanding immediate impact effects. It is much less informative about the long-term effects. Here the evidence is far more difficult to discern.[30]

As figure 8.5 illustrates, yields on 10-year inflation-indexed Treasury bonds rose on balance during each of the Federal Reserve's three tranches of quantitative easing and then began to fall as the purchases came to an end. They continued to fall after. Of course, this correlation is very superficial, and it is possible that there are complex lag effects, but it is also true that many other factors affected long-term yields during this period. These include uncertainties in the Eurozone and more recently in Asia, and in general a reduction in medium-term global growth expectations.

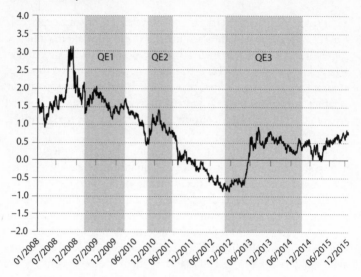

Figure 8.5: Ten-year Treasury inflation-indexed security, constant maturity.
Note: Shaded areas represent quantitative easing purchase periods. Source: Board
of Governors of the Federal Reserve (from Federal Reserve Economic Data at the St. Louis
Federal Reserve).

In light of such tectonic shifts, it is hard to rigorously sort out the
relative importance of different effects. And remember, we are only
discussing interest rates here and not the ultimate effect on the real
economy, where it is even harder to show an effect.

Quantitative Easing and Escaping from the Zero Bound Sand Trap

Despite all the theoretical and empirical uncertainties, many economists have argued that QE might have been more effective in lifting economies out of low inflation if only central banks had been
willing to use it more aggressively, and perhaps with clearer sense
of purpose, especially by forcefully expressing the willingness to
allow an inflation overshoot. One can think of the zero bound as
analogous to being caught in a sand trap in golf.[31] If you just tap

the ball, it is not going anywhere. One needs instead to (skillfully) take a full swing. Once the ball is out of the sand trap, even if in the rough, then it is possible to gain control again. If monetary policy is too aggressive at the zero bound and inflation expectations start to rise, so too will interest rates. Like the golfer back on grass, the central bank can then use normal interest rate policy to rein things in. It is indeed possible that the main problem with QE, as it has been practiced over the past few years, is precisely that central banks have been reluctant to take a full swing, doing "whatever it takes" (a phrase made famous by ECB president Mario Draghi) to restore inflation expectations.[32] The recent Japanese experience is particularly interesting in this respect, with the Bank of Japan amassing government bonds equal to more than 70% of GDP, far greater than any other central bank has tried. To date, the effects on short- and long-term inflation have been mildly disappointing. I believe that the Bank of Japan's quantitative easing policy would have been more effective had it communicated a willingness to allow inflation to overshoot targets for an extended period if necessary. This approach would be more in line with the analogy of escape from a sand trap.

Quantitative easing does create some vulnerabilities, and these do need to be acknowledged in balancing the costs and benefits of a more aggressive policy. Suppose, for some unexpected reason, that global real interest rates rise sharply due to factors outside the United States (or the country in question), and suddenly the demand for bank reserves starts falling. I realize some people think this is impossible, but if we do not completely understand why real interest rates have fallen so much, then we cannot be completely sure that they will not turn around and significantly rise at some point. The Fed undoubtedly has many instruments with which it could soak up the excess liquidity, including reversing QE (selling off long-term bonds to soak up excess currency). The Fed can also raise interest rates on bank reserves to maintain demand. However, either policy will add to the government's (consolidated) debt-servicing costs and will serve to raise real interest rates more quickly in private markets. If the economy is weak at just the moment the Fed needs to act decisively to contain inflation, it might feel constrained in doing so, and unwinding its balance sheet might prove much more difficult than anticipated.[33]

One sometimes hears the question of why government debt held by the central bank matters at all in a zero bound environment. Why doesn't the Federal Reserve just tear up its holdings of long-term government debt instead of going through the charade of collecting interest from the Treasury and then remitting back its profits? Then people would realize that the true level of government debt is lower than it seems and not worry about it so much. This scheme may sound good, but there is a small glitch. To buy government debt, the Federal Reserve has to issue bank reserves on the other side of the balance sheet; these are not included in the federal debt. In a zero interest rate environment, the bank reserves cost virtually nothing to carry, and therefore are seemingly irrelevant. But as we have just discussed, if the global economy picks up, the Fed will have to do something, and if it has torn up its Treasury debt, it won't be able to use Treasury debt to soak up the excess liquidity and contain inflation. It may be a smart move to borrow short in a historically low nominal interest rate environment, but it is risky. Indeed, one might well ask why, instead of overnight debt, the government is not issuing 100-year debt to lock in near-historic low rates.

In sum, quantitative easing is likely a significantly weaker instrument than conventional monetary policy. Given its rarity and relative newness, it is hard to be sure of the effects of QE or the channels through which it operates. This uncertainty feeds concerns that QE might be planting the seeds of asset market instability that we do not fully understand. Moreover, despite empirical evidence that QE reduces long-term interest rates in the very short run, the fact that it has occurred against a backdrop of falling global real interest rates makes it rather problematic to sort out its long-term effects. Indeed, it is not even clear how much QE has affected inflation, even though the huge increase in bank reserves it generates would normally create enormous upward pressures on prices. As discussed at the outset of this chapter, electronic bank reserves and very short-term Treasury bills become virtually perfect substitutes at the zero bound, so that injections of reserves do not necessarily create pressures on banks to lend more funds to the economy. Most central bankers would use QE again if there were no other options, but they would prefer to find more effective, clear-cut, and transparent instruments to use in the future.

FORWARD GUIDANCE

In addition to quantitative easing, some mention must be made of forward guidance, a term advanced by Columbia economics professor and central banking guru Michael Woodford. The basic idea is one we have already discussed earlier in this chapter: if the central bank cannot reduce the nominal interest rate at the zero bound, it can try to lower real interest rates by manipulating inflation expectations.[34] The problem is that such policies are not necessarily credible if they involve allowing future inflation to drift above target, especially if the public believes that central banks have a strong aversion to inflation. The idea of forward guidance is to find practical ways to make the promise of inflation more concrete and easier to understand, and perhaps therefore more credible.

Crudely put, forward guidance has the central bank telling markets, "We might not be able to lower interest rates now because of the zero bound, but we promise not to raise them later until our output and inflation projections become substantially stronger. Even then we won't raise them as fast as we usually would." Ideally, this reassurance is accompanied by concrete guideposts. This type of forward guidance is sometimes referred to as data-dependent forward guidance, because it basically aims to specify a reaction function to the data. There is also calendar-based forward guidance, where the central bank says, "We promise not to raise policy rates for at least 6 months" or, as in 2015, many Fed officials insisted, "Rates will begin rising away from the zero bound before the end of this year," as in fact they did in December 2015.[35]

The main practical problem with both types of forward guidance is that it is hard for the central bank to credibly make promises in a world where there is regular turnover of policy board members, not to mention of the politicians who ultimately oversee central banks. Perhaps even more importantly, it is difficult to anticipate, even qualitatively, the kind of pressures that might buffet the economy over any medium-term horizon. For example, in the aftermath of the financial crisis, policymakers certainly did not anticipate the long sustained drop in global real interest rates that forced repeated reassessment of what normal policy rates should look like.

In essence, forward guidance attempts to lever the increased credibility and status central banks have achieved in the past 20 years. It asks markets to believe that the central bank will honor its promise of higher inflation in the future by providing specific guideposts for judging its performance. Over the past 5 years, the often huge chasm between Federal Reserve's published predictions of its own interest rate policy and market judgments about future interest rates suggests that forward guidance has been of only limited help, certainly not enough to eschew the potential of open-ended negative rate policy, were it feasible.[36]

Finally, when comparing negative interest rate policy to much weaker tools like quantitative easing and forward guidance, it is important to recognize that any new tool will require a transition period as central banks adjust. It often takes decades of experience with any new tool, be it quantitative easing or negative interest rates, before economists can really form a strong and durable consensus. Theory does suggest that negative rates would be by far the most potent instrument available to central bankers, assuming all necessary preparations are made. But until we have accrued much more experience with all the new instruments, it will be hard to know.

CHAPTER 9

Higher Inflation Targets, Nominal GDP, Escape Clauses, and Fiscal Policy

We next turn to other ideas for dealing with the zero bound problem that might be tried in the future, other than open-ended negative interest rate policy. Of these, perhaps the most straightforward alternative to negative rates involves raising the central bank's target rate of inflation from the near-universal advanced-country norm of 2% to a higher level, say, 4%. The justification for a higher target is predicated on the view that it is not the average rate of inflation that matters for causing economic distortions but only the volatility of inflation. In theory, 2%, 4%, or 20% inflation targets should produce similar outcomes for the real economy as long as the central bank strives to make policy equally stable and predictable in all cases. This proposition may not have the ring of common sense to most people, probably because high rates of inflation are seldom as stable as low rates in practice, and frankly, there are good political economy reasons for that difference in stability. Nevertheless, some well-regarded scholars have vigorously advocated the idea of a higher inflation target.

The principle is that with a higher rate of expected inflation embedded across the whole spectrum of nominal interest rates, the central bank is less likely to run out of bullets (i.e., interest rate cuts) before hitting the zero bound. Let's compare the world we live in of 2% targets with a parallel universe in which everything else is the same except by a quirk of fate, central banks targeted a 4% inflation rate. Assuming the targets are believed (the Fed certainly has solid credibility), real interest rates in both universes should be the same, because in the long run, monetary policy does not affect the real economy. But in the universe with 4% inflation targets, all interest rates, from overnight to 30 years, will be 2% higher. Thus in the parallel universe, monetary authorities should have 2% more in interest rates cuts to play with before hitting the zero bound.[1] That's the idea, although as we shall see, things are a little more complicated, because people might behave differently and adhere to different social conventions in a world with 4% inflation targets than they would in a world with 2% inflation targets. Also, there might be more drawbacks to having 4% inflation as opposed to 2% inflation than proponents of higher targets sometimes acknowledge.

At the end of the chapter, we briefly take up fiscal policy. Of course, discretionary fiscal policy should be used to supplement monetary policy, as a second line of defense, when fighting recessions. A role exists for fiscal policy, even though it is subject to long implementation lags, is more cumbersome, and is politically divisive. At the zero bound, with monetary policy paralyzed, the case for fiscal policy becomes stronger. This does not imply, of course, that hyperactive fiscal policy is anywhere near a complete substitute for being able to use monetary policy also, as would be the case if the zero bound could be finessed.

RAISING TARGET INFLATION FROM 2% TO 4%

As already explained, the basic idea of higher inflation targets derives from the well-accepted notion that over the long run, monetary policy has no effect on real rates (i.e., nominal interest rates adjusted for inflation expectations). Put another way, fully anticipated monetary policy is "neutral" even in a Keynesian model. In particular, a different average rate of inflation will not affect real interest rates over the long run after everyone has adjusted to it.

The idea of having a target inflation rate above 2% is hardly sacrilege and has been kicking around since the early 1990s, back when central banks around the world were just starting to coalesce around the now-ubiquitous 2% target.[2] Many emerging markets and developing nations already have higher targets; Korea and Mexico, for example, have targets centered on 3%.

However, if we are going to take the 4% inflation target idea seriously, it's important to break it up into two distinct questions, which unfortunately often get confounded in the debate. First, suppose that we had a time machine and could go back to the mid-1980s, and do a complete reset of the whole inflation targeting movement. Would it have been better to choose 4% instead of 2%, especially given what we now know about the zero bound? Would economies with 4% inflation have outperformed the world of 2%? This is a much weaker test to pass than switching now from 2% to 4%; even so, the answer is not at all obvious. Stanley Fischer, presently vice chair of the United States Federal Reserve, is also former number two at the International Monetary Fund. He has had extensive experience working in high-inflation countries. Fischer has maintained that when average inflation hits 4%, people not only start changing prices more often, they also start indexing.[3] Either way, monetary policy becomes less effective. If prices and wages are indexed to inflation, then, in the limit, monetary policy does nothing. Loosely put, with a 4% inflation target as opposed to 2%, the central bank might have more room to cut interest rates, but it might need this room, too. Admittedly, it is hard to explore this conjecture empirically, because we do not live in a world where inflation has ever been stable at 4% over a sufficiently long period to say with any confidence how wage-setting and other conventions would adjust.

Another drawback to high inflation is that it potentially creates greater random dispersion among relative prices and wages, because various agents across the economy do not coordinate wage and price changes. The higher the inflation rate becomes, the bigger the adjustment needed, and therefore the bigger the gap between firms that have recently reset their prices and firms that have not done so for a long time. Although the quantitative significance of this effect is a matter of dispute,[4] many standard models suggest that the price distortions rise with inflation, and the negative effect on the economy can be considerable.[5] Moreover, the distortionary costs of high inflation are borne all the time, not just during recessions.

There are other downsides to higher inflation as well, and these also cannot be lightly dismissed. First and perhaps foremost, central banks can explain 2% inflation as the moral equivalent of zero. The logic is that with a constant supply of new products and goods, the published consumer price index tends to overstate inflation; the bias is probably more like 1% than 2%—no one knows for sure—but it is still close enough to zero that people don't need to worry about it. Having to think about inflation may not matter to economists, who think about prices all the time, but it matters a lot to ordinary people, who would prefer not to. This is not an idle objection. Zero inflation (or its moral equivalent) is easy to understand and relatively easy for the public to accept as a long-term commitment. In game theory jargon, zero inflation—price stability—is a natural focal point. Four percent inflation is a far more arbitrary choice (why not 3% or 5% or, indeed, 8%?), and therefore it might be far harder to tightly anchor expectations on it, even after adjusting to any transition period.

The biggest problem with a shift in inflation targets, though, is the way it would undermine central bank credibility. After years of telling the public that 2% inflation is nirvana, how easy will it be for a central banker to turn around and say, "Oops, we meant to say 4% is nirvana. Truly sorry that we have just upended the core expectations underlying every debt and wage contract in the economy. Our bad." Aside from setting off a level of turmoil that might well tip into financial crisis, everyone will naturally be wondering later what is to stop central bankers from changing their minds again in the future, and choosing, say, 3% or 5% inflation targets. It could take years for the trauma and uncertainty to settle down, under the best of circumstances. This is a big risk to take, especially when it is far from obvious that benefits from having more monetary bullets might turn out to be far less effective than expected (as explained above), when higher inflation targets are more difficult to make fully credible on a long-term basis, and when there are other significant distortions associated with higher inflation.

Let's not consign the 4% solution to the dustbin of intellectual history, however. Someday, maybe a sudden change in circumstances will necessitate a dramatic increase in defense spending that sets off an inflationary spiral. If and when that day ever comes, it will not be a pretty picture. But it will be an opportunity to rethink the inflation target, and which universe we really want to live in. Of course, once negative interest rates become feasible, it becomes unnecessary to raise inflation targets, and the central bank could even target 1% inflation, though for reasons just discussed, it would be better to preserve the 2% target.

TARGETING NOMINAL GDP

Another set of ideas surrounds changing the central bank's target qualitatively and not just quantitatively, for example, by targeting nominal GDP, an idea first proposed (in different terminology) by Nobel Prize winner James Meade in 1977.[6] To be clear, nominal GDP is the value of gross domestic product measured in current dollars. So a growth target for nominal GDP implicitly embodies a target for both inflation and real output growth. The idea is two-fold. First, in the long run after everyone has adjusted to the new target, the approach has the advantage of offering some automatic stabilization. For example, if output falls below trend, then monetary policy will have to aim for higher inflation to compensate for lower real growth. Second, given that monetary policy cannot significantly affect long-run growth trends of the real economy, a nominal GDP target is consistent with stable long-term inflation expectations as well.

It is an interesting idea, and in fact one I explored in a paper 30 years ago that also introduced the general idea of inflation targeting.[7] My paper recognized the stabilization advantages of nominal GDP targeting but argued that it might put the central bank under direct political pressure to achieve an unrealistic and unsustainable level of output. As a consequence, nominal GDP targeting might lead to an upward bias in inflation, greater volatility of output, and risks to central bank independence. Another fundamental issue is that GDP is a variable that is measured very imperfectly, with government statisticians often considerably updating their estimates over time, sometimes years later, sometimes quite dramatically.[8] For example, the number of technical recessions experienced by the United Kingdom between 1955 and 1995 (defining a technical recession as two consecutive quarters of GDP reduction) is ten if we use the 1996 official UK historical GDP series, but it drops to seven if we use the 2012 official series.[9] (Note we are counting recessions prior to 1996—or trying to count them, anyway.) Such measurement difficulties are another important factor weighing against having nominal GDP as a fixed target in the central bank's objective function.

As with a shift to a 4% inflation target, it would not be easy to explain to markets a shift to nominal GDP, and the transition would likely involve a long period of volatility. And there are other reasons to be skeptical: most people have no idea what nominal GDP is, making monetary policy much harder to understand than targets based on inflation and unemployment, which people already have enough trouble with. Markets would likely learn and adjust eventually, but it might take a long time.

RELAXING THE RIGIDITY OF THE INFLATION-TARGETING FRAMEWORK

As we have seen, when determining whether the zero bound is a major problem, a critical issue is the extent to which the central bank can manipulate the real interest rate by means of future inflation expectations, which in turn depends on its ability to make credible commitments. The question is why central banks have not been able to do that when faced with the zero bound in practice, at least not to any great effect. Part of the answer, of course, is they lacked an instrument that could credibly deliver the inflation being promised; allowing for negative interest rates would address that shortcoming. Part of the problem, though, might lie in overly zealous implementation of inflation targeting and a series of institutional changes since the mid-1980s that were all aimed at making inflation as low as possible. In constructing this new regime to fortify against a relapse into the high-inflation 1970s, insufficient attention was given to outside-the-box events that might make low inflation a problem. As a result, even after the long period of undesired ultra-low inflation that followed the financial crisis of 2008, no major central bank has been willing to come out and admit that a few years of mildly elevated inflation would not be such a bad thing.[10] Instead, as inflation has collapsed, most central banks remain satisfied to say that more effort is needed to raise inflation upward to 2%.

For example, when in 2012 the Federal Reserve specified triggers that it would consider in deciding when to end quantitative easing, it picked an upper bound inflation rate of 2.5%. Why not pick 3%, or better, 4%? When the Bank of Japan adopted its radical monetary stimulus program in April 2013, there was never any discussion of possibly allowing a significant inflation overshoot. Other central banks, including the Bank of England, have also made clear that they are aiming to avoid any significant overshoot of inflation. The problem is closely akin to the sand trap analogy discussed in chapter 8; central banks need to allow some inflation overshoot to reach escape velocity from the zero bound. Put another way, markets understand that the Fed has only very imperfect control of inflation, so by putting such a low cap on its threshold for overshooting, the Fed was effectively telling markets that it would prefer to miss its inflation target on the downside.

Targeting temporarily elevated inflation might well have been a powerful tool in the aftermath of the financial crisis. Had it been done forcefully and early on, and especially coincident with the large initial fiscal impulse, a higher inflation target might have helped sustain enough momentum to avoid the liquidity trap that ultimately ensnared so many countries. Higher inflation would have helped both to stimulate demand through lower real interest rates and to mitigate adverse debt deflation dynamics. And it was not necessary to do this on a permanent basis: the key was responding quickly to the crisis.[11]

True, a large branch of the zero bound literature is predicated on the view that the inability to promise higher inflation, even when essential, is inherently an intractable credibility problem. That seems far too strong; it echoes the view from the 1980s that central banks could never convince people that they *wouldn't* inflate. In fact, the extreme difficulties many countries have experienced might better be chalked up to the result of flaws in institutional design that can—and almost certainly will be—fixed at some point. A short section in the appendix looks at the development of the literature on inflation targeting and problems with the pre-crisis triumphalism. As things now stand, the trade-off between credibility and flexibility, which central banks thought they had solved, now appears far out of kilter. In fighting the last war, central bank designers may have gone too far putting themselves into an overly inflexible regime.

USING OPPORTUNISTIC FISCAL POLICY
AND DRONE MONEY

A strong case can be made for using activist fiscal policy in an economy constrained by the zero bound. One must distinguish, however, between second-best opportunistic (or one might say hyperactive) fiscal policy, and fiscal policy that would be justified even in the presence of the fully functioning monetary policy stabilization that would be possible in a world with no constraints on negative interest rate policy.

The basic idea of using opportunistic fiscal policy to escape the zero bound is simple, though there are several variants that depend on the exact nature of the rigidities and imperfections one assumes.[12] In general, the optimal policy involves using both fiscal and monetary policies. There are a couple caveats, however, that often get lost in polemic debates. First, the canonical Keynesian model of fiscal stimulus at the zero bound assumes a closed economy and ignores the fact that a part of the fiscal stimulus is likely to dissipate abroad. One of John Maynard Keynes's brilliant simplifying assumptions was to assume a closed economy and ignore the rest of the world. The closed economy assumption is analytically elegant but not very realistic, even for the United States. Open economy spillovers imply that for fiscal stimulus policies to be fully effective, coordinated action across nations may be needed. Experience suggests, however, that this is easier said than done, especially when some countries have less faith in the Keynesian model than others. Second, the impact effect of fiscal policy can be sensitive to expectations about whether the fiscal impulse is temporary or permanent; a permanent shift implies higher future taxes and is more likely to crowd out private consumption. More precisely, a fiscal stimulus that is expected to be withdrawn once the interest rate rises above zero can have a large multiplier effect on output, but a fiscal stimulus that is expected to last beyond the exit from the zero bound has a much smaller effect. This issue is significant, because in practice, it can be hard to credibly promise that a new fiscal program will be temporary: if people don't believe the program will be withdrawn in a timely manner, the stimulus effect on impact may well be quite modest.[13]

One idea that has gained some traction is for the central bank to print money and hand it out to consumers. Ben Bernanke suggested this perfectly reasonable paradigm when he was a Fed governor back in 2002 as a solution for Japan's deflation problem. No good deed goes unpunished, and some critics starting calling him "Helicopter Ben," because his advice for Japan drew on Milton Friedman's analogy to dropping money from a helicopter. Lately, the idea has become fashionable again. Lord Adair Turner, former chairman of the United Kingdom's Financial Services Authority, has advocated central bank–financed transfers in his 2015 book on debt, and the helicopter money often appears in op-eds and the blogosphere as a growth elixir.[14] There is nothing fundamentally wrong with the idea.[15] However, it is important to realize that helicopter money does not really add any new instruments to the arsenal of macroeconomic stabilization tools. Because there is so much confusion surrounding helicopter money, it is worth pausing on this point for a moment.

If the economy is not at the zero bound, helicopter money is essentially the same as having the Treasury present a $500 check to every household (or person), paying for it by issuing debt, and then having the Federal Reserve buy up the debt in full by using standard open market purchases of bonds. On impact, the private sector ends up with higher wealth in the form of cash, and there is no increase in bonds. If the economy *is* at the zero interest rate bound, the only difference is that the central bank would use quantitative easing to mop up the newly issued debt. Helicopter money can only expand the options if it is accompanied by some other institutional change. For example, if the introduction of helicopter money is accompanied by a change in the central bank's inflation-targeting preferences, then of course there will be added effects. Equivalently, if the advent of helicopter money is accompanied by new legislation that somehow helps the central bank to commit to inflationary finance in the future, that too would make an important difference. In both cases, helicopter money is just a gimmick to effect a policy change that might not otherwise be politically feasible, perhaps leveraging the central bank's reputation for being conservative to help make fiscal policy more accommodative. Put this way, it is clear there are trade-offs that need to be considered.[16]

If the central bank is going to leverage its reputation, then today's technology offers another analogy: "drone money." Instead of dropping currency indiscriminately from a helicopter, the government could use drones to target low-income households. Targeted money transfers are likely to have a much bigger bang for the buck in a Keynesian sense, because most of the money will be spent rather than saved, and such transfers would likely make particular sense in situations where the aim is both to stimulate demand and to address inequality simultaneously.

In sum, fiscal stabilization policy can be a perfectly good idea, but if the central bank could engage in negative interest rate policy, then this would be a superior first step, assuming all necessary preparations were made. This step would clear the air, remove the need for fiscal policy to serve as a second-best substitute for monetary policy, and allow policymakers to assess fiscal policy on normal grounds of needs, efficiency, and distribution of income. However, beware of any smoke-and-mirrors substitute for getting around the zero bound constraint. To expand the policy options, it is necessary to make a more fundamental change.

USING CONSUMPTION TAXES

For completeness, this section briefly mentions Martin Feldstein's proposal to use the tax system to stimulate prices and demand at the zero bound:

The first option would increase consumer spending. The government of Japan has said for some time that it wants to reduce its reliance on the income tax and increase its reliance on its value added tax. The Japanese government could announce that it will raise the current 5 percent value added tax by 1 percent per quarter and simultaneously reduce the income tax rates to keep revenue unchanged, continuing this for several years until the VAT reaches 20 percent. This revenue neutral policy would imply consumer prices rising at the rate of four percent a year.[17]

A central element of Feldstein's approach is that it creates expected inflation in the after-tax prices that consumers face but does not introduce distorting inflation into producer prices as, for example, central bank promises of future general inflation would do. In principle, fiscally engineered inflation is a workable idea, though later research has shown that it is important to deal with some nuances, including calibrating the right offsetting tax on labor income. In addition, in practice, the length of time over which the zero bound will be binding is unknown, so a more sophisticated version of the proposal has the sales tax increases and income tax cuts go away when the zero bound is no longer binding.[18] Perhaps the most serious objection to the approach is that real-world fiscal policy invariably involves redistribution; for example, the sales tax and income tax affect different groups differently, and actual tax rates represent a political equilibrium and not just an economic one. Thus, in practice, it might be extremely difficult to make any of the required promises credible, rendering the policy ineffective.

CHAPTER 10

Other Paths to Negative Interest Rates

Is it absolutely necessary to phase out paper currency to clear the way for negative interest rates? The short answer is no. Actually, there are a few other workable options—and in principle combinations among them—each with its own advantages and disadvantages, and it is important to consider them.

The first idea is for central banks to just tiptoe into negative rates, hoping to keep the interest penalty small enough that it will not set off a potentially chaotic run into cash, and hoping that no technical problem interferes with normal market functioning. Several central banks are at this point today, and they continue to wade into the water. A second idea, advanced more than a century ago by maverick German economist Silvio Gesell, is to make people pay small periodic taxes on the cash they hold. Although it seemed rather impractical when he proposed it, the idea was tried during the Great Depression, and thanks to modern technology, there might be much less burdensome ways to implement it today.[1]

The third idea is the Kublai Khan–Eisler–Buiter–Kimball dual currency model, which imposes a (time-varying) fee for converting wholesale cash deposits to electronic bank reserves at the central bank. The fee would create a wedge between the value of an electronic dollar and a paper dollar, and central bank policy would involve managing both the interest rate on electronic currency and its exchange rate with paper. If it sounds inordinately complicated, it is not. If anything, the idea is ingenious. With sufficient institutional and legal preparation, a wholesale cash deposit fee could likely work, either on its own or as part of a transition to phasing out most paper currency, which remains the most attractive long-term solution.

We take these ideas up in order of conceptual complexity, particularly as each variant motivates the next.

NEGATIVE POLICY RATES WITHOUT MAJOR INSTITUTIONAL CHANGES

Given current institutional and legal arrangements, no one knows how far central banks can effectively push nominal policy interest rates into negative territory. Is it –1%, –1.25%, or even –2%? No central bank wants to be the first to find out the hard way. The main issue is the risk of a run from bank accounts and Treasury bills into cash, wreaking havoc with the system, and ultimately making it impossible to take interest rates any lower. The most pressing issue for central banks is not so much that cash holders might be subsidized.[2] The real issue is that neither central banks nor law enforcement agencies are really prepared for having to deal with the logistics of an unprecedented surge in cash demand, and that the run into cash might significantly hamper the normal monetary transmission mechanism. If investors pull their money out of the financial system and put it into paper currency, then borrowers won't benefit from negative rates.

It is true that the system smoothly handled the modest and relatively short-lived runs into cash that occurred in many countries at the peak of the financial crisis of 2008.[3] But the scale of short-term government debt is vastly greater than the amount of cash, so with very negative policy interest rates, the potential exists for a far larger run into cash than anything previously witnessed.

As rates go increasingly negative, the question arises of whether other frictions in the system would limit the effectiveness of negative rate policy even before any absolute lower bound were reached. For example, if banks cannot easily pass negative rate charges on to their retail clients, or if legal and institutional conventions on how debt contracts are written cannot readily be adapted to allow for negative rates, the normal impact of monetary policy would be impeded.

The pass-through issue arises because central banks basically deal only with financial institutions and not with retail clients.

Among the early adopters (e.g., Denmark, Switzerland, and Sweden), the general experience is that private banks have been able to pass negative rates on to their large clients (including big corporations, insurance companies, and pension funds) without too much fuss. But they have not yet dared charge negative rates to their ordinary retail customers, at least not in a transparent fashion. Presumably, in the background, banks have to recoup their costs somehow, either by charging customers more for other services or by tacking the added cost on to loans.[4]

The experience of the Swiss National Bank, whose policy interest rate reached –0.75% in January 2015, is a good case in point. Authorities are keeping a watchful eye but, as of this writing, so far no run into cash has occurred. True, many pension funds and financial firms have seriously explored schemes for hoarding physical cash; most seem to have concluded that at –0.75%, the costs still outweigh the benefits.

Storing, handling, and insuring cash is an expensive proposition, even for an efficient large-scale operator, even with the huge convenience of 1,000–Swiss franc mega-notes. If a financial firm wants to withdraw, say, a billion Swiss francs from the central bank, it needs to send armored trucks, carefully monitoring and insuring everything. In an expedition like this, one has to guard the guards. Labor in Switzerland is not cheap. Once the transfer is complete, it still would be necessary to pay to store the paper currency inside an amply guarded, high-tech, humidity-controlled Swiss vault. And even with all this care and protection, almost any financial institution is going to be required to get insurance against fire, theft, and so forth. Early estimates of the storage and insurance costs were in the range of 0.5%. Another problem is that it is hard to know how long interest rates will be negative. This makes it extremely difficult to assess the possibilities for amortizing the fixed costs of transferring cash from the central bank into storage.

It is an open question whether private-sector innovations will develop over time that drive down the cost of storing currency, much as the Swiss have mastered the art of storing valuable paintings and gold. Governments could discourage large-scale currency storage by banning it or by imposing a tax on storage over a certain amount. This would hardly discourage criminals and tax evaders, who are already quite expert at storing large amounts of cash, but it would sharply reduce or eliminate storage by financial firms, pension funds, and the like. Needless to say, even if such a ban were legally feasible (which is far from clear in many countries), it would not prevent smaller-scale storage at levels just below the threshold.

To further discourage banks from storing large amounts of paper currency in their vaults, and to help cushion bank balance sheets, the Swiss National Bank and the Bank of Japan have both adopted a tiered approach to negative interest rate charges. The Bank of Japan's (January 2016) approach, for example, gives banks a zero percentage rate on required reserves (that have to be held against deposits), a positive 0.1% rate on excess reserves held prior to the implementation of negative rates, and a negative 0.1% on any further increase in reserve holdings. In principle, this policy strengthens the effect of future quantitative easing policies, because banks would have a stronger incentive to lend out any new funds rather than let them sit at the Bank of Japan earning a negative nominal return. The tiered interest approach has the advantage of cushioning bank balance sheets from the initial impact of negative interest rates and at the same time still discourages them from converting their existing reserves into paper currency. However, it falls far short of the kind of policy that would be needed to deal with the overhang of Treasury bills if interest rates went too negative.[5] As already observed in chapter 6, Japan's net debt as a percentage of its GDP is more than 130%.[6]

A flight from bank accounts and Treasury bills into cash is the main concern with negative interest rates, but there are others, and early experiments with mild negative rates have revealed a host of other potential complications. These other issues don't necessarily prevent rates from going below zero, but they do potentially create significant distortions that need to be addressed, especially if rates are ever to go deeply negative. [7] The basic problem is that societies have built up a wide range of social conventions, laws, and financial systems predicated on the idea that after someone issues a bond, the stream of subsequent payments are always going from borrower to lender. However, most of these obstacles are minor conceptually and could be easily fixed in the long run.

One practical problem that came up very quickly is that many bank computer systems were designed with the idea that interest rates can never go below zero. This might sound ridiculous to young people familiar with modern database programs, but financial firms try hard to avoid changing software systems too often, and some of the systems are surprisingly antiquated.

One only has to recall the "Y2K" computer problem that arose at the turn of the century. In the run-up to New Year's Day in January 2000, software engineers around the world scrambled to patch software, because many legacy computer systems defined years by two digits instead of four, making it impossible for the year 2000 to be distinguished from the year 1900. (A bit like when Romanian gymnast Nadia Comaneci scored the first perfect 10.00 in the 1976 Olympics, but the crowd was momentarily silenced when the scoreboard registered her majestic performance as only 1.00. The scoreboard had just three digits instead of four, because it had never occurred to its Swiss designers that anyone might ever achieve a perfect score.)

In a sense, Y2K for negative interest rates has already come and gone. When Denmark's central bank, Danmarks Nationalbank, implemented negative interest rates in July 2012, many private financial institutions were forced to enter negative rate trades manually, because they were totally unprepared, as their systems were not ready. This affected not only banks in Denmark, but also in Sweden and anywhere else that intermediated trades in Danish currency and bonds. It was an expense and an inconvenience, but Scandinavian banks managed and have now converted their systems.

Also important are laws governing bond payments that never envisioned that, in some periods, coupons might be negative. Fortunately, the economics of paying negative coupons is not so complicated. For a fixed rate bond with negative yield, the contract can be designed either so that the lender actually makes payments to the borrower along the way, or the amounts can be deducted from the final principal payment. It gets a little more complicated with floating rate bonds, where the interest rate varies over time, and in fact this problem came up quickly in the early adopter countries. Again, though, the lender could make a payment, or the appropriate amount could be deducted from the final principal payment. It seems complicated, but it's not. Initially, in Sweden, there was some uncertainty about how the legal system would handle the problem, but a solution was found.[8] When the Eurozone first instituted an extremely mild negative rate (–0.1%) in June 2014, concerns arose that it might interfere with the functioning of swap markets, but again, no major problems materialized. Given the vast size and liquidity of the European markets, the Eurozone experience with (slightly) negative rates is having a powerful demonstration effect and is being scrutinized particularly closely by other central banks.

Nevertheless, these early experiences cannot be regarded as a true test of unfettered negative rate policy. There is a big difference between being able only to tiptoe into negative rates and being able to tell markets that the central bank is prepared to do "whatever it takes," say, to end deflation. If negative interest rate policy is to have a decisive effect on inflation expectations and dynamics, it needs to be a bazooka, not a water pistol.[9] In sum, although no fundamental conceptual issue exists for how monetary policy would work under negative rates, countries may need to lay the groundwork for them to be fully effective. We will return to this issue in chapter 11.

We now turn to two ideas that, in principle, would allow central banks to go much deeper into negative interest rate territory.

SILVIO GESELL'S STAMP TAX

One approach is to literally make people pay interest on paper currency. The idea of paying negative interest rates on money was first floated by a German economist in a series of papers published in the late nineteenth century and early twentieth century.[10] Silvio Gesell was a merchant, economist, and social activist, who believed that if interest rates could temporarily be very low, even negative, it would help spur growth. It is unclear whether Gesell understood the fundamental principle that money is neutral in the long run. In normal times, excessive monetary expansion ratchets up inflation expectations in a way that ultimately must be painfully reversed. Gesell, however, definitely understood the zero bound on nominal interest rates. His completely outside-the-box solution was to create "stamp money," where the owner periodically had to buy stamps and place them on the back of the currency to maintain its value. The requirement that people have to periodically buy and affix stamps on money would effectively give it a negative nominal interest rate.

During the Great Depression, leading thinkers from John Maynard Keynes to Irving Fisher became greatly enamored of Gesell's idea. They recognized that negative interest rates could be a powerful tool for lifting the world's economies out of deflation. Fisher, in particular, was so completely fascinated that he wrote a short book in 1933 about stamp money. Ultimately, and after much anguish, Gesell's ideas were basically rejected as impractical, and the world found another way (abandoning the gold standard). Keynes actually devotes a long section to Gesell's idea in his magnum opus, *The General Theory*, which is well worth reading and also shows the importance the idea reached in the depths of the Great Depression. Despite praising Gesell as "an unduly neglected prophet . . . whose work contained flashes of deep insight," Keynes nevertheless concludes:

> The idea behind stamped money is sound. It is, indeed, possible that means might be found to apply it in practice on a modest scale. But it would encounter many difficulties that Gesell did not face. In particular, he was unaware that money was not unique in having a liquidity premium attached to it, but differed only in degree from many other articles, deriving its importance from having a greater liquidity premium than any other article. Thus if currency notes were to be deprived of their liquidity premium by the stamping system, a long series of substitutes would step into their shoes—bank money, debts at call, foreign money, jewelry and the precious metals generally, and so forth.[11]

Some small experiments with negative interest rates were conducted during the Great Depression, with perhaps the seminal one being the local stamp currency issued in Wörgl, Austria, a town of

2,000 inhabitants. Every month, inhabitants had to buy stamps of 1% of the value of the note to maintain its validity; the notes ranged from 1 to 10 schillings. The experiment ran for just over a year, until stamped monies were banned by the Austrian government. Some small municipalities across the United States also experimented with stamped money during the Great Depression, as did the Canadian province of Alberta in 1936.[12]

The idea might sound just ridiculous to people today, but I am old enough to remember when my mother used to collect "Green Stamps," once a popular rewards program at supermarkets. Although it was very time consuming to put stamps into the little books, we did it, and so did most of the other families we knew. Thus, from a cultural perspective, stamped money was not quite so crazy when Gesell proposed the idea as it might seem today. Still, the original proposal was pretty impractical. The problem with stamped money, as Keynes noted, is that it severely compromises the liquidity role of currency.

There are other variants, such as creating currency that has an expiration date, and then requiring that it be exchanged for new notes at a discount. Of course, the practice of monarchs during the Middle Ages of periodically calling in coins and handing back smaller ones with less precious metal content was a way of taxing currency. Another common practice, even more directly analogous to a Gesell tax, was to force people to hand in coins and then give them back a smaller number of coins similar in weight and content, for example, handing in four coins and getting back three.[13]

Many other ways can be used to implement a crude Gesell tax. At the improbable (but instructive) end of the spectrum is the idea of creating short-stick lotteries advanced by my Harvard colleague N. Gregory Mankiw, who attributes the idea to a graduate student. Mankiw proposed that the central bank run regular lotteries based on the serial numbers of currency in circulation. Notes with the losing numbers become completely worthless. The problem is that after a couple dozen lotteries, it would be pretty difficult to identify worthless notes without a tedious serial number cross-check against the official list. This inconvenience would, in turn, once again greatly diminish the liquidity of currency.

Perhaps the first vaguely practical idea for implementing a Gesell tax was proposed by Richmond Federal Reserve economist Marvin Goodfriend, who suggested putting magnetic strips on currency.[14] Any time a note was turned in at a bank, it would be run through a machine that would identify the individual note and calculate a tax based on how long it had been in circulation. The burden of identifying the bill and collecting the tax would be borne by banks, who presumably would find ways to pass the costs on to their customers. Importantly, the magnetic strip technology could also be used to pay positive interest on currency, though that was not Goodfriend's main focus.

For the moment, Goodfriend's idea is not quite feasible, or at least economically viable, but the time for it might not be far off. Indeed, periodic bouts of consternation have roiled the underground economy on rumors that the government is putting active transmitting radio-frequency identification (RFID) chips into currency, to be able to detect large bags of cash in airports and elsewhere. One can find videos online that show how to put currency in a microwave to fry any embedded chips. The implication is that if an RFID chip is embedded, the microwave might burn a hole in the note, but that is better than getting caught with a big bag of illicit cash. In fact, as of yet there are no embedded chips in US currency, though paper-thin chips are being developed that might make it possible someday, if the government chose to do so.[15]

Embedded chips (or magnetic strips) may prove unnecessary in any event, given the development of increasingly low-cost cash processors that can scan serial numbers at extremely high speeds. The technology already exists in high-end currency-sorting machines that many banks and law enforcement agencies already have access to (as mentioned in chapter 3). The scanners work particularly well with high-tech polymer plaster currencies that don't crinkle and bend as easily as paper. As costs fall sufficiently, serial number scanners can in principle be embedded in standard retail cash registers.

That the Gesell solution might be technologically feasible someday does not make it elegant. It would still be a problem that when a note is circulating outside the banking system, retailers would need to be able to figure out how much of a discount to assign to it. Fresh notes would be worth par, but notes that have been outside the banking system for a long time would have significant tax due. Having to deal with this issue, even if feasible, would detract from the liquidity and homogeneity that are fundamental to a good currency. Thus, even a high-tech implementation of the Gesell currency tax seems problematic for much the same reasons as Keynes critiqued stamp money.

Parenthetically, if the day ever comes when serial numbers can be read and processed at low cost in retail cash machines that time-stamp transactions, then the anonymity of currency could be significantly compromised. Authorities could match up time-stamped security camera photos with transactions. Alternatively, the government could require retailers to ask cash customers to sign receipts with serial numbers when making cash payments.[16]

Gesell's idea is a brilliant insight but is only part of the solution. The fully workable solution requires a further leap.

ROBERT EISLER'S TWO-CURRENCY SYSTEM: THE KUBLAI KHAN–EISLER–BUITER–KIMBALL APPROACH

The critical challenge then, is how to collect tax on individual notes that differs according to how long a note has been circulating, and yet at the same time make all currency completely homogenous. The brilliant solution was first proposed by Depression-era economist Robert Eisler (1933); it has since been rediscovered and significantly refined by a group of economists including Stephen Davies, Willem Buiter, Ruchir Agarwal, and Miles Kimball.[17] It is intriguing and should be taken quite seriously. Although the latest and most refined version (due to Agarwal and Kimball) is actually quite simple, a brief discussion of the intellectual history is immensely helpful in understanding the essential elements as well as the underlying elements for how it works.

Without question, the early modern-day pioneer is Willem Buiter, a highly regarded academic economist well known for his outspoken policy positions and out-of-the box ideas. Buiter, however, credits a discussion by Stephen Davies for pointing him to Eisler's solution to the heterogeneity problem inherent in the Gesell tax.[18] Eisler himself, who was also a historian, points to inspiration from the "tabular standard" introduced by the Massachusetts Bay Colony in 1747 during the colonial inflation era.[19] The approach very cleverly offers a way to give a negative nominal return on paper currency without separately tracking and taxing individual notes. There is no need to look at the back to see when a note was last stamped or to run it through an electronic reader to see how much cumulated interest is owed.

Robert Eisler's original 1933 formulation imagined a world with a global gold standard, and his framework for understanding inflation is flawed. The key insight in his proposal, however, stands. The insight is that countries should essentially have two currencies instead of one, an accounting-book currency for use inside the banking system, and a paper currency outside it. Eisler called the interbank accounting currency "money banco," intended as a dig at the snobbery of elite London bankers, who he hoped would be offended by its Italian name. Money banco would have most of the functions normal money has: it would be the unit of account and the currency accepted for taxes, repayment of all debts (legal tender), and the unit in which financial transactions would be cleared. It would be money in every sense, except that it would have no physical form. Money banco would only be a bookkeeping entry, which back then meant paper accounting books, not electronic ones. The government would issue a separate paper currency "current money" that would be used for ordinary retail transactions. It would not, however, be a unit of account and, critically, current money and money banco would have an exchange rate between them.

The Eisler concept is not quite so far from our world today as it might seem. Central banks actually already do issue two types of money, as recorded, for example, on the Federal Reserve's balance sheet. One is the paper currency stored in bank vaults and held by the public at large. The other is an electronic currency (a virtual currency), which banks can hold at the central bank. For all intents and purposes, it is already the case that electronic bank reserves are the part of the money supply that matters most for the legal economy. Unlike paper currency, electronic bank reserves (I resist the temptation to rename them "virtual currency banco") can pay positive or negative interest, depending on central bank policy. The big difference between today's world and the Eisler world is that today, central banks stand ready to trade electronic currency and paper currency at the rate of one to one. In the Eisler world, when interest rates are negative, this would not be the case.

Buiter's adaptation of Eisler starts by having the central bank withdraw all currency from circulation (let's say all euros) and replace it with a new currency, which he christens the WIM, after fellow Dutchman Wim Duisenberg, who served as the first president of the European Central Bank (ECB). Electronic euros (including bank reserves, bank accounts, and so forth) would be unaffected, and all legal contracts would continue to hold in electronic euros. (Buiter fully recognized that this is far from a minor assumption, because private parties can contract in anything they want, but let's put that aside for now.) Initially, the WIM would trade at par against the euro, but after that, the exchange rate would be set each period by the ECB, which would also set the path for the exchange rate between electronic and paper currencies.

In Buiter's setup, the ECB has three instruments: the interest rate on euro reserves (which can be positive or negative), the current spot exchange rate (the rate at which banks can trade WIM paper currency for euro electronic currency at the ECB), and the forward exchange rate (the rate at which the ECB offers to trade WIM for euros in a future period, say, 1 month hence). Of course, specifying how many euros you can get for a WIM today and how many euros you can get tomorrow is exactly the same as specifying a nominal interest rate on WIMs across the two periods, so in essence the central bank has only two independent instruments. If 1 WIM equals 1 euro today and then only 0.95 euros in a year, then this is the same as charging a 5% interest rate on WIMs.

Now we are ready to see the big trick. (My apologies to professional magicians who, I have learned, generally prefer the term "effect," because "trick" has negative connotations. Eisler's trick is magic in the most positive sense of the word.) Obviously, there is no longer any difficulty in charging a significant negative interest rate on the electronic euro, let's say as large as 5% per year. All these accounts are electronic, and collecting a tax is trivial. But won't everyone just convert all their electronic currency euros into paper currency WIMs? No, not if the central bank sets the WIM–euro exchange rate to fall by 5% per year at the same time. It does not have to be exactly the same rate, because as discussed earlier in the chapter, physical cash has both storage costs and differential transaction usages that allow it to pay a slightly different interest rate than electronic money.

In this scenario, the central bank collects tax on paper currency whenever financial institutions go to the central bank to exchange notes for electronic reserves. The central bank collects the tax by exchanging WIMs at a discount according to its WIM depreciation schedule. The fundamental difference from the Goodfriend scheme is that *all currency notes trade at the same discount*. All anyone in the retail world needs to know is the exchange rate between the country's two currencies. The Buiter-Eisler scheme is vastly simpler than the Gesell solution, once one accepts that each country has separate electronic and physical currency units.

Doesn't this seem really inconvenient for merchants and banks, which are dealing with both electronic and paper currency payments? One answer is that if negative interest rate periods are relatively short lived and never too deeply negative, then merchants might just eat the cost the way they now absorb credit card fees. Also, because the exchange rate is being set by the central bank and is easily ascertained, the calculation would be child's play for modern electric cash registers.

In principle, the Buiter-Eisler dual currency formulation slickly eliminates the zero bound while retaining cash, albeit with the net minuses discussed in part I of this book. However, there is an important qualification. For monetary policy to be fully effective when negative interest rates on the electronic euro are in place, it is critical that a large fraction of private contracts be indexed to the electronic euro and not to the paper WIM. Bonds denominated in WIMs will still be governed by the zero bound, and if enough of the economy is indexed to the WIM, the monetary authority will still be constrained by how much WIM inflation it can achieve. This is somewhat akin to the fact that for the United States, exchange rate changes have surprisingly little short-run effect on the relative price of imports and exports, because such an overwhelming percentage of both are priced in dollars.[20]

Stephen Davies, in his original discussion, suggested having the government simply dictate that the electronic euro has to be the unit of the account in contracts. In most countries, however, the government has only limited legal power in this respect.[21] It can certainly denominate all government liabilities, pay employees and suppliers, and collect taxes in electronic euros. This practice might help make denomination in electronic euros what game theorists term a "focal point" for private contracting. But if a large share of private transactions is being conducted in the paper currency WIM, then WIMs might be the natural focal point for many private financial contracts, and the zero bound would remain. Laws could be changed to strengthen the government's ability to dictate the indexation of contracts, but this extreme solution could spin off many other problems. My strong hunch is that this indexation problem would not be paralyzing, but it is a risk, and it does slightly weaken the case for the two-currency system versus simply phasing out (most) paper currency.

Buiter's work is important for carefully laying out the theoretical foundations of the Eisler approach, but the idea has gained greater traction through the advocacy of economist Miles Kimball, who has also refined its implementation and, together with Ruchar Agarwal, has written a working paper on the topic.[22]

The Agarwal and Kimball formulation, though perhaps only a small tweak of Buiter's from a theoretical perspective, makes the whole approach seem simpler and less forbidding. First, Agarwal and Kimball do not envision retiring the existing paper currency. Second, they implement the discount on paper currency in a slightly different way that is isomorphic to Buiter's approach but easier to explain to laypersons. Instead of announcing a forward exchange rate, they would have the central bank (equivalently) announce the interest rate path for paper currency, which is collected only when banks bring currency to the central bank.

So when people bring currency to the deposit window of a private bank, they get paid according to the exchange rate, but the private bank is not required at any point to collect tax to turn over to the government. Again, the Agarwal-Kimball variant is virtually the same as Buiter's (no pun intended), but operationally, it is easier to explain.

Agarwal and Kimball also take up an issue that would be quite critical in practice, should the Buiter-Eisler approach ever be implemented. Suppose after a year where the interest rate on the euro electronic currency is –3%, deflation is defeated, and the central bank is again raising interest rates above zero. By this time, the central bank will be trading paper for electronic currency at (roughly) a 3% discount. If the emergency negative interest rate situation is over, it might be desirable to bring the paper currency and the electronic currency exchange rate back to par (one to one). The government does not have to do this—it can leave the paper currency at 0.97, or it can just keep on pushing down the exchange rate for paper currency as a way to collect more seigniorage tax. However, it would certainly be convenient in terms of the payment system to bring the exchange rate back to one, especially if negative interest rate episodes are few and far between. Then, in normal times, the distinction between paper and electronic currency is not anything that anyone would have to worry about.

Bringing the paper currency back to parity, however, is trickier than it seems. If the central bank tries to return paper to parity too quickly, say within 6 months, it would mean that paper currency would effectively pay a 6% interest, and this would likely conflict with monetary objectives. So the exchange rate would need to return to par more gradually. One might think the central bank could get around the problem of return to parity by doing it suddenly and out of the blue. Unfortunately, people will anticipate this move, and it could cause serious problems exactly during the period when the central bank is trying to hold the interest rate down. The challenge of returning to parity exemplifies the kind of practical question that might not seem obvious at first sight, but would absolutely need to be negotiated in practice, ideally without excessive experimentation. Although arguably a minor issue, at least compared to dealing with a decade at the zero bound, this kind of problem nevertheless further supports the view that phasing out currency is much the neatest long-run solution.

I appreciate that many readers' minds are by now dizzy with the idea that a country should have two currencies with an exchange rate between them and the apparent complications such a system would engender. One shouldn't overstate either the legal or conceptual obstacles, however, and most advanced countries have had far more complicated systems in place at one time or another in the post–World War II era. During the 1950s and in some cases into the 1960s, most European countries implemented complex multiple exchange rate systems. People managed. (Technically speaking, the United States had two currencies and an exchange rate between them during its 1860s Civil War and the ensuing Reconstruction. The "greenback" paper currency could be used for almost everything. However, customs duties, which back then were a principal source of federal revenue, had to be paid in gold. One reason for this system was to maintain a steady flow of hard currency to keep down bond interest rates while the paper greenback floundered in high inflation, since the government redeemed its debt in gold.[23])

If the gain is large enough to overcome political obstacles, then in principle, the Eisler approach can be implemented fairly quickly, albeit the Eurozone, with its diverse legal frameworks, might present more significant challenges than, say, the United States, Japan, Canada, or the United Kingdom might face.

The conclusion of this chapter is that it is completely possible, and completely workable, for countries to break the zero bound without eliminating paper currency, just as it is possible for countries to phase out paper currency without having negative interest rates. The Eisler-Buiter-Kimball approach especially merits serious attention and must be understood as a real option, if possibly only as part of a transition to a less-cash society.

It is also worth noting that there is a definite family resemblance of the Eisler-Buiter-Kimball proposal to the Kublai Khan two-currency model discussed in chapter 2, where a tax had to be paid to convert paper currency back to silver at the "bank" (the Mongol treasury). As the reader will recall, The Great Khan (Marco Polo's term) circulated paper notes for use by his minions. One note was stamped as worth equal to one ounce of silver, the unit of account and the medium of exchange in high-level court transactions. But if a merchant wanted to redeem the currency for silver (the bank money of the day), a merchant would need to tender two paper silver notes to receive one ounce of real silver, a practice that monetary historian Gordon Tullock describes as quite unique.[24] Hence the moniker "Kublai Khan–Eisler–Buiter–Kimball" for the idea of charging a fee to convert cash at the central bank.

As a final point, if paper currency is only partially phased out (say, if $5 or $10 bills remained per the blueprint in chapter 7), some lower limit to negative rates would still exist, though a much lower one than with big notes, because transportation, handling, and storage costs would be so much larger. The effective lower bound should be sufficiently negative in this case that it is not really an obstacle, but if it did become one, there are several possible solutions, including forcing bulk holders of cash to pay a fee to redeposit funds. Uncertainty over the likely duration of any negative rate episode will discourage potential hoarders from paying large fixed costs for bulk storage. Hoarders will also have difficulty insuring large quantities of cash. All in all, eliminating large bills alone should be sufficient to pave the way for invoking deeply negative policy interest rates in response to a financial crisis or a very deep recession but, as we have seen in this chapter, it is not the only approach.

CHAPTER 11

Other Possible Downsides to Negative Nominal Policy Rates

The fact is that negative interest rates are still very much an experimental policy, and although they can work wonders in theory, no one can be sure what issues might arise in practice, especially if rates become significantly negative. Even if one solves the hoarding problem, either by phasing out cash or adopting one of the clever mechanisms discussed in chapter 10, the question still remains of whether other complications might arise, ranging from tax matters to legal obstacles to financial stability concerns.[1]

The concern that various frictions might become worse as policymakers wade deeper into negative interest rate territory can be seen by analogy to an individual standing at the edge of the water on a beach. As the person ventures slowly into the water, she will still have sand under her feet and only gentle resistance from the water. As she wades in deeper, however, the resistance from the water increases until it becomes far more difficult to move. At the same time, instead of sand below her feet, she may begin to encounter sharp rocks, barnacles, and jellyfish, and it could get hard to see clearly enough to avoid them. Continuing the analogy, our fearless bather can get swept out to sea by an underwater ocean current, or bitten by a shark lurking below the surface. The implication is that even if a few central banks have successfully tiptoed into negative rate waters, things might get much more complicated and risky if they try to do too much more.

The beach analogy may sound pretty forbidding, but maybe the moral should be that there is a big benefit to learning how to swim, that is, to adjusting to life with occasionally negative rates. This chapter discusses a host of concerns and reaches the conclusion that the frictions one might worry about are fairly superficial, and most can be easily dealt with, given a long transition time.

FINANCIAL STABILITY AND NEGATIVE RATES

One of the central debates in monetary theory over the past 20 years has been to what extent the central bank should focus solely on stabilizing output and inflation when setting interest rates, and to what extent interest rate policy should take into account broader financial stability considerations. Many finance economists have argued that due to a mix of psychology and market imperfections, long periods of ultra-easy monetary policy—whether through ultra-low interest rates or quantitative easing or both—invariably lead to speculative excesses that can reach systemic proportions. Presumably, those already concerned about quantitative easing or extended periods of near-zero interest rates will be even more concerned about deeply negative interest rates.

This is an old debate, going back at least to the 1990s, when Alan Greenspan was chair of the Federal Reserve. The classical point of view, embodied in Ben Bernanke (Fed chair after Greenspan) and Mark Gertler's well-known 1999 Jackson Hole conference paper, is that monetary authorities should take into account financial stability risks only to the extent that these risks affect their forecasts for primary target variables, such as inflation and output.[2] The reasoning is that the monetary authorities are not any better at predicting asset prices than are markets, and therefore have no special way to tell whether a large run-up in housing prices or stock prices is a bubble. Moreover, it is unclear just how much high asset prices spill over into real activity. All a central banker can do is to try to maintain stable inflation, and if the economy blows up, clean up the mess. An alternative view, championed by William White and other economists at the Bank for International Settlements, is that debt-fueled bubbles are predictably problematic. So if the monetary authorities see a sharp rise in asset prices that is accompanied by a sharp rise in private debt, it should be a concern. (It must be said that the theoretical case that looser monetary policy necessarily implies greater aggregate risk taking is not nearly so black and white as it is often made out to be. When the central bank lowers its policy interest rate, it may lead to a great demand for risky loans, but it also leads to lower supply from lenders, and the overall effect on aggregate risky leverage buildup can be ambiguous.[3])

The classical hands-off approach still leaves open the question of what should be done to manage the risk of systemic financial crises. Ben Bernanke has argued forcefully that the right remedy for dealing with debt buildups is so-called macroprudential regulation, for example, putting limits on loan-to-value ratios in housing loans.[4] But this is easier said than done. After many years of a long boom, there are strong political economy pressures on regulators to ease up on markets that seem to be doing just fine. Yet it is exactly toward the end of long booms that risks start becoming the greatest, as Carmen Reinhart and I emphasize in our 2009 book on eight centuries of financial crises.[5]

Beyond that, crafting good financial regulation is not easy, and there will inevitably be important omissions, especially as the private sector will constantly be looking for weak links. The case for using interest rate policy to lean against the wind of a debt-fueled asset-price bubble was perhaps made most eloquently by former Fed governor Jeremy Stein, who said that, unlike macroprudential policy, interest rate policy gets in the "cracks" of the financial system. The Bernanke-Greenspan answer to this critique is that in a true asset-price boom, small interest rate changes won't burst a bubble. One can argue that they downplay too much the possibility that letting out a little steam from a bubble still might help make the cleanup easier.

For example, Bernanke and Greenspan have both pointed to the UK experience as illustrating that small interest rate hikes don't help much. In the run-up to 2008, the Bank of England prophylactically raised rates slightly to take froth off a real estate bubble, including housing but also parts of commercial real estate, such as a strip mall building boom. Bernanke and Greenspan are right that the hikes did not spare the United Kingdom the financial crisis, but it is hard to know whether they helped mitigate the costs. Cross-country comparisons are inherently difficult. The financial sector accounts for a larger share of output in the United Kingdom than in the United States (in 2008, it was 10% and 8%, respectively).[6] The United Kingdom was also far more exposed to the Eurozone debt crisis than the United States was through its links in banking and trade. In contrast, the housing bubble never burst in the United Kingdom the way it did in the United States, given land use restrictions, especially around London, that create a chronic housing shortage. Thus one cannot be sure that the modest pre-crisis interest rate hikes didn't help; it is difficult to disentangle cause and effect.

Anyone who has followed the debate on quantitative easing, which, after all, is a weak substitute for negative interest rates, will recognize broadly parallel arguments. The concern is that QE bids up the general level of asset prices, and if it goes too far for too long, systemic risks might arise. Though I tend to think the risks associated with QE in most countries have been justified, the fact is that economists don't fully understand the channels through which QE works, a problem I highlighted in chapter 8.

My conjecture is that the risks associated with periods of negative interest rates are going to be more like the risks associated with conventional easy monetary policy. I don't see any compelling reason for a discontinuity in the risk taken when interest rates are lowered from, say, 2% to 1% as when they are lowered from –1% to –2%, particularly after institutional frictions are addressed. The early experiences of Sweden, Denmark, Switzerland, and the Eurozone (albeit less so Japan) support the notion that there is no great discontinuity in financial stability, although the continuing existence of large notes and other impediments has severely circumscribed these efforts.

Of course, everything will be better to the extent that financial regulation is strengthened, with or without negative rates. Even with the huge intensification of financial regulation after the financial crisis of 2008, there is great scope for improvement. Perhaps the most compelling idea is to require banks to hold significantly more equity, but this debate does not turn critically on the zero bound.

Let us also remember that the whole premise of (significant) negative rates is to turbocharge the economy out of a deflationary recession. If being able to do "whatever it takes" with negative interest rates leads to a much shorter period of ultra-easy monetary policy, then the financial stability effects may turn out to be much smaller than after the, say, 7 or 8 years of near-zero interest rates that many countries have experienced.[7] To some degree, the financial stability argument might have it backward: if central banks could quickly exit deflation (stubbornly low inflation) using negative rates, they could normalize the economy more quickly, decreasing risks of financial instability, not increasing them.

TECHNICAL ISSUES WITH NEGATIVE RATES

Aside from financial stability, most other objections that have been raised to negative interest rates on currency relate to possible loopholes and technical challenges. We have considered some issues already in chapter 10, including the costs of transitioning legacy computer systems not designed to deal with negative interest rates, but there are many others.

For example, in the United States, self-employed individuals are supposed to pay taxes on a quarterly basis. With negative interest rates, there might be an incentive to overpay and later claim a zero interest refund. Maybe, but this seems to be truly a red herring and can be dealt with easily.

It seems quite a stretch to worry that some billionaire is going to arbitrage borrowing $100 million at a negative interest rate (presumably a bit higher than the rate the government pays), overpay estimated taxes by $100 million, and then claim it as a refund, creating a sort of "carry trade." Of course, in the unlikely event that negative interest rates sit at –4% for years on end, this would be an issue. But in that case, the government can easily make adjustments to discourage the practice at the margin. Current tax law already specifies an overpayment rate that is a function of short-term borrowing rates, and there is little reason in principle that this rate cannot be set to a negative value by the secretary of the Treasury.[8] Let's also bear in mind that the objective of negative interest rate policy is primarily macroeconomic stabilization, not raising revenue. Indeed, one suspects it must already be the case that those filing for very large tax refunds run a higher risk of audit. That risk should be more than enough to discourage your average billionaire from this practice. On top of that, the Internal Revenue Service exercises considerable discretion over the timing of the refund; it is hardly a fully liquid asset. There are many solutions to the tax prepayment problem, and it is just not a serious obstacle.

We discussed in chapter 10 the logistical complications that negative rates could create for bond issuers, and how they might be resolved. Relatedly, interest rate swap markets have become a key element of the financial ecosystem, allowing firms to conveniently hedge interest rate risk. A world of negative rates might require a restructuring of some of the institutions and legal frameworks surrounding these markets, but again, early experience in Europe suggests that this issue may not be nearly as problematic as some feared.

Some worry that in a world of negative interest rates, the custom of allowing the recipient of a check to decide when to cash it could be problematic. In other words, if you write me a check, I might wait to cash it until I need the money, forcing you to pay the negative interest rate "carry" in the meantime. Again, this seems a trivial problem. First, electronic payments can take this issue off the table. Second, and more importantly, the simple device of writing "not valid after 30 days" pretty much covers the problem. People can start having a time limit printed routinely on their checks, as many companies already do. Another problem along the same lines is that many contracts allow for prepayment of debts, and this calculus could change if there were negative interest rates. Again this is a minor issue and could be dealt with, for example, by introducing prepayment penalties, as is already the case with some mortgages. There is no big legal obstacle. The same reasoning extends to virtually every other private savings device. For example, it is no trouble for banks to add monthly service charges or other mechanisms to ensure negative effective interest rates on prepaid cards.

Would negative rates harm the health of financial intermediaries? As mentioned in chapter 10, if banks cannot pass the negative rates on to their depositors, they might have to add the charges to loans, so that interest rate cuts into negative territory did not feed through to the real economy. As pass-through does not seem to be a problem for the bank's larger customers, and the central bank can exempt some share of the smaller accounts through exemptions for individuals, the pass-through problem would not seem to be terribly difficult to overcome in due time. Clearly, it would be helpful to have legal and financial experts examine every aspect of negative rates to make a transition as smooth as possible.

Finally, when thinking about these hurdles, it is again important to bear in mind that part of the idea of employing negative short-term policy rates is to raise current and future expected inflation, thereby raising long-term rates and tilting the yield curve up. Even if short rates were expected to remain negative for a year or even two, one would not expect long-term nominal rates to be negative if the central bank seems determined to create inflation. Admittedly, it is difficult to know how aggressively the central bank will need to move to dislodge deflationary expectations. Especially when negative rates are a new tool, an overshoot may be necessary, but with such a powerful instrument, the central bank should be able to move the dial on expectations pretty quickly.

CHAPTER 12

Negative Interest Rates as a Violation of Trust and a Step Away from Rule-Based Systems

At this point, some readers may be asking themselves, "Do we really want to give the government the right to 'tax' currency?" Sure, maybe negative rates might be useful in periods of deflation and severe recession, but does anyone really trust a revenue-hungry government not to abuse this privilege in normal times? Shouldn't we worry that a government will invoke negative rates whenever it feels like it needs more money or is under pressure to repay high debts? One can quibble about the semantics of whether negative interest rates should be viewed as a tax or as a by-product of macroeconomic stabilization policy. Either way, many people will likely regard negative interest rates as a violation of the trust citizens place in their government by giving it a monopoly over the currency supply.

To see negative nominal interest rates as *unholy* but moderate inflation as just *bad* is to suffer what economists call "money illusion." In principle, there is no reason that currency holders should prefer a world with 2% inflation and a zero interest rate on currency to a world with zero inflation and a –2% interest rate on currency. Either way, the real rate of return on currency is –2%. (I am deliberately abstracting from the possibly different tax implications for ease of exposition.) A –2% rate of return may seem incredibly unattractive, but compared to the high-inflation 1970s, when the negative rate of return on holding currency hit double-digit levels, a –2% real return seems positively wonderful.

To mitigate concerns that money illusion would create broad-based populist protests against negative rates, and to avoid exacerbating inequality, there is no compelling reason that negative interest rates have to be passed on to small depositors. As discussed earlier, the government can provide an exemption for average daily deposit balances up to, say, $1,000 or $2,000, with individuals being allowed to register only one account. The central bank would provide the requisite subsidy in bulk to banks. Remember, the point of negative interest rates is to stimulate the economy on the margin, not to generate revenue.

If the concern is that negative interest rates will make it just too easy for governments to inflate, perhaps a brief discussion of modern monetary history will put that notion to rest. The simple fact is that if a central bank wants to debase your money, it already has all the tools it needs for doing so and can make it happen pretty darn fast. Even in an economy at the zero bound, a government intent on creating inflation at all costs can generate as much as it wants by just using the printing press to fund arbitrarily large government deficits (albeit a qualification is that even money-financed deficits won't work at the zero bound if the public is sufficiently concerned about the future tax liabilities inherent in government debt; recall the matryoshka doll discussion from chapter 8).[1]

Young people today in the advanced world have grown up without experiencing substantial inflation, but one hardly has to reach deep into the history books to find remarkable examples. As recently as the 1970s, double-digit inflation was the scourge of advanced economies, reaching 13% in the United States in 1980 and 23% in Japan in 1974.[2] Even as late as 1992, there were 44 countries with inflation above 40%.[3]

And 40% is nothing compared to hyperinflations of 2,000% per year or more. Table 12.1 shows the effects of modern-day hyperinflations on the value of currencies in emerging markets between 1970 and 2001. The Congo, with three bouts of hyperinflation (or near hyperinflation) during this period, and Brazil, with two, top the list. In the case of the Congo, for example, the cumulative inflation rate is almost 10 quadrillion (10 thousand trillion) percent (as proxied by exchange rate depreciation against the dollar).

The most famous hyperinflation is the one in post–World War I Germany, which reached 22 billion percent in 1923. There are stories of how children would meet their fathers at the factory gate

Table 12.1: Cumulative change in the currency's value versus the US dollar, January 1970–December 2001

Country	Cumulative percentage change
Congo, Democratic Republic of	9,924,011,976,047,800
Brazil	124,316,767,667,574
Argentina	2,855,714,286,430
Turkey	7,500,585
Mexico	77,249
Indonesia	2,798

Source: Reinhart and Rogoff (2002, table A1).

on payday, then race by bicycle to spend the money in town before it became worthless. The twenty-first-century record appears to belong to Zimbabwe, where inflation reached an annual rate of more than 24,000% in 2008 and a far higher rate than that at its peak.[4] (I had an undergraduate student from Zimbabwe at the time who commented that she could not figure out how the government calculated the official price level, as there was nothing to buy in the stores anyway.) Of course, there are still countries with very high inflation even today. The International Monetary Fund is already forecasting inflation of more than 1000% in governance-challenged Venezuela, which may prove optimistic.

All of this carnage was achieved without negative interest rates. Any government that cannot control its appetite for inflation finance is not easily contained once it has the printing press.

The change in inflation possibilities wrought by the printing press cannot be overstated. Most people associate King Henry VIII of England with beheading his wives, but monetary historians also know him for what he did to the country's coinage, reducing the silver content of the 1-pence coin by 67% between 1541 and 1547, a fall considered quite spectacular and damaging at the time.[5] One can only imagine what would have happened if he had discovered the joys of paper currency.

In modern economies, the real reason governments might be tempted to ramp up inflation is to default on debt, not to collect an inflation tax from currency. The currency supply in advanced economies runs from 5% to 10% of GDP, but net general government debt is far higher, 70% of GDP in the Eurozone and 83% among the G7 countries.[6] Won't having negative interest rates make it tempting for governments to try to fine-tune the inflation rate as a backdoor to partial default? Possibly, but it is not as easy for an advanced economy to inflate away a large part of its debt as one might think. The basic problem is that ramping up inflation takes time, because goods markets and labor markets adjust much more slowly than financial markets do. This differential makes it much harder to use modest shifts in monetary policy to significantly default on government debt. It is not as if the government can just push a money creation button and achieve surgically precise defaults through inflation. If the government appears to be starting a significant run-up in inflation, investors will start charging a premium immediately, long before inflation actually rises. Put differently, the slow adjustment of goods markets works in favor of a monetary policy aimed at short-run stimulus, precisely because prices and wages take time to adjust. But it works against a government that might be trying to use inflation to take the edge off of high debt levels, particularly if a large proportion of government debt is short term and needs to be frequently rolled over at new interest rates. As long as a government is constrained to pay market rates, its options are limited unless a large share of the debt is long term, in which case it has the luxury of ramping up inflation more slowly and still effectively defaulting (in real terms) on a large proportion of its debt.

The same basic argument applies if the government attempts to use inflationary policy to reduce the value of private debt. This is not to deny that a monetary loosening is good for debtors and bad for creditors. To get a dramatic effect, however, requires such a high and sudden surge in inflation that it would destroy the financial system and be self-defeating. A developing country under extreme fiscal duress and with a very small financial system might contemplate such a trade-off (as table 12.1 illustrates), but modern advanced countries really cannot, albeit many experienced extremely high inflation rates in the immediate aftermath of World War II.[7]

There is one way that an advanced-country government can reliably engage in partial default: through what is sometimes termed
"financial repression." Financial repression in this context means
quite simply that the government rams debt down the private-
sector's throat without paying market interest rates. At low inflation rates, this tactic doesn't accomplish very much very fast, but
if the inflation rate is 8% and the government forces banks, insurance companies, and pension funds to hold large amounts of non-
marketable government debt at a controlled interest rate of 2%,
then financial repression can bring the real value of government
debt down very fast. If you think this doesn't happen, think again:
a combination of interest rate controls and inflation played a huge
role in helping advanced countries bring their debt-to-income ratios down after World War II.[8] The widespread view that advanced
countries escaped their debts mainly through high growth ignores
the massive implicit taxes that financial repression imposed on
government debt holders.

It is true that the existing literature does not encompass the case
where the government has the option of setting interest rates at a
negative level, and it is an open question whether the additional
option could make a difference. At first blush, it would seem the
answer is no. Both printing currency (which increases supply) and
administratively lowering the interest rate on currency (which lowers demand) will create an incipient excess supply and ultimately
lead to a higher price level. (If there are short-run nominal price rigidities, then short-run output and employment effects also exist.)
Both approaches adversely impact the real value of government
bonds. However, this superficial equivalence probably requires
deeper exploration than is possible to provide here. Obviously,
with negative rates, the government can default almost instantaneously on currency, but the size of bond debt is much larger, and
that is the main issue.

The most important concern probably relates to whether negative rates might create greater temptations to engage in severe
financial repression. In classic financial repression, the government sets the interest rate at a positive level, then inflates and
forces captive savers to accept a significantly negative real rate of
interest. With the option of negative nominal rates, the government

could collect large financial repression revenues without having any inflation. And yes, this temptation could be a problem for revenue-starved governments, and could in principle lead to significant distortions. True, modern advanced economies have by and large learned to strike a balance between necessary financial regulation and distortionary financial repression, and it seems unlikely that negative rates would decisively tilt that balance. Nevertheless, it is an issue to be monitored. A good defense would simply be to insist that the central bank aim to use negative interest effectively and in a way that lifts the economy back to positive nominal rates reasonably quickly.

All in all, modern central banks have learned to contain inflation expectations effectively through a variety of innovations relating to independence, transparency, targeting, and communication. Ultimately, in any modern monetary regime, the public has to trust the central bank's intentions. If the central bank announces that it is aiming for 2% inflation, the public must trust that it will operate competently and responsibly to try to achieve that goal. From this perspective, the possibility of paying interest on currency (positive or negative) should be viewed as an improvement in the toolkit of the central bank without fundamentally altering the political economy that governs its actions.

One cannot deny that some people will think that negative interest rates are immoral, and explaining that they are victims of money illusion will do little to dissuade them. Then again, some people also feel very strongly about inflation, and negative interest rates can in principle allow economies to operate at a much lower average level of inflation by taking the zero bound off the table. As for default on government debt, modern governments already have extensive tools for achieving partial default through financial repression. Negative rates do expand the government's options, and it will be important to monitor abuse, but this seems like a relatively small price for having the capacity to break the zero bound in deep recessions and to restore the full efficacy of monetary policy in normal recessions. Nevertheless, the question of whether negative rates might create instability in monetary policy is likely to concern many people, so we pursue it in greater depth in the next section.

WILL NEGATIVE RATES UNDERMINE RULE-BASED MONETARY SYSTEMS?

Up to this point, we have looked at some visceral issues related to negative interest rates, namely, the question of whether they constitute a breach of trust, and whether a shift to negative rates would be a precursor to a new era of ultra-high inflation. We next take up the issue of whether allowing for negative interest rates would make it harder for the monetary authorities to maintain an effective rule-based monetary system. Even without negative interest rates, the debate over discretion and rules became intense over the course of the financial crisis. The disagreement really centers on the question of how much flexibility a central bank needs to retain in order to deal with out-of-the-box surprises and events that are difficult to incorporate into rules. In a sense, the topic of flexibility versus commitment in monetary policy is far broader than the scope of this book, but it is a hot-button issue that is arguably magnified by negative rates, so it is important to discuss it here.

Since 2001, and particularly since the financial crisis of 2008, leading monetary scholars such as John Taylor and Allan Meltzer have strongly criticized central banks for departing too much from rule-based systems by keeping interest rates too low for too long. There is in fact a long history of debate over whether the government should be trusted with discretionary monetary policy at all. The great monetarist economist Milton Friedman was convinced that a stable long-term relationship existed among base money, inflation, and economic growth, a relationship documented in his magisterial book with Anna Schwartz, *A Monetary History of the United States*.[9] Motivated by his research, Friedman argued that the best way to ensure stable growth and inflation was simply to keep the money supply on a steady, predictable growth path.

Friedman perfectly well understood that monetary policy could be a potent tool for economic stabilization, but he argued that central banks were so incompetent and so prone to inflationary finance that life would be simpler and better if the whole concept of Keynesian activist monetary policy was simply forgotten. More- over, he argued, the best way to guarantee a passive monetary policy was to pass a constitutional amendment that would fix the rate of money supply expansion in perpetuity. Friedman began espousing the idea of a constant money growth rule in the 1960s[10] and had many influential followers in the 1970s and 1980s, most notably Nobel Prize winner Robert Lucas. Lucas developed a theoretical framework showing that, under certain assumptions, activist monetary policy created random noise that made it more difficult for consumers to sort out movements in relative prices across diverse goods from generalized inflation.

The late 1970s and early 1980s were perhaps the peak period of Friedman's direct influence on monetary policy. His view that real-world activist monetary policy usually does more harm than good seemed to be utterly corroborated by blundering central bankers, who badly mishandled the 1970s breakup of the Bretton Woods system of fixed exchange rates, as well as the sharp concomitant rise in global commodity prices. The United States, which was supposed to make the US dollar the bedrock of the international financial system, was at the epicenter of the problem. Instead of maintaining a stable money supply and inflation rate, the Federal Reserve massively increased the money supply in the run-up to the 1972 presidential election, in part to stimulate growth and help incumbent US president Richard Nixon get re-elected. (As Allan Meltzer documents in his research on the history of the Federal Reserve System, one can actually listen to the Watergate tapes and hear Nixon crudely pressure Fed chairman Arthur Burns to pump-prime the economy.)[11] Nixon won the election in a landslide, but afterward inflation soared. Burns was succeeded by William Miller who, in his brief tenure from March 1978 to August 1979, managed to make things even worse. Miller made the fundamental mistake of focusing only on short-term stimulus while not paying attention to anchoring long-term expectations. Only when Paul Volcker came in as Fed chairman in August 1979 did inflation start to stabilize, and then only after a painful recession as the economy adjusted to a lower inflation rate.

At the time, the common assessment was that Volcker had simply implemented Friedman's policy; after all, the Volcker Fed used money supply targets to help justify the tight interest rate policy needed to bring down inflation. It was, again, a high-water mark for monetarism. But curiously, around the same time, the tight link between the money supply and inflation that Friedman emphasized began to disappear. The problem, emphasized in Princeton professor Steve Goldfeld's 1976 paper "The Case of the Missing Money" was not hard to ascertain.[12] Thanks to a mix of new technologies (the growth of credit cards), financial liberalization (particularly the end of restrictions on the interest rates banks could pay), and deregulation that created new instruments like money market funds, the relationship between Friedman's notion of "money" and inflation began to fray badly. For a time, the Federal Reserve tried to find a link between money and prices by developing ever more expansive measures of "money," for example, incorporating money market funds in addition to checking and savings accounts, with the aim of trying to find some notion of money that still had a stable reliable relationship with the price level. But such efforts were largely to no avail.

In the event, Friedman's measure of money grew far more slowly at times than inflation, because as the economy adjusted to new technologies, it simply was not necessary to have as much currency (or any form of older payment technology, e.g., checking accounts) to achieve the same level of transactions. High inflation was also a factor. Ironically, Friedman's fixed money supply rule might have led to the very kind of inflation he was aiming to control. Had Friedman's constitutional amendment for fixed money growth been put into effect, the world might have experienced extremely erratic inflation rates.

What happened instead is that central banks changed the way they did business, paying much more attention to long-run expectations. A key development that made this possible was a generalized move to make central banks more independent, sparked by academic research that explained why the ability to resist short-run political pressures to cut short-term interest rates was actually the key to keeping down long-term interest rates. Nowadays, many central banks around the world enjoy substantial independence, but that was not the case 30 years ago. Back in the early 1980s, it was really only the Bundesbank and the Federal Reserve that could claim significant independence among the major central banks.

At the Federal Reserve, I got to see the transition between William Miller and Paul Volcker close up. Watching the incorruptible Volcker's success unfold after the pliant Miller's failure greatly influenced my research. The experience prompted me, in the early 1980s, to develop a theory on why it might make sense for society to make its central banks independent, and for the central banks to choose targets that would help stabilize long-term inflation expectations, not just targets that would promote short-term growth. Starting in the late 1980s, many countries across the world began to make their central banks more independent and much more focused on inflation stabilization.

Yes, many countries still struggle with achieving low and stable inflation, for example, Brazil, Russia, Vietnam, and Turkey. But even in these countries, the issues pale next to the very high inflation these countries once experienced as recently as the 1990s.

Yet there are still those who, in the tradition of Friedman, remain convinced that it would be better to dispense with activist monetary policy and have central banks focus just on price stability and nothing else. In his politically influential 2009 best seller *End the Fed*, Texas congressman Ron Paul argued that the financial crisis revealed the US central bank to be undemocratic and favoring the Wall Street elite. Through its quantitative easing polices, the Fed was massively raising the money supply (we have already noted why this characterization is incredibly misleading at the zero bound), and ultimately the United States would experience hyperinflation. Paul argues for abolishing the Federal Reserve and returning to some form of the gold standard. Paul's book inspired a wave of venom being hurled at the Fed, culminating with Texas Governor Rick Perry's attack on Fed chair Ben Bernanke in the 2012 Republican presidential primaries, where Perry stated, "Printing more money to play politics at this particular time in American history is almost treasonous."[13]

THE WIZARD OF OZ AND THE POLITICS OF MONEY

It is hardly the first time in US history that the debate over the monetary system has spilled over into presidential politics. In July

1832, President Andrew Jackson killed the Second Bank of the United States by vetoing a bill to renew its charter, saying that "the rich and powerful bend the acts of the government to their selfish purposes."[14] The United States did not again have anything resembling a central bank until Congress created the Federal Reserve System in 1913. And the Free Silver movement was an expansionary-currency philosophy espoused by the populist candidate William Jennings Bryan at the Democratic convention in 1896. In this era, the concern was that the gold supply was inadequate to keep up with the fast rate of growth in the United States, leading to a deflationary spiral. The Free Silver advocates wanted to be able to have money backed by silver at the ratio of 16 to 1 versus gold. This change would have raised inflation and helped out heavily indebted farmers, who were suffering under mortgage payments that remained fixed even as the prices of their agricultural goods fell.

There is a fascinating debate about whether Frank Baum's magnificent children's tale *The Wonderful Wizard of Oz* was really intended as an allegory for the gold standard. The book, of course, formed the basis for the classic 1939 Judy Garland movie of the same name. The notion that the story might be an allegory was first raised by high school teacher Henry Littlefield in 1964, and later taken further by other authors, most notably economist Hugh Rockoff in a 1990 *Journal of Political Economy* piece. Whether right or not, the allegory is often used as a teaching tool for efficient introduction to monetary economics concepts. Littlefield draws the remarkable connection between the characters in the book and the main players in the 1890's populist movement. The Scarecrow represents the farmers, the Tin Man represents industrial workers, and the Cowardly Lion is William Jennings Bryan. The characters in the Emerald City see everything through green glasses (green paper currency), and the yellow brick road is a narrow trap. Importantly, in the book version, Dorothy has silver slippers, not ruby ones. At the end of the story, Dorothy learns that to return safely to her family farm, all she needs to do is tap her shoes together, signifying the simple answer of the Free Silver movement.

Regardless of author Frank Baum's intentions, there is little doubt that deflation occurred at times under the gold standard, and the problem illustrates some of the drawbacks of any commodity-backed currency. Indeed, the idea that the gold standard produced spectacular stability is a fantasy and a false image of what the gold standard was really like. The gold standard era was punctuated by deep recessions (the recession of 1893 was in some ways almost as profound as the Great Depression of the 1930s). There were bank runs and long bouts of deflation. Nothing stopped governments from abandoning the gold standard when they desperately needed funding to pay for World War I. Once citizens realized that the gold standard might not go on forever, it proved extremely fragile. There is little reason to believe that a modern-day gold standard would fare any better.

Efforts to design an alternative rule-based monetary system have proved elusive, although some progress has been made. Virtually every central bank in the world today says it is engaged in some form of inflation targeting, albeit the interpretation is broad and diverse, so that in practice, the moniker has only limited meaning. Some central banks take a rather rigid view of inflation targets (in principle, the charter of the European Central Bank (ECB) directs it to look only at inflation). Others, such as the United States Federal Reserve, practice flexible inflation targeting, which tends to mean that inflation is a factor in the central bank's interest rate decision, but not necessarily to the exclusion of other macroeconomic variables, notably output and employment.

Among modern-day monetary rules that take multiple factors into account, perhaps the best known is the Taylor rule (discussed in the section on Taylor's rule in the appendix), which posits that the central bank should set its policy interest rate according to deviations of output from its full-employment level and inflation from its target level. The Taylor rule has many virtues and is certainly a quantum improvement over the gold standard or the Friedman rule. But even the original Taylor rule, which had proved a very useful device for many years, is not reliable enough to enshrine in any kind of rigid law for central banks. Indeed, in the aftermath of the financial crisis of 2008, central banks held interest rates at zero for much longer than a mechanical interpretation of the Taylor rule would have suggested, yet inflation remained stubbornly low anyway. Simple rules may perform well for long periods, but a mechanism is needed for an escape clause, especially during catastrophic events that fall far outside the historical norm, such as the financial crisis of 2008.

Again, our long digression into rule-based alternatives to the current monetary regime is to address objections from people who do not entirely trust the central bank to protect the value of their money, and perhaps share the Friedman-Lucas view that activist monetary policy likely does more harm than good. So they would almost surely look askance at giving the central bank the power to charge negative interest rates if the main idea is to enhance the bank's capacity for countercyclical policy.

My 1985 paper (inspired by the contrast between Miller and Volcker) raised the idea that the ideal monetary system is one that balances flexibility and commitment. This is really the most critical element in central bank design. Just as the experience of the 1980s showed what can go wrong when there is too little commitment to keeping inflation low in the long term, the recent financial crisis and its aftermath has arguably illustrated what can go wrong when there is too much. Yes, many authors have since written papers that argue how in a perfect world, it is always possible to find a system that gets it just right and involves no compromises. And unfortunately, during the 1990s and early 2000s, many central banks bought into the idea that they could find an ideal rule that dispensed with any trade-offs.

But just as it is hard to design a rule that is always just right, it is hard to design any incentive mechanism or institutional set of rules that is always going to look optimal ex post. Hence, despite the inevitability of having some human error, it is probably ideal to have a system that tries to balance flexibility and commitment. In my view, the modern central bank has suffered from an overshoot in the weight put on rigidity versus flexibility; central bankers were too ready to believe that inflation targeting and simple rules would essentially eliminate any need for trade-offs. The experience of the past 8 years has shown how wrong that view is. Although allowing for negative interest rates would help alleviate the need for flexibility by taking away the zero bound, it is important to be prepared for other outside-the-box surprises in the future.[15]

Still, although there is clearly room for improvement, the modern-day system of having independent central banks run by technocratic central bankers has worked far better than any other system so far, certainly better than a gold standard would. In the context of today's broadly competent and independent central banks, introducing the possibility of negative interest rates should not be a big problem. And if negative interest rates are viewed as posing an inflation risk at the margin, the right remedy is to strengthen central bank independence, not to undermine it. In today's context, the advent of negative interest rates should be viewed as a technical fix, and certainly not an occasion to question the broad principle of central bank independence.

CONCLUSION TO PART II

The issue of negative rates is an extremely complex one that hits on many of the challenges and problems facing monetary policy in general. Even during the period of early experimentation with negative rates by several European countries and Japan, the topic has brought up heated debate. In part II of this book, we have gone through the case for facilitating the use of negative interest rates. We have explored some alternative ways to mitigate the zero bound, including other ways to clear the path for unlimited negative interest rate policy without phasing out paper currency. We have also analyzed objections that negative interest rate policy might lead to price instability, financial instability, and a departure from rule-based monetary policy.

In brief, although there are a host of issues and objections, the case for properly designed negative interest rate policy is a strong one. If central banks had the option of setting interest rates to negative levels without limit, they would have far more scope than they do today for pushing an economy quickly out of a deflationary spiral and for counteracting the effects of credit contraction after a systemic financial crisis. Lowering interest rates to negative levels would temporarily raise aggregate demand and strongly incentivize banks to lend out excess reserves. But for such efforts to be truly effective, it is necessary to clear the path fully for negative interest rates. First and foremost, this means taking away (or substantially taking away) incentives to hoard cash when interest rates are negative, incentives that presently put a huge check on the effectiveness of policy. It also means preparing all the "plumbing" for negative rates in terms of legal, tax, and institutional changes. Again, the present experience of tiptoeing into negative rates cannot be viewed as a decisive test of how they might work after the necessary preparations have been made, because many issues have yet to be dealt with, especially finding a way to deal with a run into cash.

A true shift to a world where negative interest policy is possible will be transformative, comparable to moving off the gold standard in the 1930s, moving off fixed exchange rates in the 1970s, and the advent of modern independent central banks around the world in the 1980s and 1990s. Like all of these changes, there will be uncertainties during the transition, but after awhile, central banks and financial market participants likely won't be able to imagine doing things any other way.

Lastly, let's understand that negative interest rates are no panacea for all of an economy's ills. They do not substitute for education and infrastructure investment, nor market-friendly reforms, nor rational countercyclical fiscal policy. But they can restore the effectiveness of monetary policy at the zero bound, and clear the air of confusion in the policy debate.

PART III

International Dimensions and Digital Currencies

CHAPTER 13

International Dimensions to Phasing Out Paper Currency

In this last and relatively brief part of the book, we take up a couple of important questions that have been treated somewhat cursorily until now: the international dimensions of phasing out paper currency, and the implications of digital currencies. These are both substantial topics that can fill many books on their own, and they certainly appear to raise objections to phasing out paper currency, at least at a superficial level. On closer inspection though, neither consideration raises challenges that cannot be met or that trump the main case I have presented thus far.

We begin with the important question of whether the phaseout of paper currency will need to be coordinated internationally. If criminals in the United States can't use $100 bills, won't they just conduct transactions with large Canadian-dollar, yen, and euro notes? Relatedly, wouldn't it be foolish for one region (say, the United States or the Eurozone) to unilaterally give up its share of the profits to be garnered by supplying paper currency to international criminals? What about emerging markets or developing economies—should any of them be thinking about a paperless world? Also, what if some advanced countries succeed in defanging the zero bound, but others remain stuck there?

WOULDN'T FOREIGN NOTES SUBSTITUTE FOR DOMESTIC ONES?

Let me be clear: foreign paper currency would hardly take the US underground by storm after a phaseout of US notes. The most important point is that foreign notes would be difficult to recycle into the legal domestic US economy, and it is neither easy nor cheap to move large quantities in and out.

The experience of the United Kingdom is a good case in point, because in a sense, it has already faced the problem of being a relatively small-note country situated next to a mega-note neighbor. Recall that the largest actively printed Bank of England note is only 50 pounds (about $75), and the United Kingdom is just a channel away from the Eurozone, with its big notes (a 500-euro note is worth about $570).[1] Brexit will not change this.

Back in 2010, the United Kingdom's Serious Organised Crime Agency (SOCA) pointed to the scourge of the 500-euro note in the UK underground economy.[2] The agency's name sounds like something out of a James Bond film, but SOCA really did exist from 2006 to 2013. Their annual reports provide a veritable handbook on the problem of money laundering and cash in the underground economy for anyone who wants to take the issue seriously. SOCA's research, involving multiple law enforcement agencies, showed that more than 90% of UK demand for the 500-euro note came from criminals. Working in conjunction with experts from the financial industry and elsewhere, SOCA concluded that "there was no credible legitimate use for the 500-euro note in the United Kingdom in the volumes being supplied, and that easy access to it was a key enabler of criminal activity, since it allowed criminals to move large volumes of cash effectively."[3]

Thanks to SOCA, and in coordination with the UK Treasury, private note wholesalers were persuaded to stop providing 500-euro notes in the United Kingdom, making them hard to obtain through a bank, for example. It is not illegal to hold 500-euro notes in the United Kingdom, but it has become a lot riskier to hold significant quantities without raising suspicion. In due time, the United Kingdom will have to take similar actions with respect to 100- and 200-euro notes, especially now that the European Central Bank (ECB) has finally been persuaded to phase out the 500-euro note.

As the United Kingdom did with large-denomination euro notes, any country that phases out cash unilaterally will need to put in place obstacles to moving large amounts of foreign currency in and out of the domestic financial system. Those obstacles, however, already exist in spades, with the various anti-money-laundering regulations. Anyone taking more than $10,000 worth of currency in or out of the United States needs to report it; in the European Union, the limit is 10,000 euros; most other countries now have similar strictures. Anyone making substantial cash deposits and withdrawals of foreign currency (or domestic currency) needs to fill out paperwork, and banks are required to report large transactions. And cash limits can be lowered in the future.

In a world where ordinary retailers are not accepting euros, and where paper dollars have been (mostly) phased out, laundering paper euro notes is not going to be easy. True, there is no law stopping a US store or restaurant from taking payment in euros. (The legal tender status of the dollar only requires that it be accepted as payment of debts.[4]) But any US business that comes to the bank each week with a pile of euros might as well have "money laundering operation" emblazoned on its stationery. It will draw attention. Yes, it will also be important to stop casinos from laundering wholesale quantities of euros, but this can be accomplished easily enough as well.

What if big euro notes just sat in the underground economy, facilitating crime and trade, without ever entering the legal economy? For example, a black market could develop for large-denomination euro notes on the darknet, effectively allowing a 100-, 200- or 500-euro note to be used multiple times before being smuggled out of the United States. I have addressed this basic point before in chapters 5 and 7, but repeat it here, because it is fundamental. Any bills that can be used only in the underground economy would sell at steep discounts, because they would be costly and difficult to use. For tax evaders and even criminals, high transactions costs and illiquidity would be significant impediments akin to the problems with uncut diamonds; they want to spend their money in retail stores and online, like everyone else. Last but not least, if the bills did retain high value, counterfeits would eventually intrude once innovation in the notes' security features had stopped.

FORGONE PROFITS FROM SUPPLYING THE WORLD UNDERGROUND WITH THEIR FAVORED TRANSACTIONS TECHNOLOGY

Next we turn to the question of all the income the United States (or the Eurozone) makes by supplying a universally accepted anonymous transaction medium to the world underground economy. We have looked at estimates of foreign holdings of dollars and euros in chapter 3, and certainly they are significant, accounting for perhaps as much as half of the United States' profits from selling paper currency. I have also argued, however, that the entire amount of seigniorage revenue loss is likely canceled out by indirect benefits due to higher tax revenues from the underground economy, not to mention all the ancillary benefits in terms of crime reduction. If the United States phases out paper currency (except perhaps for small bills and/or coins, as per chapter 7), the euro's share would rise, though probably not proportionately. For countries like Mexico, Colombia, and Argentina, underground US dollars are far more liquid than underground euro notes, given the frequent back-and-forth exchange of goods and people with the United States. Sure, the Eurozone would get some new business from drug lords and human traffickers who had been relying on dollars, and would thus be a beneficiary. Hopefully, they are not going to want this business, especially if European leaders begin to better appreciate the role cash plays in financing illegal immigration and terrorist activities, not to mention facilitating tax evasion.

Yes, in an ideal world, the rest of the G7 countries, and eventually even safe-haven countries with large notes (e.g., Switzerland, Singapore, and Hong Kong), would do the same. One benefit of coordinated action is that it might simply be easier to sell politically. It would also be the most effective means of addressing global crime. Global criminals could and would use alternative currencies, for example, yuan and rubles, but these are vastly less liquid (consider China's capital controls) and are hardly a perfect substitute for the world's key currencies. Moreover, China's largest note, the 100 yuan, is equal to only $16 (although larger notes are reportedly being considered).[5]

Admittedly, some would argue that large US notes are a powerful force for good in countries like Russia, where paper dollars give ordinary citizens refuge from corrupt government officials. Realtors in Moscow think nothing of someone buying an apartment with a suitcase full of $100 bills. Unfortunately, for every case where dollar or euro paper currency is facilitating a transaction that Americans might somehow judge morally desirable, there are probably many more cases where they would not, for example, human trafficking in young Russian and Ukrainian girls to France and the Middle East. Closer to home, the drug lords in Colombia and Mexico receive dollars from their US sales, and they pay dollars to buy weapons and to corrupt politicians, police, and customs agents. On balance, even taking into account instances where dollarization helps support economic activity when the local currency is not trusted (a situation several Latin American countries have found themselves in),[6] the foreign policy argument for keeping paper currency is extremely dubious.

So far, the discussion has centered on the United States dollar. What about other countries' currencies? Each country has its own legal and cultural institutions, but broadly speaking, the case for phasing out paper currency is actually even stronger than for the United States.

For Japan, the question of loss of seigniorage from the international criminal mafia is not terribly relevant, as the yen is little used outside Japan. Indeed, Japan should be considered a prime candidate to be the first large country to phase out paper currency, given the country's long battle with ultra-low inflation and the weak credibility of the Bank of Japan's long-term inflation targets. Whatever happens over the next few years, Japan is clearly highly vulnerable to the kind of deflation relapse it has experienced repeatedly over the past two decades. As noted in chapter 7, a few smaller advanced economies, such as Sweden and Denmark, have already taken significant steps toward sharply reducing the use of cash in their economies.

There is a somewhat different set of concerns in the United Kingdom, where euros move particularly easily in and out of the country, despite the restriction that all travelers carrying more than 10,000 euros are supposed to fill out a form reporting their cash holdings. European citizens have easy access in and out of the UK, and will surely continue to do so in any future regime. By some estimates, there are as many as 300,000–400,000 French citizens living in London, leading London's mayor, Boris Johnson, in 2013 to observe that he was mayor of the sixth-largest French city.[7] For the United Kingdom, it certainly will be much easier to phase out paper currency (soon to be plastic currency) in coordination with Europe. However, controls of the type SOCA and the Treasury have already implemented could easily be extended to other large-denomination foreign notes.

EMERGING MARKETS

Most emerging markets would likely be large net beneficiaries if advanced countries phased out their own paper currencies, especially the large-denomination notes so prevalent in corruption and crime. But for most, it is far too soon to contemplate phasing out their own currencies. For one thing, most emerging markets are not anywhere near the zero bound on interest rates; many are working hard to keep inflation rates in single digits, and most are forced to pay risk premiums on their bonds. So the need for negative interest rates to promote the smooth functioning of monetary policy is just not an urgent one. In addition, although some emerging markets are ahead of the curve on cell phone banking, their overall financial infrastructures are much less developed, with a high proportion of people still being unbanked (e.g., roughly 50% in Colombia). So the burden of providing free universal debit cards far exceeds what it would be in a country such as the United States or Germany. In China, in particular, a large share of the population still lives in relatively poor agricultural communities, so even if the major coastal cities could go cash free, the whole of China cannot. The challenges in India, which is growing but still significantly lags China in economic development, are even greater.

Perhaps most importantly, for emerging markets and developing economies, it is far from clear that measures to reduce the size of the informal economy by reducing the use of cash will be a net benefit. A great deal of informal employment makes use of workers with low human capital who could not clear the threshold for employment in the formal sector and could not be easily absorbed by firms required to bear the costs of dealing with weak government institutions.

That said, many emerging markets have profound corruption problems, which are a central cause of the weak institutions that are holding back development.[8] A case in point is Brazil's spectacular recent oil and construction corruption scandal, where the total amount for bribes and kickbacks is reported to have exceeded $3 billion and counting, and corruption allegations have reached the highest level.[9] Of course, corruption on this scale takes many forms besides cash, but cash still features in many reports. Even if it is far too soon for emerging markets to contemplate phasing out their own currencies, there is a case for phasing out large notes. At the present, given the very weak exchange rate of the Brazilian real to the dollar, the largest note (100 reais) is worth only $30, but just a few years back, it was worth closer to $60.

DO NEGATIVE INTEREST RATES REQUIRE INTERNATIONAL COORDINATION?

So far this chapter has been dealing with international issues arising from phasing out paper currency, but what about spillovers from negative policy interest rates? For concreteness, suppose the Federal Reserve is the first major central bank to completely remove the zero bound barrier, with other advanced countries only able to tiptoe into negative rate territory because of paper currency. In normal circumstances, with positive interest rates, the need for international monetary policy coordination among advanced economies appears to be relatively minor. Yes, spillovers do occur, but they appear to be second order.[10] As long as countries keep their own monetary houses in order, the system will work relatively well. (There are a variety of qualifiers to this broad claim, particularly if a major country faces severe distortions that can be mitigated by activist monetary policy, but we need not get into them here.)[11]

The monetary policy coordination literature, however, by and large does not take account of the zero bound and assumes that every country is able to move its interest rate as necessary to balance inflation and output deviations. Only recently have economists started to study seriously how the zero bound affects the usual results. Some new research has suggested how a large central bank mired in the quicksand of the liquidity trap can pull down a lot of other countries with it, and when several countries are trapped, it can set off a round of competitive exchange rate devaluations as the last resort of monetary policy.[12]

In principle, one can extend this analysis to address the question of what happens if policy interest rates in all major regions have collapsed to zero, but some central banks have the capacity to go deeply negative when others do not. Suppose, for example, a global recession collapses all major central bank policy interest rates to zero, but the United States has phased out paper currency, while other central banks have not. This would allow the Federal Reserve to take its interest rate deeply negative, while others would remain stuck at the effective lower bound. The drop in US interest rates will be a net positive contribution to global demand, but the concomitant exchange rate depreciation will shift global demand toward the United States. At a minimum, the United States will benefit disproportionately, and in principle it is possible other countries might actually be worse off than if the US were stuck at the zero bound like everyone else. This is an open research question, but it is easy to imagine that spillovers of unilateral negative rate policy could be first order and could produce great tensions.

In some sense, the world has already had a version of this asymmetry. In the decade before the financial crisis of 2008, the Bank of Japan alone was stuck at the zero bound, while other central banks were not. The decade did not go well for Japan, though it is hard to isolate the extent to which a lack of international monetary policy coordination played a role.

So far we have focused on monetary policy cooperation across advanced economies, where spillovers might be modest. The same cannot be said for emerging markets. Emerging markets are profoundly affected by US monetary policy, with shocks to US interest rates having a marked impact on their equity and bond markets. London School of Economics professor Hélène Rey has argued that this vulnerability to global capital market conditions seems to affect emerging markets whether they choose to be on fixed or flexible exchange rates.[13] On the face of it, allowing for negative interest rates in the United States would seem to exacerbate the problem by amplifying US interest rate cycles. However, if the tool of negative rates allowed the United States to escape much more quickly from a liquidity trap, it is possible that the spillovers would be lessened.

As things currently stand, the Federal Reserve does not directly weigh the welfare of other countries when determining its policy; they count only to the extent that any adverse effects might rebound back on the United States. This is hardly a desirable state of global governance but is not an issue I aim to tackle here.

CHAPTER 14

Digital Currencies and Gold

When I suggest to people that there might be benefits to phasing out paper currency, they almost invariably assume I am advocating a cryptocurrency like Bitcoin and are a bit disappointed to find out otherwise.[1] No doubt anyone who looks at distributed-ledger technologies has to be excited about their potential applications in financial services and record keeping in general. For the foreseeable future, however, the best system is one in which a government-issued currency is the unit of account, though of course it will eventually morph into a fully electronic one.

I appreciate that many leaders in the alternative payment space hold the libertarian view that new web-based transaction technologies can free people from the tyranny of government currency and regulation. They have deep conviction that with encrypted digital currencies like Bitcoin, someday no one will have to trust banks, either. For true believers in the promise of cryptocurrencies, trying to find ways of improving the current system, as this book aims to do, is a waste of time. Better to fast-forward to the brave new world where governments are no longer in the payments picture and no longer even control the unit of account.

With all due respect to promising security advances offered by public ledger technology and the ingenious algorithms embodied in some of the new "currencies," the view that Bitcoin—or any other cryptocurrency—is going to replace the dollar anytime soon is quite naive. As currency innovators have learned over the millennia, it is hard to stay on top of the government indefinitely in a game where the latter can keep adjusting the rules until it wins. If the private sector comes up with a much better way of doing things, the government will eventually adapt and regulate as necessary to eventually win out. Even if (for argument's sake), cryptocurrency technology proved unstoppable, the winner (say,

Bitcoin 3.0) would only end up being a precursor to a government-controlled "Bencoin" (after Benjamin Franklin, who now adorns the US $100 bill).

It is not because modern-day governments are so worried about seigniorage revenues from currency; at least that should not be their main concern. The real issues involve the ability to use monetary policy to (1) stabilize the private economy, (2) issue credit in response to financial crises (act as a lender of last resort), and (3) be able to inflate the price level in an emergency where it is necessary to engage in partial default (in real terms) on government debt. To achieve these ends effectively, it is extremely helpful for the government to control the unit of account and the currency to which most private contracts are indexed.

If the world ends up on a private-sector currency standard, and there is a run on banks, who is going to bail out the banks? Yes, historically, the private sector has occasionally organized bailouts. New York banker J. P. Morgan famously helped stem the panic of 1907, which occurred before the Federal Reserve was created in 1913. Morgan pledged large sums of his own money and convinced other New York bankers to do the same, enabling them to shore up the banks. This is just not going to work in today's globalized world, certainly not in a really deep systemic crisis. The government is going to have to step in, if not to bail out financial markets, then to organize an orderly default.

It is critical that the government be able to draw on large pools of liquidity in the event of a war, pandemic, or other crisis that creates large unexpected short-term funding needs. There are several dimensions to maintaining "fiscal space," including prudent debt management, but being able to control the unit of account is an extremely important safety valve. It is especially useful if a country's debt is denominated in its own currency, giving the government the option of partial default through inflation. On top of dealing with outright catastrophes, a country that does not control its own currency is unable to use modern monetary stabilization policy.

Multiple units of account may coexist, and one can find many small economies where both the local currency and the dollar (or euro) are widely accepted. But, in general, the unit of account is a natural monopoly that a well-run government with strong legal and fiscal institutions is uniquely well poised to control. If the US government ever decides to oversee a Bencoin, it can use seigniorage profits to help defray costs of maintaining the system, and it can use tax revenues to ensure that the system never becomes insolvent. These are advantages a private currency cannot compete with. Even more importantly, it can use laws, regulations, and outright coercion to come out on top: a determined government is always going to win the battle for currency supremacy, at least in the long run. Other transaction media may thrive, but the government currency will be at the center.

Regardless of whether the first generation of cryptocurrencies survives the next decade, the public ledger encryption technology they pioneer just might provide a road map to better security over a broad range of financial transactions. The basic idea, in a nutshell, is to create a system in which diverse private-sector individuals (or entities) are incentivized to maintain independent ledgers of transaction trees (or blockchains), and new transactions cannot clear the books without achieving a critical mass of third-party acceptance. A fair dose of encryption technology is also included, and in Bitcoin, for example, individuals are allowed to use aliases with passcode-protected accounts to make it difficult to determine their identities. A lot of truly fascinating science supports the different systems, and one can find many excellent treatments.[2]

Governments around the world have already begun regulating cryptocurrencies more aggressively. In the United States, Bitcoin wallets must now comply with anti-money-laundering rules, and the Internal Revenue Service has begun to issue rulings on how Bitcoin earnings should be taxed. The European Union, too, is in the process of intensifying its regulations. Where governments have the greatest leverage is in regulating how financial institutions interact with cryptocurrencies. In China, although trading in cryptocurrencies between individuals is legal at present, financial institutions are proscribed from buying, selling, and insuring these currencies or any derivative products. Advanced countries have temporarily taken a more hands-off approach, but this will not last forever. By controlling the gateway into the financial system and the legal economy, governments have tremendous leverage to undermine the value and liquidity of any alternative currency scheme that attempts to avoid regulation permanently.

This recurrent theme parallels the discussion from chapter 7, where I asked what would happen if $100 bills continued to circulate in the underground economy long after they had been phased out of the legal economy. A cryptocurrency that cannot be used for legal retail purchases or converted at banks might have a longer life than a defunct $100 bill, but its reach, importance, and usefulness would likely be distinctly limited.

Plenty of other targets in the transaction ecosystem in theory could be overtaken by digital currencies, even after adjusting to regulation. The huge fees collected by credit card agencies, wire services, and other extant electronic transaction technologies make these media extremely vulnerable to disruptive innovators. Already, digital currencies are far cheaper for transmitting money internationally than wire services, where the charges can often run as much as 10–15% of the amount transmitted. And some applications of distributed-ledger technology offer the promise of cutting out intermediaries in transactions between, say, two banks. This would substantially reduce costs, particularly in international transactions. The approach can also be used to save on legal contracting costs. Some of Bitcoin's competitors, notably the newer Ethereum platform, aim to offer the possibility of creating secure exchanges for transactions of almost any type.

People sometimes ask whether the cryptocurrency Bitcoin *could* be a currency (supposing that the government does not interfere). The answer is certainly yes, Bitcoin (or perhaps one of its present or future competitors) can fulfill many of the basic functions of currency, including unit of account and medium of exchange, with or without government adherence.[3] In fact, digital currencies in some ways offer the capacity for much more complex kinds of transactions and contracts than traditional paper currency offers, precisely because the former embed so much information, including the history of transactions. Already, markets are forming to exploit this capacity, for example, in applications surrounding Ethereum.[4]

That distributed-ledger technology could in theory someday produce a superior currency, however, hardly means that the world is already there in practice. One problem is that the value of Bitcoin 1.0 fluctuates wildly (figure 14.1), so it hardly fulfills the function of a stable store of value. In principle, it could become more stable if it gained more widespread monetary acceptance. Figure 14.2

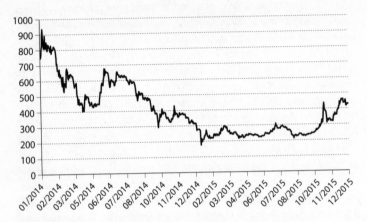

Figure 14.1: Market price of bitcoins (US dollars). Source: Blockchain.info.

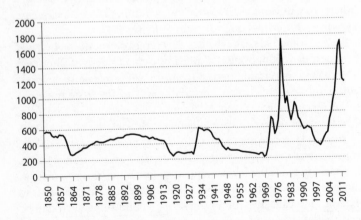

Figure 14.2: Real gold price (US dollars). Source: 1850–1920, National Mining Association; 1921–2015, Bloomberg.

shows that the price of gold in terms of dollars was much more stable under the gold standard, even in real (purchasing-power) terms. Whether this could happen without a government that aimed to stabilize the value of Bitcoin 1.0 is at best a conjecture.

Another major concern under a Bitcoin currency standard (or any digital currency) is inflation. It is true that the supply of bitcoins has been capped at 21 million coins, a limit that is expected to be reached sometime in the twenty-second century. Some people worry that this cap will eventually imply deflation, if world growth continues but the supply of bitcoins is fixed. They should be much more worried about inflation than about deflation. How is that? Because Bitcoin does not have a monopoly on the underlying technology, imitators can appear, and indeed they already have. Over time, Bitcoin 1.0's first-mover advantage may fade, especially if Bitcoin 2.0 or Bitcoin 3.0 offers a superior mechanism (e.g., much lower maintenance costs and more surefire anonymity). If so, the problem will be inflation, not deflation.

Can the government really copy the new technologies to create a superior clearing mechanism for its own electronic currency? Federal Reserve Bank of St. Louis vice president and research director David Andolfatto has noted that there are in fact stronger parallels between the Federal Reserve's existing monetary system and Bitcoin than are commonly recognized, starting with the fact that both are basically computer programs. He has argued that the Federal Reserve might have the potential someday to adopt a similar blockchain public ledger technology in its own accounting.[5] For the moment, there are just too many uncertainties, but over a long enough time frame, it is not hard to imagine that this kind of idea, or perhaps a later generation approach to digital currencies, will make the case for a digital government currency compelling.

If there ever is a government-supervised digital currency—say, a Bencoin—the potential impact on the financial system could be quite dramatic, significantly impinging on private banks' ability to engage in liquidity transformation. Individuals would effectively be able to hold accounts and conduct transactions without any need to depend on a private intermediary. In a sense, it would be as if individuals could bypass banks and hold accounts directly at the

Federal Reserve. In the extreme, the quantitative effect of a Bencoin on banks' lending capacities could be absolutely as dramatic as the Chicago plan (chapter 6) that effectively forces all private money substitutes to be 100% backed by government debt. Much would depend on regulation, however, including what alternatives private financial institutions were allowed to offer.

CRYPTOCURRENCIES AND PRIVACY

You might be wondering why I have framed the discussion of cryptocurrencies in terms of their security protocol and not their privacy features. It is true that much of the early publicity for Bitcoin surrounded dodgy retail merchants or underworld marketplaces, such as Silk Road, but the landscape is constantly evolving. For example, for many years, people regarded Bitcoin as a way to do anonymous transactions that the government can never detect. That is part of the reason it was a popular means of payment on the heavily encrypted darknet, even if such purchases were never at the center of its use. Yet the public ledger (the blockchain) contains a record of all transactions, and even though these are pseudonymous, the government can use other pieces of information surrounding the transactions to try to deconstruct them and pull out identities. In fact, there is a fair chance that the government has already done so in many cases. It is not simply a matter of the fact that Silk Road 1.0 and Silk Road 2.0 have been busted; there are always vulnerabilities, human or otherwise. This is a good example where a technology gives a measure of protection against government detection, but it is not perfect and does not necessarily last forever.

At the end of the day, governments will not lightly tolerate financial transactions that protect the anonymity of criminals and terrorists (unless, it seems, it is their own paper currency being used). To the extent that new approaches to financial transactions are developed that evade government efforts to root out their sources, they will be met with a stiff hand. There may be an important scope, however, for designing a regulatory regime for cryptocurrencies that allows only relatively small anonymous transactions. For the moment, this question remains open.

GOLD

In the spirit of this book's back-to-the-future proposal for phasing out paper currency but leaving coinage, it is helpful to discuss the future monetary role of gold, which might increase absent paper currency. It is certainly true that gold is valued at far more than it might otherwise be worth because of its history as a monetary asset. Some would say the high price of gold is a huge bubble.[6] That is one interpretation, but the history of money suggests another: gold is valuable, because a society needs to have a currency, and gold has proven an attractive option for a very long time. That gold has monetary value is not an accident of history or a freak of culture; gold filled a critical void in the technology of currency. Gold fulfills essentially all the characteristics of Jevons's (the nineteenth-century monetary theorist first cited in chapter 2) list, including portability, homogeneity (in coin or certified bar form), and durability, and yet is valuable because it is in relatively scarce, but not extremely scarce, supply.[7] Sure, gold has its flaws as a monetary asset: it is not useful for small change. It is inferior to paper currency and electronic currency, no matter how much some conservative politicians pine for a return to a gold standard. Nevertheless, given that no alternative is perfect, gold remains relevant as a secondary or tertiary monetary asset, not least for anonymity.

Gold is already valued in many places precisely for all the reasons $100 bills are valued. Gold may be only a deep backup currency, but in some places, you need a deep backup currency. In a country like India, gold jewelry has long been considered one of the few investments that citizens can safely hide from the government, and demand is also high in other financially repressed economies, such as that of China. Indeed, of the almost 3,000 tons of gold mined each year, jewelry typically constitutes more than half the demand, with bars and coins another 30%.[8]

As paper currency is phased out, it is likely that gold prices will rise, but an increased monetary use of gold is unlikely to undermine significantly the overall goal of reducing tax evasion and crime. As with large foreign notes, it will still be difficult to use gold in common circulation, and the same laws that require the reporting of large cash imports and exports already apply to gold.

By the way, a strong case can be made that central banks should consider using gold more than they already do now as a reserve asset, especially given concern over a shortage of "safe assets" that some would argue plagues the global monetary system.

In closing this chapter, it is important to be clear that one should not regard the current monetary system as a structure that can or should last forever. I have no idea what will come next, but the overwhelming presumption is that the age of (government-run!) electronic currencies will be with us for a very long time. But who knows? Most, but not all, science fiction writers have long envisioned some kind of electronic currency credits as the payment vehicle of the future. There are, however, exceptions. In *Star Trek: The Next Generation*, the Ferengi—an extraterrestrial race that is famed for its entrepreneurship—make payments in "latinum," a highly volatile liquid substance that needs to be encased in otherwise relatively worthless gold to preserve its stability.[9]

CONCLUSION TO PART III

International factors are important and potentially affect the design and implementation of any plan to phase out paper currency. Well-designed international coordination to eliminate large-denomination bills would be a good place to start, and issues in international monetary policy should be looked at afresh in a world where negative interest rate policy is possible. But overall, international issues do not overturn the basic calculus, whereby the domestic benefits are likely to be more than enough to offset the costs, even for the United States.

Nor does the advent of digital currencies change this conclusion. Digital currencies indeed have important implications for financial technology going forward, and they raise important questions and challenges for regulation. However, they are simply not central to the case for drastically scaling back paper currency now.

AFTERWORD TO THE PAPERBACK EDITION

If anyone had doubted the need to thoroughly analyze the role of cash in society, the events of the past year, most dramatically India's radical experiment with demonetization, should have settled the matter. In this afterword, I will address the Indian experience and other major recent developments since the book first went to press in May 2016. Not least, these include the election of Donald Trump as president of the United States, who came to office on the back of a promise to find ways to better control US borders from illegal immigration. Yet there is little recognition that a central magnet for the whole process is the ability of employers to make payments anonymously and off the books by using cash.

There is a plethora of nonsense on the Internet from polemicists who think in absolutist terms. Many commentators do not grasp the fundamental difference between a "less-cash" society (which this book argues for) and a completely cashless society (which it does not). Serious discussion of the potential for large-denomination notes to facilitate tax evasion, crime, and corruption, and to paralyze monetary policy during a financial crisis, should not be drowned out by vacuous hyperbole.

I'll begin here by addressing the nonsensical argument that fighting the large-scale use of cash in crime and tax evasion means taking cash away from ordinary citizens. I then turn to India, Trump, and other recent developments, and reiterate some key points concerning negative interest rates, touching upon an August 2016 analysis by Fed chair Janet Yellen of the way that effective negative interest rate policy might work in practice. In the last section, I briefly update some key data from the book.

LESS CASH IS NOT EQUIVALENT TO CASHLESS

I have attempted throughout to give the reader context concerning the past, present, and possible future of cash usage, and to explain that while cash remains very useful for many purposes, the current system is badly out of kilter. It should be perfectly possible to allow ordinary people to continue using cash pretty much as they do now, while making cash less convenient for those engaged in large-scale crime and tax evasion operations. The simplest place to start is by gradually removing the large notes that are used only to a small degree for legitimate purposes, but where the main demand comes from the underground economy. Of course, a multipronged approach, for example curtailing very large retail cash transactions as well as addressing digital security and financial inclusion, would ultimately be the most effective.

Most readers, as well as reviewers who read the book, have not had much difficulty discerning the essential difference between a less-cash society and a cashless one. Yet some commentators insist on creating the straw man of "cashless" as a reason to be outraged, worrying for example that if the plan if this book is implemented, people won't be able to pay for prostitutes or illicit drugs. Others say it will make it too hard to give money to homeless people. Seriously? Overwhelming evidence shows that most people have little essential need for big bills, even those who rely heavily on cash.

A subtler line of argument is that removing big bills is a slippery slope. Once the government phases out big bills, won't it quickly turn to phasing out small bills as well? This is a little like the gun lobby argument that if we allow the government to ban semi-automatic weapons, hunting rifles are sure to follow. Indeed, a remarkably large number of commentators mention guns and cash in the same breadth. A September 2016 *American Thinker* piece claims: "Washington's Endgame: First Your Guns Then Your Cash."[1] I can only say that I am not very sympathetic.

One MIT professor recently told me she had once bought an apartment in an institution-challenged emerging market using $30,000 in hundred dollar bills. But the same amount in $10 bills would weigh less than seven pounds and could be carried around in a normal-size purse. And how often must ordinary people engage in transactions of this scale? Admittedly, I have received correspondence from individuals claiming they routinely do transactions in cash for $10,000 to $50,000, and would sorely miss

$100 bills. Curiously, though, they never seem to say exactly what business they are engaged in. A couple people have told me they like to hand out $100 bills to homeless people, but I am sure five $20s or ten $10s would be even more welcome. Of course, there are billionaires who just like using hundreds, because they can. Indeed, at least before becoming president, Donald Trump was apparently fond of giving tips with $100 bills.[2] While we can applaud such generosity, billionaires can presumably substitute into multiple smaller bills or use new technologies to express their generosity.

On the opposite side of the spectrum, the knee-jerk reaction from many well-intentioned liberals is: "What about poor people who rely on cash? Won't they suffer mightily in the cashless economy?" Once again, the book does not advocate going cashless in the foreseeable future; the poor are not the heavy users of large-denomination notes. Indeed, the poor suffer disproportionately from the crime large notes help to facilitate and, in any event, the chapter 7 blueprint includes an extremely straightforward and relatively low-cost path to universal financial inclusion. True, some poor and low-income individuals use cash to underreport their true incomes and thereby receive greater subsidies from means-tested transfer programs, but large-denomination notes are hardly essential. I still remember sitting in my grandmother's modest Brooklyn studio apartment when I was perhaps eight years old. She explained how she was happy to be paid in cash in her job as a clerk at a local department store, as otherwise the government might find out, and then cut her social security benefits. By and large I have downplayed underreporting of income by transfer recipients because, however one feels about it, eliminating large denomination notes is unlikely to have much impact, and going cashless is still far too high a cost to consider.

Some argue that if we take away $100 bills, criminals and tax evaders are just going to find other ways to make anonymous payments. True, per the observations of John Maynard Keynes (quoted in chapter 10), cash is only one of a continuum of liquid assets. Maybe so, but when it comes to liquidity and universal acceptance, cash towers above the rest. Gold coins must be weighed and assayed, and can hardly be spent at the tobacco shop. Indeed, as the price of precious metals has risen, the problem of counterfeit gold coins has increased considerably, with gold-plated tungsten coins (often made in China) requiring considerable expertise to discern. Uncut diamonds are even less liquid. Bitcoin is pseudonymous (albeit traceable in many instances), but governments are likely to continue putting up all sorts of tax rules and restrictions on financial institutions that will ensure that it remains a very poor substitute for cash. A government cannot stand by idly and allow people to evade tax laws and regulations en masse. It is one thing to look away while a promising new multipurpose technology evolves; it is another thing for the government to allow its ability to govern to be eviscerated. As chapter 2 illustrates, the long history of cash shows that even if new transactions technologies are developed in the private sector, they are inevitably regulated and often appropriated by governments.

Although this book emphasizes one blueprint for dealing with problems in the current cash system, it also discusses and encourages the reader not be wedded to any single scheme. Phasing out big bills is perhaps the most light-handed approach, which is why it seems like the right place to start. But it can in principle be supplemented by other approaches. These include a prohibition on large cash transactions that many European countries have adopted (Table 5.1), installing tamper-proof recording boxes in cash registers, and altering regulations so that not all bank branches carry cash (Box 7.1), etc.

Each of these steps has an impact. For example, a limit on cash transactions does not prevent people from doing large payments illegally, but it does make the funds less liquid, that is less useful to the individual who ultimately intends to spend them. A successful Hollywood couple I know told me they were offered $8 million for their Beverly Hills house where the asking price was only $6 million. However, to get $8 million, they had to be willing to accept the full payment in $100 bills, and to sign official papers indicating a much lower transaction price. My friends passed on this under-the-table offer, but this kind of transaction still happens routinely in Los Angeles, Miami, New York and cities all over the world. Limits on the size of retail transactions may seem crude, but they do appear to have had some effect in European countries where they have been tried. Yes, there are still Americans who buy $12,000 used cars in cash, but nowadays there are plenty of alternatives for executing real-time clearing of transactions and the options are rapidly improving and evolving.

There is also the carrot of facilitating new technologies and of providing universal financial inclusion. Fundamentally, the aim of this book is to identify the issues, not to advance a one-size-fits-all solution. My guess is that, per the blueprint of chapter 7, some form of physical currency will likely be necessary into the very distant future. Exactly where one draws the line (for example, what should be the largest currency note a couple decades from now) is certainly open for discussion, and the line is likely to shift as technology evolves.

In sum, despite the obvious distinction between a less-cash society and a cashless society, it is stunning how many writers (and editors) choose to believe that this book must be advocating the complete abolition of cash. These writers then go on to speak about the Orwellian society that cashless will bring, and insist not another word be uttered. Talking about such extremes might help generate more spectacular headlines, garner more hits, and increase Twitter followers. As one journalist remarked to me, "cashless society" is just a much better headline than "less-cash society." As for people who get the idea, but are still incensed about getting rid of $100s, why not bring back the $1,000? Well, let's talk about that next.

JAMES HENRY'S PIONEERING WORK AND THE CASE FOR SUDDENNESS INSTEAD OF GRADUALISM

Speaking of $1,000 bills, as we know, the United States once printed large-denomination notes including $500 and $1,000 bills—as well as $5,000 and $10,000 and even briefly a $100,000 bill. Before the days of electronic transfers, these were mainly used in transactions among financial firms and sometimes in large-scale real estate sales.

Mega-bills did occasionally appear in other contexts, perhaps most famously in the classic gritty short stories of Damon Runyon about life on Broadway. In his 1930 piece "Blood Pressure" a few big-time gamblers carry around "G notes" (slang for one grand or $1,000 bills).[3] Runyon's celebrated 1930 short story later provided some of the core material for the hit musical *Guys and Dolls*, which first appeared on Broadway in 1950 and later as the 1955 Joseph Mankiewicz film starring Marlon Brando and Frank Sinatra.[4] To put things in perspective, $1,000 in 1930 was worth between $14,000 and $30,000 to a consumer today; and even in 1950, it was still worth between $9,000 and $15,000.[5] And, of course, this comparison neglects that back in 1930, real per capita income and wealth was far lower than today, so Runyon's gamblers were indeed truly high rollers.

For the first couple decades after mega-notes ceased to be printed, banks continued to recycle them. In 1969, however, US president Nixon decided to start having them recalled and destroyed as they migrated back into the banking system. Nixon believed that these $500 and $1,000 notes had come to be heavily used in the drug trade. (Larger notes were scarce and of little significance.) Nixon's edict, however, left mega-notes as legal tender. This contrasts with the blueprint of chapter 7, which makes large notes invalid after several years.[6]

During the 1970s, former McKinsey chief economist James Henry, in a pioneering short article that anticipates some of the core ideas in this book, advocated going much farther and faster than Nixon ever did (Henry, 1976). Henry argued for having the United States call in all $50 and $100 bills at short notice, and force people to exchange them into smaller bills.[7] Much like Indian Prime Minister Modi in 2016, Henry envisioned having tax and legal authorities carefully vet anyone bringing in large amounts, causing holders of "black money" to choose between a high risk of prison and penalties, or just forfeiting their cash.

Henry pointed to precedents such as schemes in West Germany in 1948, France in 1959, and the sudden recall of military scrip in the United States during the Vietnam War in the 1970s. Executing a recall in a peacetime economy with moderate inflation, however, is completely different from doing it in a postwar economy with very high inflation. My preference for a vastly slower approach, as detailed in chapter 7, is five-fold. First, some 40–50% of all US paper currency is held abroad, and any abrupt demonetization of large notes could feel precariously close to a default to foreign holders of dollars. Second, although holdings of $100s in the legal, tax-compliant economy is likely small compared to the underground economy, it is still significant. One does not want to penalize, for example, an elderly person who prefers $100s and does not keep up with the news.

Third, printing the new currency in secret is easier said than done, as again India learned. It takes six months to a year to print new currency, and the scale of production, in terms of physical bills, would have to be a huge multiple of today's production.[8] (The government must make five $20s for every $100 it is replacing. Moreover, the government would be replacing over a trillion dollars, an order of magnitude greater than a typical year's currency production.) Fourth, the idea that the tax and legal authorities have the personnel capacity to handle vetting a large sudden recall is fanciful. The government would have to gear up training for a couple years and by then the plan would be no surprise at all. Of course, compared to the mid-1970s, there is now a much stricter anti–money laundering regime in place, with deposits over $10,000 requiring reporting to the IRS. But banks, who already struggle with the considerable reporting requirements involved in reporting large cash transactions, are also limited in their legal and institutional capability for dealing with a massive sudden currency conversion. Finally, in a country like the United States, a dramatic currency reform would normally be preceded by a study commission and public hearings, again making a surprise move impossible.

While it would be desirable to nab all the crooks who have been using cash to hide ill-gotten gains, the more modest aim of sharply increasing transaction costs for porting, hoarding, and hiding illegitimate transactions seems a better plan. India's experience illustrates some of the potential pitfalls with a rapid recall.

INDIA

On November 8, 2016, the same day that Americans were electing Donald Trump as president of the United States, India's prime minister, Narendra Modi, took to national TV to make a stunning announcement. As of midnight, India's two highest-denomination bills, the 500- and 1000-rupee notes (worth roughly $7.50 and $15.00) would no longer be legal tender; citizens would have 50 days to deposit their old notes in the bank or to trade them for new ones. The two notes accounted for 86% of currency supply in a country where cash accounts for roughly 90% of transactions. In many ways, Modi's demonetization has proven the most dramatic and far-reaching macroeconomic event to affect this fast-growing nation of 1.3 billion people since the IMF-driven reforms of the early 1990s.

To add to the sense of drama, the prime minister forced his cabinet to surrender their cell phones before informing them of his decision, presumably to assure the public that none of his own minsters would profit by it. Modi's stated aim was to fight "black money," that is, cash used for tax evasion, crime, terror, and corruption. It was a bold, audacious move intended to radically alter the mindset of an economy where less than 2% of citizens pay income tax, and where official corruption is endemic.[9] It is important to emphasize, however, that whereas the litany of problems with cash listed by the Indian prime minister is essentially the same as in *The Curse of Cash*, the setting and tactics of implementation are vastly different.

This book has argued that emerging markets need to be cautious in moving to less-cash societies, in part because they lack the necessary financial infrastructure (chapter 13). Also, there are manifold reasons for moving slowly and deliberately: "Gradualism helps avoid excessive disruption and gives institutions and individuals time to adapt. It puts authorities in a position to make adjustments as issues arise" (chapter 7).

Another distinction is that India's largest notes were already modest-sized by international standards, with the 1000-rupee note being worth less than $15 at the time. The banning of the 500-rupee note, which was in widespread use by ordinary people, was particularly inconvenient, comparable to having the United States ban the $20 bill at short notice. Indeed, the replacement notes included a new 2000-rupee note, which will presumably be even more valuable in black economy transactions than the old notes it replaced. India's demonetization was clearly targeted at capturing the existing stock of black money, but in practice this is very difficult for reasons we have already discussed. A much more practical plan is to find ways to raise transactions costs for those engaged in tax evasion, corruption and criminal activity.

But none of these objections captures what was no doubt the single biggest challenge India faced, which is that it did not have nearly enough new notes on hand to exchange for the old ones that had just been demonetized. Evidently, the government had been concerned that if people found out that it was printing new notes, crooks would be given too much time to launder their ill-gotten currency. Although a rapid recall would have created massive logistical problems in the best of circumstances, it was the need for currency-rationing that led to the most severe dislocations, particularly in the agricultural and rural sectors where business is done almost entirely in cash. Although official figures suggest that the disruption was not as bad as some had initially feared (official GDP still grew at 6.5%, about a 1% drop from the pre-demonetization baseline), this is surely a significant understatement. Even if output in the formal sector really did dip only 1%, the effect on the informal sector—which even in some advanced economies equals 20–25% of GDP (chapter 5)—was surely an order of magnitude larger.

Ironically, precisely because the method of demonetization caused so much collateral damage, the Indian authorities had little scope or capacity to sort out black money from white money. Instead, the government and banks were forced to concentrate on remonetizing the economy as quickly as possible. Efforts were made to report any large and suspicious sequence of deposits, but overwhelmed banks were hardly able to do extensive enforcement. The Indian authorities claim they plan to look closely at bank deposit records in the aftermath of the demonetization, and that this will offer a second chance to detect illicit deposits. Whether this approach will have a significant yield remains to be seen.

Will India's demonetization yield long-term benefits? The answer, of course, depends on the implementation of other government policies to fight black money and corruption, and on how well it succeeds in accelerating progress towards financial inclusion. For example, India's new gross sales tax may make tax enforcement somewhat easier, and the government has been engaging in financial information treaties with other countries to make off-shore laundering more difficult. And make no mistake, several of India's policies to promote financial inclusion and to move towards a less-cash society have already borne fruit. In the text, we discussed the Modi government's move to have license fees paid online instead of by cash. The provision of free (or heavily subsidized) bank accounts linked to biometric data has helped even illiterate citizens have the possibility of financial inclusion. Interestingly, biometric security has also made it more difficult for corrupt bank employees and state officials to siphon off money into fake accounts, because they cannot so easily produce the biometric signatures required to withdraw funds.[10]

Perhaps surprisingly, India's demonetization, no matter how much criticized by economists, has been broadly popular in a country where people are deeply frustrated by endemic corruption, and appreciate the government's broad efforts to fight it. Hopefully, the government will be able to build on this good will to implement a basket of policies that will help reduce corruption and crime over time. Certainly, demonetization has greatly accelerated financial inclusion, with hundreds of millions of Indians now taking advantage of heavily subsidized basic debit accounts, a program that until now, had been developing relatively slowly. There is little doubt that multitudes of papers will be written on India's demonetization, but it could take years to untangle its full effects, which have as much to do with psychology as economics.

SELECTED CURRENCY DEVELOPMENTS ELSEWHERE

Compared to India, other developments in currency over the past year are less dramatic, but nevertheless underscore growing policy interest in dealing with cash. The European Central Bank's May 4, 2016, official announcement that production of the euro 500 note will be stopped "around the end of 2018" was noted briefly in the first printing of this book, which was going to press at just that time.[11] ECB President Mario Draghi testified in the European Parliament in February 2016 that the 500-euro note was an instrument for illegal activities and cited "increasing conviction in world opinion" that it is used almost exclusively for criminal purposes.[12] Concern about terrorist financing arising especially after the November 13, 2015, Paris terrorist attacks also reportedly played a role. Nevertheless, the ECB is initially moving at a very slow pace, declaring that the note would "always retain its value" and "can be exchanged at national central banks of the Euro system for an unlimited period of time." It is still not clear when the ECB will start requiring banks to surrender 500-euro notes for destruction as they re-enter the banking system, à la Nixon. Absent such enforcement, there is little incentive for banks to remove the rationed notes from circulation since they may well eventually trade at a premium. Presumably the ECB must do more at some point. Otherwise, 500-euro notes, which today constitute over 30% of the euro currency supply, will continue to cause problems for decades to come.

In December 2016, the Australian government stirred up a great deal of controversy by announcing the formation of a task force to study the role of cash in the underground or black economy.[13] Among other ideas, the task force is to consider phasing out the Australian $100 bill (and presumably eventually the $50), as well as other restrictions and regulations aimed at reducing the use of cash for tax evasion and crime.

As we have seen in chapter 3, large-denomination notes dominate the Australian currency supply; $50 and $100 notes account for 93% of the value of currency, which in turn is roughly 4% of

GDP. There are (approximately) fourteen $100 bills and twenty-seven $50s per capita. As in most other advanced economies, cash remains important for small transactions in Australia, accounting for 70% of transactions under $20, per an April 2016 report by the Australian National Audit Office.[14] But the importance of cash drops sharply for larger transactions, and most of the large-denomination notes are unaccounted for. In addition to crime and tax evasion, some Australian authorities have pointed to hoarding of large-denomination notes by pensioners to game Australia's means-tested pension system.[15] The study commission is due to issue its report in late 2017.

The Nordic countries continue to lead the way in phasing out cash, using a multipronged approach (per Box 7.1). Although Sweden has now re-introduced the 1000-krona bill in a new design, it still forms a relatively small share of the currency supply, in part because many banks do not carry it, and in part because the Riksbank does not encourage it. Anti–money laundering rules also make it difficult for hoarders to restock quickly. In general, the Nordic country experiences are important in that they show how a multipronged approach is likely best for moving to a less-cash society.

The Swedish central bank is among several central banks openly considering issuing its own digital currency. Others include China, South Africa, and the United Kingdom. Indeed, many other central banks are looking at similar ideas although they are reluctant to disclose their efforts publicly. The long-term development of central bank digital currency is already foreseen in chapter 14 where the key issues are discussed. One point to reiterate is that even after central banks issue retail digital currencies (this could be decades away), society will still want to retain a properly calibrated physical currency for purposes of privacy and robustness to power outages.

Progressive politicians around the world are always pointing to Denmark, Sweden, and other Nordic countries as models of good governance. Less so Venezuela, which has also gotten into the act of late. In mid-December 2016, Venezuelan President Nicolás Maduro pulled the 100-bolivar note, the country's largest, which constituted 75% of the nation's currency supply. The president's stated aim was to fight profiteering by criminal gangs on the Colombian border.[16] The edict was almost comical in a country already nearing hyperinflation territory, where people were already doing everything possible to avoid holding the currency, and where the 100-bolivar note was worth only two cents outside government stores. As with India, Venezuela did not have an adequate supply of new notes on hand, though it is hard to call the policy a disaster in a country already mired in macroeconomic and political meltdown anyway.

The United States is not Venezuela, but the election of Donald Trump has certainly opened the door to unconventional policies, and we turn to the United States next.

TRUMP'S PROPOSED WALL AND ILLEGAL IMMIGRATION

During its first few months in office, the Trump administration has not signaled any interest in paper currency management or monetary policy at the zero bound. In principle, the administration ought to be interested in an idea that could reduce crime and tax evasion, thereby both providing a safer environment and creating fiscal space for tax rate cuts. There is always going to be opposition from the cash lobby, which certainly includes people who benefit from increased ability to evade taxes under the status quo, and as already mentioned there seems to be some overlap with the gun lobby. But $100 bills are far less widely held than guns. More than one in three Americans holds at least one firearm.[17] But only a few percent of Americans admit to occasional possession of even one $100 bill, much less 35 of them.[18] So the notion that support for big bills is a natural populist position is perhaps quite wrong.

The Trump administration has, however, insisted that the United States will build a wall across the US–Mexican border to forestall illegal immigration. If built, such a wall could have a significant effect on some classes of illegal immigrants. Illegal immigration is a complex, multilayered issue that defies any single simplistic solution. As this Afterword is being written, there is a fierce struggle between the Trump administration and "sanctuary cities," such as San Francisco, Los Angeles, Chicago, New York, and Washington, who resist enforcing federal immigration laws that their leaders feel to be unjust. But it is important to recognize that the main magnet for illegal immigration is the offer of jobs with private employers who often make payments in cash to avoid detection and labor laws. Failure to address this issue ignores the root of the problem.

Unfortunately, phasing out large bills will have only a modest effect, even if there is anecdotal evidence of illegal immigrants being paid in $100s in some instances, particularly in the construction industry. A more direct approach would be to tighten and enforce existing anti–money laundering regulations. These already require banks to report the identification of individuals or businesses making large withdrawals and deposits (at present the threshold for both is $10,000 per day). In principle, this kind of data could also be used by authorities to investigate reports of large-scale employment of illegal workers. Yes, there are other ways for employers to make off-book payments (for example prepaid bank cards or Amazon gift cards). But as argued in the text, none of these can begin to supplant cash, especially for use on a large scale over long periods.

There are a plethora of other, rather straightforward ways to deal with illegal immigration besides reigning in cash, e.g., a stricter policy forcing employers to verify social security numbers. Each raises its own concerns about balancing privacy and public interest. As mentioned in the text, India has already gathered biometric data for (now) over a billion people. The main sticking point, of course, is dealing humanely with the existing stock of illegal immigrants, but presumably it would be much easier to make the case for relatively generous amnesty policies if voters knew the government had a coherent plan for discouraging illegal immigration in the future. Dealing with the problem of cash payments by employers ought to be a piece of any such plan.

NEGATIVE RATES

Another area where a lot of emotional nonsense has been written concerns negative interest rates. Much of the confusion stems from a failure to understand that if *effective* negative interest rate policy were possible in a financial crisis or in a deep recession (cash being the major obstacle standing in the way), then the episode would not necessarily be long-lived. In contrast to the recent post–financial crisis experience where overnight policy rates sat near the zero bound for six years or more, effective negative interest rate policy would allow the central bank to reflate the economy far more quickly than otherwise and to bring interest rates back above zero much faster than otherwise. In fact, long-term interest rates could even rise as the central bank steers very short-term rates deeply into negative territory, because of the expectation that normal growth and inflation would be restored more quickly.[19]

Misunderstanding of when and how negative interest rate policy might be applied similarly underlies the blunt claim that a negative rate is unambiguously bad for savers. As far as small retail savers go, the chapter 7 plan already provides an exclusion; the object of negative rate policy is to help with inflation-targeting and macroeconomic stabilization in an economy under extreme duress. It is not to raise revenue. Indeed, financial repression is a far more effective instrument for exploiting savers if raising revenue is the government's main objective, and it does not require negative rates. In fact, employing effective negative interest rate policy to combat a financial crisis would not only drive up very long-term rates, it would also lead to higher housing and equity prices. And although monetary policy is not a panacea, decisively breaking the zero bound should help bring back jobs more quickly than otherwise. Thus, the suggestion that negative rates are just a tool to rob savers is empty polemic. As chapters 8 and 9 discuss, existing instruments for dealing with the zero bound in the next financial crisis are thoroughly inadequate, while other proposals for combatting the zero bound are either dubious (e.g., increasing trade protectionism, forgoing structural reform, dropping helicopter money, conducting countercyclical fiscal policy on steroids), or a distant second-best to effective negative rate policy (e.g., raising central bank inflation targets to 4%).

Central banks, of course, do not want to admit their impotency at the zero bound. In her August 2016 speech to the world's leading central bankers at Jackson Hole, Wyoming, Federal Reserve chair Janet Yellen demonstrated how monetary policy would work (in theory) in a world where (implicitly) all the legal, institutional, and tax frictions that impede monetary policy from engaging in effective negative interest rate policy had been removed, including the problem of cash hoarding (presumably either by a phase-out of large notes—if necessary combined with a charge for redepositing large sums of cash—or by implementing the dual currency system discussed in chapter 10). Her simulations assumed that the US was facing a severe recessionary shock, albeit not as severe as the Fed faced in the 2008 financial crisis. In the simulations, constructed using the Federal Reserve's quantitative model, optimal monetary policy (unconstrained by the zero bound) would slowly take the overnight interest rate down to negative six percent, but policy rates would rise above zero faster than if the Fed did not breach the zero bound, and correspondingly the ten-year interest rate would rise above baseline considerably faster. Yellen also showed simulations attempting to quantify an alternative policy where the Fed left the policy interest rate at zero, but used quantitative easing and forward guidance to ease monetary policy, instead of negative interest rates. Her claim that QE and forward guidance could perform as well as deeply negative interest rate policy is not entirely convincing, and one hopes that by the time another deep systemic financial crisis arises, the way will have been paved for deeply negative rate policy.

The financial industry lobbies heavily against the whole idea of negative rates. Leading financial newspapers regularly publish articles by banking industry proponents that argue how negative rates will deter governments from pursuing structural reform. In the long run, banks shouldn't lose from negative rates. After all, they make money off the difference between the rates they pay to borrow and the rates they charge to lend, and once the preparations are made, they should not have cause to complain. In fact, the banking system will benefit by having more effective protection against systemic crisis. Bank lobbyists, of course, are not focused on long-run policy as this book is, but on very short run policy, and on early experimentation with very slight negative rates in Europe and Japan. Unfortunately, these monetary policies have often run ahead of making the various adjustments needed to make negative interest rate policy effective. Indeed, given the failure to make comprehensive changes in laws, institutions, and tax policies, not to mention minimal progress on paper currency, one simply cannot read much into the early experiments with negative rates; they do not illustrate how unfettered effective negative rate policy would work. Very small doses of negative rates are in some ways akin to using a drug in subclinical doses, possibly enough to get side effects but not enough to cure the disease.

Another vocal opposition group to negative rates are gold bugs who believe in an idyllic return to the days when the dollar was fixed in terms of gold. Chapter 12 thoroughly dispenses with this spectacularly naïve and uninformed view. Contrary to the idealized image, the gold standard era was punctuated by severe financial crises, and the fact that the United States grew strongly most of the time says little more about how the gold standard would work today than China's fast growth says about its system of significant financial repression.

Lastly, readers of the text will understand that the idea of phasing out large notes and the implementation of negative interest rates are two related topics, but they are hardly the same thing. The Kublai Khan–Eisler–Buiter–Kimball dual currency system allows one to have very large negative interest rates while keeping the current cash system completely intact (or even to issue larger-denomination notes). Getting rid of large-denomination notes would allow the central bank to reach significantly more-negative interest rates (by raising the cost of storage), and may well be sufficient for achieving as deeply negative rates as necessary in the next financial crisis, understanding that the period of negative rates is likely to be relatively short-lived. If necessary, central banks can also implement charges for redepositing bulk quantities of cash, or incorporate the Eisler scheme, thereby clearing the path to even larger negative rates for even longer periods (assuming all other frictions were dealt with).

In the end, if global real interest rates stay low for the next decade, there will likely be occasional periods of negative rates during recessions in most advanced economies, whether we like it or not. Part II of the book explains how to make negative rate policy much better and more effective. My strong guess is that in the coming decade, several governments around the world will in fact figure out how to implement effective negative interest rate policy as an emergency measure in the next deep systemic financial crisis. Economists now know how to solve the problem Keynes thought to be intractable. The zero bound should no longer be considered an insurmountable obstacle, provided governments start planning now for the inevitable next financial crisis. Readers can make up their own minds, but surely it is better to try to understand and prepare for this new world than to follow polemic commentators in the press and on the Internet who reject modern central banking and still harbor deeply uninformed fantasies about a blissful return to the gold standard era.

DATA UPDATE

The data, including all figures, tables and spreadsheets for the book, are posted on my Harvard University and author webpages. The reader can look there for updates of many of the figures and tables from the first printing. A few highlights:

By the end of 2016, currency in circulation in the United States had risen to roughly $4400 per person, up from $4200 end 2015. The ratio of currency to GDP was 7.9% compared to 7.4% end 2015.

End 2016, 81% of the value of US currency in circulation was in $100 bills (up from 80%). 87% of the value of US currency was in $100s and $50s, up from 84%.[20]

The US had almost as many $100 bills in circulation (1.15 trillion) end 2016 as $1 bills (1.17 trillion). There were over 35 $100 bills per capita.

There were approximately 3300 euro per capita, up from 3200 end 2015. The share of 500-euro notes, which the ECB announced a plan to stop printing in May 2016, had dropped slightly. The ratio of euro paper currency to euro-area GDP was 10.6%.

In Japan, the ratio of currency to GDP had risen to 21.2% of GDP from 19.2%. Using end-2016 exchange rates, yen currency issuance amounted to $7300 per capita.

For 2016, the yearly average of Swedish kronor in circulation was 65 billion, down from 77 billion in 2015, and equal to 1.5% of GDP; so far in 2017, kronor demand continues to drop rapidly. Take-up of the new 1000-krona note (issued to replace the old demonetized note) remains under 6% of the currency supply, partly because many banks have chosen not to carry it. Much of the drop in currency demand comes from a fall in holdings of 500-krona notes; a new note was issued in October 2016, the old 500-krona note will be invalid after June 30, 2017. Again, the Nordic experience suggests that a multipronged approach to discouraging cash use, including both obstacles to making large anonymous cash payments and innovation in alternative payments mechanisms, is the most effective approach.

Although the Nordic countries lead the way, the use of cash in legal transactions continues to drop rapidly in most advanced economies as well as in many developing economies. Preliminary results for the United States from the newly released *2015 Diary of Consumer Payment Choice* survey show the share of cash in transactions fell from 14% by value in the 2012 survey to 9% by value in 2015; the percentage of transactions (not weighted by value) fell from 40% to 32%. If this trend were to continue, one would expect cash payments in legal tax-compliant transactions to fall to today's Nordic levels within the next five years.

No doubt the use of cash will continue to evolve in both expected and unexpected ways over the next decade. Regardless, I hope the analysis in this book has persuaded the reader that it is time to start thinking more concretely about the ramifications of cash for modern macroeconomic policy, and that the topic of paper currency should no longer be considered a backwater of economics, an inconvenient sideshow in the world of monetary economics. That view has never been right, today more so than ever.

FINAL THOUGHTS
—

Phasing out cash is not a free lunch. The government monopoly on paper currency is a very lucrative business to surrender. The United States, for example, has been averaging profits of 0.4% of GDP annually in recent years. If the US government had to issue bonds to buy back the entire supply of dollar paper currency, it could add more than 7% of GDP to the national debt. For the Eurozone, the corresponding figures are 0.55% of GDP for annual profits from printing currency and 10.1% of GDP to buy back all paper currency. On top of that, paper currency has some special qualities which at present no other transaction medium quite duplicates: near total privacy, near instantaneous clearing of transactions, robustness to power outages, and of course, deep penetration into social consciousness and culture.

But if one looks more deeply, it becomes apparent that the virtues of paper currency open the door to many vices. Large-denomination notes, which constitute 80–90% of the global hard currency supply, largely circulate in the underground economy, helping facilitate tax evasion, crime, and corruption, and on a big scale. Tax evasion at all levels is more than 3% of GDP in the United States, and likely much higher in most European countries. No one likes taxes, but if the government is able to collect more revenue from tax evaders, it will be in a position to collect less taxes from everyone else.

Although far more difficult to quantify, the direct and indirect social costs of criminal activity are potentially far more important than tax evasion. If scaling back paper currency leads to even a marginal reduction in illicit activities, it would be a huge benefit. Sure, there are substitutes for cash in all underground transactions. But cash is king for good reasons, and there is no substitute on the horizon. If one appears, governments have ways to marginalize it, as emphasized throughout this book. Circumscribing cash will not end crime and terrorism, but it will deal them a significant blow. Moreover, scaling back on cash is probably the single most effective step a country like the United States can take if it is interested in discouraging employers from avoiding minimum wage restrictions and social security reporting, not to mention employing illegal immigrants. Beyond the practical considerations, sharply reducing the role of cash raises a host of philosophical and practical questions that I have addressed as well.

My argument for phasing out paper currency is essentially orthogonal to the debate on cryptocurrencies. This is not a book aimed at explaining—much less evangelizing—digital cash. Phasing out paper currency would already have made a lot of sense 20 years ago, when I first started writing research papers on the topic. Yes, digital currencies raise important questions for the future, but more as competitors for other financial instruments and institutions, not so much for paper currency. In fact, all evidence suggests that the world's mountains of cash are not going to fade anytime soon, unless governments actively move to phase out paper currency. The simplest way to start would be for governments to cease printing new large-denomination notes, an action that can be taken quite straightforwardly by most treasuries and central banks. This is just a step on the road to actively phasing out most paper currency, which, as I have argued, is the right destination to aim for.

There are many casual objections to reducing the role of cash, but that is mostly what they are, casual objections. The blueprint described here, which leaves small bills around indefinitely (eventually replaced by coins) and provides for free or heavily subsidized debit cards to low-income households, answers most objections that would arise during a long transition period.

The second and distinct argument for (mostly) phasing out paper currency is that it would make it easier for central banks to invoke negative interest rates either when inflation is stuck at very low levels or, far more significantly, when the economy is in deep recession and requires substantially negative real interest rates to help stimulate demand. Paving the way for unfettered and fully effective negative interest rate policy ought to be thought of as a major collateral benefit of phasing out paper currency. It certainly would put countries in a much better position to deal with the next financial crisis, and it would be very helpful for freeing up monetary policy in ordinary recessions in a low interest rate world. I have made the case that it is not necessary to completely eliminate cash to have sufficient scope for negative rates at any level they might realistically be needed. If problems do arise, I have illustrated ways to pretty much eliminate any fears that negative rates will provoke a run into small bills, for example, by instituting a charge for banks to tender paper currency at the central bank.

Just as some believe that phasing out currency will bring untold evil into the world, there are those who believe that negative interest rate policy will undermine civilization. Up to a point, I have tried to deal with all the reasonable arguments that have been made in favor of keeping cash exactly as is. For example, financial stability is a legitimate concern, but it is fair to say that most central bankers and financial policymakers would rather suffer a short period of negative rates followed by normalization than a decade at the zero bound. Of course, various institutional and legal obstacles need to be overcome for negative rate policy to be fully effective, and we have discussed how to deal with them.

As for the international dimensions of the problem, a coordinated phaseout of currencies among advanced countries would be the most effective policy. The domestic benefits alone, however, are more than enough to justify phasing out most paper currency, even for the United States and Europe. For smaller advanced economies, and for Japan, whose currencies are not used internationally, the case for winding down paper currency is especially compelling.

The topic of paper currency may seem a mundane one, and it has long been debated only in obscure corners of monetary economics. In fact, however, it is hugely consequential. Most economists and policymakers seem content to let paper currency ride quietly into the sunset over the next 100 years or so, thinking the system works pretty well and that the issue really doesn't matter that much. They couldn't be more wrong. The massive quantities of cash circulating today, and especially large-denomination notes, are a huge public policy problem that needs to be urgently discussed, not taken as an immutable fact of life.

A postcript: As this book went to press, the European Central Bank announced that it plans to discontinue printing the 500-euro mega-note ($570), though existing bills would still remain legal tender indefinitely. Although only a small first step, it is an encouraging one for those of us who have long argued that the printing of large notes is penny-wise and pound-foolish.

ACKNOWLEDGMENTS

This book is the culmination of a project that has been many years in the making, and there are correspondingly many people whose help needs to be acknowledged. Indeed, my journey began two decades ago at a Centre for Economic Policy Research conference in Spain. There, inspired by the announcement that the Eurozone planned to issue a 500-euro note, I presented my first research paper on the dubious role of large-denomination notes. My paper, titled "Blessing or Curse? Foreign and Underground Demand for Euro Notes," was later published in the journal *Economic Policy*. I was fortunate to receive some great comments from conference participants on this early work, including a preview of some of the broad range of issues that I returned to in this book. I resumed working on the topic again during my stint as chief economist at the International Monetary Fund in the early 2000s, where my colleagues had some helpful insights, particularly about the uses of foreign currencies in developing countries.

Fast-forwarding through many twists and turns, the next major step toward this book came in 2013, when Columbia professor Mike Woodford and Princeton professor Jonathan Parker extended an invitation to give a presentation to the National Bureau of Economic Research (NBER) *Macroeconomics Annual* conference, which brings together many of the top young macroeconomics researchers, not to mention a few still very active senior ones. By that time, the issue of the zero lower bound on central bank interest rates had come to the fore, and I used the occasion to integrate my earlier work with ideas on how phasing out paper currency could open the door to more aggressive monetary policy in deep recessions. Again, the conference discussion was extremely helpful. My NBER presentation resulted in a 2014 publication that foreshadowed many ideas in this book. It also made me realize that to tackle the issues comprehensively and coherently, it would be necessary to write a book-length manuscript. I also benefited from comments after a lecture at the University of Munich in 2014, based on related ongoing work that is more technical in nature, particularly on the zero bound. Other conferences where I have presented ideas underlying this book include a Chief Economists' Workshop at the Bank of England in May 2015, where the Bank of England's Andy Haldane chaired my session. I also presented another talk that same month at a conference in London that was jointly sponsored by the Centre for Economic Policy Research, the Brevan Howard Center for Financial Analysis at Imperial College, and the Swiss National Bank. And finally, I received feedback from colleagues at the Group of 30 meeting in June 2015 in Rio de Janeiro, during extensive discussion after a presentation I gave.

Beyond these unusually fruitful lecture and seminar comments, I have benefited from the help and comments of many individuals during the writing of this book. Diana Zhu (who also worked on the 2014 NBER paper) and Scarlet Hu provided research assistance, and both also gave useful comments on an earlier draft. Leandro Gomes, Beatriz Zahran Rache de Almeida, and Le Kang also provided excellent assistance. I was very fortunate to have critical feedback from my graduate students at Harvard, Stephanie Lo, Chenzi Xu, and Max Harris, who read earlier drafts (Max read through two different drafts in great detail). I cannot count how many people over the years have given me anecdotal evidence from personal experience on cash hoarding to avoid taxes. I am grateful to Mehreen Malik for insights on the challenges that fast-growing China has faced with its paper currency.

Nicole Tateosian made useful edits on an early version, and my remarkable assistant Jane Trahan gave extremely important help throughout the writing of this book.

Beyond the comments and suggestions I received at the May 2015 Chief Economists' Workshop in London, researchers at central banks have provided helpful advice and data, including David Zhang and Scott Schuh (at Federal Reserve Bank of Boston), Ksenia Yudaeva (deputy governor of the Russian Central Bank), Edward Robinson (of the Monetary Authority of Singapore), Susanna Grufman, Jesper Lindé and Björn Segendorff (Swedish Riksbank), Ilan Steiner (Bank of Israel), Pablo García Silva (Central Bank of Chile) and José de Gregorio (former governor of the Central

Bank of Chile), and Ruth Judson (on the Board of Governors of the Federal Reserve System); Ruth is also one of the outstanding contributors to this literature.

I am also grateful to New York Univerity professor Mark Gertler for helpful discussions, and to my Harvard colleague Emmanuel Farhi for important feedback as well. My three anonymous referees at Princeton University all had constructive comments, and I particularly benefited from those of Michigan professor Miles Kimball, who chose to reveal himself. Russian and comparative literature professor Edyta Bojanowska at Rutgers helped guide me on my interpretations of popular Dostoyevsky quotations on the issue of cash. My Harvard colleague physicist Lisa Randall helped with my (mostly facetious) analogy between approaching the zero interest rate bound and approaching a black hole (though any errors are mine!).

I feel very fortunate to have once again worked with the team at Princeton University Press, including my editor, Seth Ditchik, who gave extremely useful guidance from an early stage, and Peter Dougherty, the director of Princeton University Press, who lent his strong support and encouragement. Indeed, Peter even stepped in as editor at a late stage when Seth was lured to a prominent position at another publisher. Cyd Westmoreland, the copy editor for this book, was terrific. My book agent, Andrew Wylie, was a pleasure to work with, and I am grateful to Niall Ferguson for introducing us.

It is not possible to engage in a book project of this type without strong support from one's family, including my wife, Natasha L. Rogoff, and my children, Gabriel and Juliana. In fact, I have to credit Natasha with pointing me to the artwork on the cover of the English progressive rock band Pink Floyd's single, "Money," which inspired the colors on this book's cover. Juliana, in turn, helped me arrive at the book's title, hammered out over a long walk one day. Finally, I have to thank all the many people I have met over the years, dating back to my days as a professional chess player, who have taught me a thing or two about how cash works in the real world.

APPENDIX

This appendix covers important, mildly technical material that augments the discussion in several chapters.

POSSIBLE FRAGILITIES IN THE CURRENCY SYSTEM THAT A SHIFT TO ELECTRONIC CURRENCY MIGHT EXPOSE

Is there any risk that in a paperless world, government fiat money will lose so much of its distinctive character that near-perfect substitutes will undermine the central bank's capacity to stabilize prices? This might seem like a rather abstract question, but it would be a mistake not to anticipate it and address it.

Wallace's Paradox of Fiat Currency

Here we consider the concern that if paper money disappeared entirely, it might create problems for central banks in maintaining price stability, as discussed toward the end of chapter 7. Back in the early 1980s, monetary theorist Neil Wallace argued that the only reason the government gets away with issuing non-interest-bearing fiat money is because the government makes it difficult to use interest-bearing government debt for transaction purposes. For one thing, the government issues interest-bearing bonds and notes only in large denominations. If three-month Treasury bills paid market interest and if they came in, say, $100 denominations, they might even be preferred to cash for some transactions. (Something akin to this occurred in the United States during the War of 1812, when small Treasury bills bearing interest were sometimes used as currency.[1]) Second, even if the government issues bills and bonds only in large denominations, it has to be careful to prohibit private financial firms from issuing interest-bearing paper money–like substitutes that are 100% backed by government bonds. Without the second restriction, which the government exercises through its monopoly on currency creation, intermediaries might be able to step in and basically chop up large-denomination bonds into pieces that could be used as paper money, and then sell them at profit. As we all know, the financial system is very good at that kind of game.

Wallace argued that absent these restrictions to prevent bonds from competing with currency as transaction media, any efforts by the government to issue intrinsically worthless fiat currency will always be doomed to collapse. Absent restrictions and legal regulations, the only stable system would be a currency that is 100% backed by commodities, for example, gold or silver.

At the time of Wallace's writing, institutional realities seemed to make his concerns about monetary instability far-fetched and institutionally implausible. First, paper currency is completely distinct from other transaction media, because it is anonymous. Interest-bearing Treasury bonds and bills today are registered to an owner and, to be transferred and sold, need to be registered to a new owner. And the vast bulk is now electronic. If currency becomes completely electronic, however, it will lose its distinctive anonymity properties, making it harder to differentiate money from interest-bearing electronic bonds. In the limit, bonds could undermine currency and make it difficult for the government to control the price level, essentially because too many currency-like instruments would be floating around.

Until now, there does not seem to have been a problem. Central banks have considerable capacity to stabilize prices thanks to their monopoly on currency, and they have retained this capacity even as a plethora of transaction substitutes has emerged, including credit cards, debit cards, and Apple Pay.

Is there an answer to this concern? Standard monetary theory suggests that as long as the central bank can control the overnight interest rate between banks, it will not matter if "cash" blends into other debt. But the theory does contain some subtle assumptions about price stickiness that allow the government to control inflation, even without having a currency to control.[2] A complete phaseout of all currency (paper and coins) would test this proposition, but because the proposal in chapter 7 leaves small notes or coins (or both) circulating indefinitely, it might be enough to avoid the issue, if indeed it is one.

A further idea that bears a certain family resemblance to the Wallace conjecture is the "fiscal theory of the price level," of Leeper, Sims, and Woodford,[3] which came a decade later. It also hypothesizes that the price level depends on all the nominal assets the government issues (bonds, bills, and money). The fiscal theory of the price level goes one step further and argues that the price level today also depends on the government's expected future financing needs. Quite simply, the price level has to adjust to make the government's budget constraint add up, given all its current future plans for spending and taxes (as opposed to classic monetary theory, where the price level equates the supply and demand for real money balances).

There are a number of objections to the fiscal theory of the price level. For one thing, it excludes the important possibility of default. And it seems to fly in the face of a great deal of empirical evidence that suggests that prices and exchange rates are particularly sensitive to the currency supply as opposed to the overall supply of government debt. Nevertheless, it, too, may become more relevant in an all-electronic currency world, where the liquidity and transactions distinctions between electronic money and longer-term electronic government debt start to be lost.

One's gut instinct is that shifting to electronic currency will be a fairly smooth process, though it is simply not possible to definitely rule out the possibility that it will upset social conventions and expectations and lead to an outcome that is quite different than planned. This is the kind of "known unknown" the government must plan for in making a transition, and we would be remiss to ignore it in this book.

THE TAYLOR RULE, CREDIBILITY, AND THE ZERO BOUND

This short section is for readers who are interested in more specific details of the literature on the academic debate surrounding just how serious an impediment to conventional monetary policy the zero bound actually is. As already emphasized in the text, by far the most important issue is whether the monetary authorities can make commitments. Even if the monetary authorities are unable to move the current nominal rate, they can still influence the real economy just as effectively if they can manipulate the real interest rate by operating through inflation expectations.

It is helpful to begin with policy prescriptions that are based on simple rules of thumb, rather than full-blown quantitative macroeconomic models. Although missing a lot of important ingredients, they illustrate some of the challenges that arise in much more sophisticated models.

We begin with the influential formulation of Stanford professor John Taylor, whose simple "Taylor rule" for setting the policy interest rates worked surprisingly well for describing central bank behavior in many countries during the period of the Great Moderation (from the mid-1980s until the run-up to the 2008 financial crisis). Taylor's 1993 formulation assumed equal weights on stabilizing inflation and output, with inflation deviations measured around a target level presumed to be 2%, and output deviations measured around potential output (loosely speaking, the rate of output consistent with full employment).[4] When Taylor formulated his rule in the early 1990s, it seemed reasonable for him to build his approach on the assumption that a normal Federal Reserve overnight policy interest rate would be 4%. This presumed a normal real interest rate of 2% and an assumed target inflation rate of 2%. The original Taylor rule formulation specified that the interest rate ought to be adjusted according to

$$i = 4 + 0.5(\pi - 2) + 0.5y, \qquad \text{(original Taylor formulation)}$$

where y is the deviation of output from its full employment level, and π is the expected inflation rate. Even this simple formulation has considerable room for interpretation, for example, the central bank needs to determine exactly what inflation rate it wants to target, how to figure out whether the economy is at full employment, how to measure expected inflation, and so forth.[5] There are also variants that allow for lagged output gaps.

The basic Taylor formulation would not necessarily have produced negative interest rates in the financial crisis of 2008 (except perhaps at the early peak), in part because the baseline interest rate is high (4%), and in part because it takes a really big output gap to pull rates below zero; an output gap of 8%, multiplied by 0.5, subtracts only 4% from the policy interest rate. If inflation is at target (it never moved all that far below), it is hard to get a negative number. But one can easily get much bigger negative rates if one adopts the view that (1) the equilibrium real interest rate is significantly lower than 2% and (2) output stabilization should get twice the weight of inflation stabilization, as current Fed chair Janet Yellen argued back in 2012. Her formulation would have

$$i = x + 0.5(\pi - 2) + y, \qquad \text{(Yellen's preferred formulation)}$$

where x is the equilibrium real interest rate.[6] Given the huge collapse of output during the 2008 crisis, the Yellen formulation can easily yield significantly negative rates, particularly if one throws in that the equilibrium real interest rate collapsed during the financial crisis, with investors putting a huge premium on safe assets.

Taylor rules are only a starting point for exploring the academic and policy debate on the zero bound, where the number of parameter choices and modeling decisions expands rapidly as model complexity grows. And the choice among models is dizzying. Modern macroeconomics offers a plethora of sophisticated approaches, ranging from large-scale macroeconomic models (e.g., the Federal Reserve Board's long-standing FRB/US model), to smaller-scale dynamic stochastic general equilibrium and New Keynesian models that sacrifice realism in exchange for a greater degree of coherence and internal consistency.[7] Without a structural model that specifies how the economy works, and without carefully specifying the ultimate objectives of monetary policy (ideally a welfare measure), it is impossible to answer coherently the question of just how much better things would have been if interest rates could have gone deeply negative in 2008. And needless to say, there are a raft of technical issues and modeling choices.

A representative finding is that of Roberto Billi, who compares the central bank's welfare loss (using inflation and output deviations as in the Taylor rule) in the presence of the zero bound, and finds it is three times higher in the case where the central bank cannot commit compared to the case where it can. The reader should not find this kind of result surprising, for the reason we have already discussed: if central banks can credibly commit to above-target inflation after the economy reaches full employment (i.e., commit to keep stepping on the gas after it is no longer necessary), then they can stimulate demand by lowering the real interest rate.[8] The question is how this might be achieved.

One intriguing approach for solving the commitment problem has been advanced by Gauti Eggertsson and Michael Woodford. Using a standard New Keynesian macroeconomic model, they showed that the central bank can achieve nearly optimal monetary policy through a form of price-level targeting in which the central bank targets zero average inflation over the long run. The idea is simple: if people sincerely believe that the central bank is committed to get back on its target price path after it falls off, the periods of below-normal inflation automatically raise expectations of future inflation. So in a financial crisis, when deflation sets in, it automatically generates expectation of higher inflation, lowers real interest rates, and stimulates aggregate demand. At least that is the theory. The idea is that because targeting the price level is such a simple and understandable rule, it just might be possible to make it credible without massive institutional change. Price-level targeting does not eliminate the zero bound problem, but in theory, it can mitigate it.[9]

Another fundamental point is that one needs to know the underlying friction in the economy that monetary policy is supposed to solve. Monetary policy is at its best when it can be used to offset the effect of nominal wage and price rigidities. But if financial rigidities are the main problem—and especially in a situation where a raft of bad loans hobbles the banking system—then conventional monetary policy (via interest rates rather than balance sheets) might be less effective, and other policies, such as recapitalizing banks, might be required.[10]

This literature on the costs of the zero bound is a fast-evolving one, and in the normal course of research, the debate is likely to play out for decades to come, with many twists and turns, especially as more experience accrues.

INDEPENDENT CENTRAL BANKS AND INFLATION TARGETING: AN OVERSHOOT?

One of the great institutional reforms of the post–Bretton Woods era has been the advent of modern independent central banks, designed with a view to give monetary policy a more technocratic basis and to insulate policy from short-term political pressures to inflate. But unfortunately, many central banks implemented policy regimes that were simply too inflexible. My 1985 paper introduced the idea of having an independent central bank as a solution to the inflation credibility problem first analyzed by Kydland and Prescott.[11] A critical issue my 1985 paper raises is how to balance flexibility versus commitment. A more flexible system has the advantage of allowing a better response to shocks. But it also leaves the central bank more room to cheat in normal times, when the central bank will be tempted to set interest rates too low, thereby helping lower government finance costs and raise employment. But the public will see through this temptation and adjust expectations accordingly, introducing an inflationary bias that will be built into all interest rates, prices, and wage contracts. At the other extreme, a strong commitment holds down inflation expectations but potentially leaves the central bank insufficient scope to respond to shocks. Under realistic assumptions, neither extreme—zero weight on inflation or zero weight on output stabilization—is optimal. (An intermediate idea, proposed by Susanne Lohmann (1992), is to follow a rigid rule in normal times, but retain an escape clause in extreme events.)

Later work by Carl Walsh suggested that this trade-off could be eliminated through properly designed incentive contracts for central bankers that effectively eliminated any bias toward inflation without affecting central banks' reaction to shocks.[12] Although this initial solution turned out to be extremely fragile,[13] later work by John Taylor, Lars Svennson, and others argued that any inflation bias could still be eliminated if the central bank made its policies sufficiently clear and transparent, explaining any deviation in terms of a rule that would yield target inflation on average, with no bias. Much of this literature, though, is predicated on models with no financial market imperfections and no source of "Knightian uncertainty," or "unknown unknowns," that can create problems for any fixed rule.

During the 1990s and into the 2000s, dozens of central banks adopted some form of inflation-targeting regimes.[14] Today, inflation targeting has become the norm in central banking around the world, certainly in advanced economies, and to some extent also in emerging markets and even developing countries.[15] Even the US Federal Reserve, long resistant to the trend, finally adopted inflation targeting under the leadership of Ben Bernanke, who, as an academic, had penned an important book on the topic in 2001 with Thomas Laubach, Frederic Mishkin, and Adam Posen.[16] A central question, already raised in the text, is whether practitioners have taken inflation-targeting evangelism too far, and now the approach needs to be rethought to recognize the trade-off between flexibility and commitment, once thought to be solved. Allowing for full-fledged negative interest rate policy will go a long way toward restoring balance, but even so, more flexibility is likely needed.

NOTES

___

CHAPTER 1: INTRODUCTION AND OVERVIEW

1. See, for example, Rogoff (2014), which builds on Rogoff (1998a) and anticipates the main ideas here; I have also been making these arguments in op-eds.

2. Rogoff (1998a). Henry (1980) argues for swapping out old 100s and 50s.

3. Sylvia Nasar, "Crime's Newest Cash of Choice," *New York Times*, April 28, 1998, available at http://www.nytimes.com/1998/04/26/weekinreview/ideas -trends-crime-s-newest-cash-of-choice.html.

4. I continued working on the topic while chief economist at the International Monetary Fund (e.g., Rogoff 2002), but still without many takers.

5. For example, the 2002 film *All About the Benjamins* (starring Ice Cube). The title refers to Benjamin Franklin, who currently adorns the face of the $100 bill.

6. Interest-paying anonymous bearer bonds did once exist, and they play a role in F. Scott Fitzgerald's 1925 novel *The Great Gatsby*. One finds villains still demanding them in Hollywood movies from the 1980s, like *Die Hard* and *Beverly Hills Cop*. But today they are effectively prohibited in the United States and on their way to being an extinct species in other advanced countries. In the United States, bearer bonds were made obsolete by the Tax Equity and Fiscal Responsibility Act of 1982, which removed the deduction for interest payments by the issuer. As bond recording becomes fully electronic, and with governments everywhere concerned with tax evasion and terrorism, interest-paying bearer bonds from advanced economies will not survive, regardless of what happens to paper currency.

7. Keynes (1936).

8. To a first approximation, the handling and storage costs of hoarding a billion dollars in $10 bills should be ten times the costs for $100 bills, or if $5 bills are the largest note, then 20 times larger. Storing and sorting billions of dollars in coins (the very long run of the plan in chapter 7) would be still more problematic. Given that any period of significant negative rates is likely to be both relatively short and unpredictable, the fixed costs of storage and insurance would likely be prohibitive. If even this were not enough, the government can introduce other fixed costs to redepositing funds in the banking system.

9. Dostoyevsky (1862), quoted in German newspaper FAZ, November 19, 2014.

10. Rogoff (2014) argues that phasing out paper currency can kill two birds with one stone.

11. A few very good books have been written by journalists about electronic money, including *The End of Money* by David Wolman (2012) and *The Age of Cryptocurrency* by Paul Vigna and Michael Casey (2015). But these are much more about what is happening in the world of alternative payment mechanisms rather than a fundamental rethink of the global monetary system.

CHAPTER 2: THE EARLY DEVELOPMENT OF COINS
AND PAPER CURRENCY

1. For a nuanced interpretation of the role of paper currency in Goethe's *Faust* (part II), see James (2012).

2. Grubb (2006).

3. See, for example, Davies (2002) or Ferguson (2008).

4. See, for example, Kocherlakota (1998) or Kiyotaki and Wright (1989). Kocherlakota argues that money is a primitive form of social memory; electronic money obviously offers many more possibilities for record keeping than does physical money.

5. Einzig (1966).

6. Prior to coinage, gold and silver ingots were long used as mediums of exchange by traders who recognized the need to hold stocks. Hicks (1969) thus argues that money grew out of private market activity. Bordo (2008) gives a more cautious assessment.

7. Melitz (2015).

8. For younger readers, the Battle of Salamis is the epic ancient naval battle depicted in the 2014 movie *300: Rise of an Empire*, sequel to the modern-day cult classic 2006 film *300*.

9. Davies (2002).

10. Sargent and Velde (2003).

11. See Levenson (2011), p. 62 on clipping and p. 64 on Newton's milled edges.

12. Fischer, Sahay, and Végh (2002).

13. As Rolnick, Velde, and Weber (1996) demonstrate, seigniorage revenues typically rose significantly around debasement periods.

14. Ferguson (2008).

15. This point is also emphasized by Davies (2002).

16. Tullock (1957).

17. See Morse (1906).

18. See Tullock (1957).

19. Peng (1994), Von Glahn (1996).

20. Marco Polo. 2004. *Travels of Marco Polo*, with an introduction by Milton Rugoff. New York: Signet Classics, bk. II, ch. 24.

21. Numerous later authors built on, added to, or embellished Polo's discussion of Chinese money, including Jevons (1875) in his classic work on the foundations of money. The best and most sophisticated analysis is perhaps that of Tullock (1957).

22. Davies (2002).

23. Tullock (1957).

24. For an interesting further discussion of Europe's first central banker, see Irwin (2013).

25. See Clapham (1966, p. 185). Existing private banknotes were grandfathered in England and Wales and remained in circulation for decades. Scotland and Northern Ireland banks retained the right to issue notes that can be used in transactions throughout the United Kingdom, though these are not legal tender

(and therefore do not have to be accepted in payment of debts). Importantly, the Bank of England regulates their issuance. The Bank Act of 1844 is also known as Peel's Act after the prime minister who pushed it through.

26. Rothbard (2002).

27. Franklin (1729), available at http://founders.archives.gov/documents /Franklin/01-01-02-0041.

28. Among Franklin's seemingly endless talents included being America's first widely known chess player. His tract "Morals of Chess" was reprinted in *Columbian Magazine* in 1786. The exact date it was originally written is unknown.

29. Reinhart and Rogoff (2009).

30. The assignat inflation of revolutionary France in 1795–96 was even more spectacular than the US revolutionary war inflation, with monthly inflation exceeding 50% per month (the Cagan definition of hyperinflation) for 5 months; see Capie (1991) and Sargent and Velde (2003).

31. Reinhart and Rogoff (2009).

32. Reinhart and Rogoff (2013).

33. Ahamed (2009).

34. The classic modern reference on the prewar gold standard is Eichengreen (1996).

CHAPTER 3: SIZE AND COMPOSITION OF GLOBAL CURRENCY SUPPLIES, AND THE SHARE HELD ABROAD

1. When the euro hit 1.6 dollars in July 2008, a 500-euro note was worth $800.

2. On spirit-world dollarization, see Julia Wallace, "In Cambodia, the Ghosts Prefer Dollars," *New York Times*, April 8, 2016.

3. Gross domestic product is the total value of final goods and services produced in a country, evaluated at market prices.

4. The 10,000–Singapore dollar note still circulates, but the Monetary Authority of Singapore stopped printing new ones in 2014 as a step against money laundering. Rachel Armstrong, "Singapore to Stop Issuing $10,000 Note to Prevent Money Laundering," *Reuters*, July 2, 2014. Available at http://www.reuters.com /article/singapore-regulations-idUSL4N0PD2M120140702.

5. As of the end of 2015, the Eurozone member countries consisted of Austria, Belgium, Cypress, Estonia, Finland, France, Germany, Greece, Ireland, Italy, Latvia, Lithuania, Luxembourg, Malta, the Netherlands, Portugal, Slovakia, Slovenia, and Spain.

6. Indeed, Otani and Suzuki (2008) attribute the bulk of Japan's high cash holdings to hoarding by the elderly, who might be concerned about bank stability. They point to the fact that during the same post-1990 period when there was a particularly sharp rise in Japanese currency holdings, one can also observe a sharp rise in demand deposits by the elderly. If one assumes that the ratio of currency to demand deposits is relatively stable, then currency demand must have risen as well. It is true that Japan is a relatively low-crime country, so stashing tens of thousands of dollars of cash is arguably safer than in most Western countries, but it seems like quite a stretch to assume that these two factors alone explain the

bulk of Japanese currency outstanding, especially when other studies suggest that the size of the Japanese underground economy is larger than that of the United States.

7. For example, Okamura (1993).

8. *A Taxing Woman* is a 1987 Japanese film directed by Juzo Itami, who also directed the sequel, *A Taxing Woman's Return*.

9. The currency/GDP ratios in figure 3.4 use end-of-year data and might be slightly lower if mid-year data were used instead due to difficulties in adequately controlling for seasonals. This is not a first-order issue, though.

10. Sprenkle (1993) observed that even in the early 1990s, surveys indicated that roughly 80% of the currency supply was unaccounted for.

11. Excellent discussions of why US currency might be used abroad are found in Hellerstein and Ryan (2011) and Doyle (2001).

12. Antràs and Foley (2015) investigate the detailed transactions of a major US frozen poultry exporter and find that nearly all transactions are not intermediated by banks, a fact largely driven by exports to countries with weak governance.

13. Peng and Shi (2003) estimate that 15–25% of Hong Kong's currency is held abroad. It is easy to imagine that the amount has since increased with greater integration with mainland China.

14. This approach is used in Rogoff (1998a). Doyle (2001) is perhaps the most thorough effort to apply the cross-country approach, using comparator countries that are known not to have internationally circulating currencies.

15. An excellent discussion of alternative approaches to inferring foreign holdings of domestic currency is given in Porter and Judson (1996).

16. See, for example, Alexis Akwagyiram, "Suspected Smuggler Held in Nigeria for Swallowing $111,000," *Reuters*, September 18, 2015 (available at http://af.reuters.com/article/nigeriaNews/idAFL5N11O2CE20150918), or Cesar Garcia, "Colombia Police Arrest Mule with $38,500 in Stomach," *Associated Press*, August 5, 2015 (available at http://news.yahoo.com/colombia-police-arrest-dollar-mule-38-500-stomach-175625395.html).

17. Porter (1993) and Porter and Judson (1996) introduce the seasonal approach; see also Judson (2012).

18. Porter and Judson (1996); Judson (2012).

19. Although Judson (2012) finds an estimate for foreign holdings of US currency of 50%, she argues that the ratio is somewhat larger for $100 bills.

20. United States Treasury (2006).

21. Judson (2012), Rogoff (1998a).

22. The overseas holding of dollars in figure 3.7 corresponds to the Federal Reserve's Z.1 (Flow of Funds) publication, table S9a, line 95.

23. Fischer, Köhler, and Seitz (2004). In a more recent effort, based on a very different approach, the European Central Bank took surveys after the financial crisis (European Central Bank 2011) and obtained broadly similar estimates, suggesting that demand for euros in the legal domestic economy may account for roughly one-third of total euro notes outstanding. Finally, Bartzsch, Rösl, and Seitz (2011) look at euro notes issued by the Bundesbank and find that between 40% and 55% are held outside Eurozone countries.

CHAPTER 4: HOLDINGS OF CURRENCY IN THE DOMESTIC, LEGAL, TAX-PAYING ECONOMY

1. Porter and Judson (1996); Sumner (1990).

2. Of course, conventions and definitions vary across countries; see the central bank sources for the tables, but the basic orders of magnitude given here for business and bank holdings of cash are still relatively small across advanced countries.

3. Federal Reserve release H3 table 2, available at http://www.federalreserve .gov/releases/h3/current/.

4. Though there are slight accounting differences across countries, currency in circulation generally excludes currency held at the treasuries and central banks and in required reserves. Bennett and Peristiani (2002) note that the ability to include cash in ATMs has made bank reserve requirements virtually nonbinding.

5. The higher end of the range is consistent with the estimates of "The 2013 Survey of Consumer Payment Choice" (Schuh and Stavins 2015, fn. 25), which estimates that if very large cash holdings are included, then from 2008 to 2013, total cash held by consumers averaged 18.2% of all cash that is estimated to be held domestically (i.e., excluding estimated foreign holdings). See also Feige (2012a,b). Of course, as the survey acknowledges, there is no way to be sure that cash reported by survey participants is all going to fully tax-compliant legal activities.

6. Survey and diary approaches are informative but must be viewed with caution, because they are based on small samples with all kinds of potential reporting issues. The 2013 US "Survey of Consumer Payment Choice" (Federal Reserve Bank of Boston 2013), for example, had 2,089 respondents; this is a healthy number but still small given the huge diversity of the US economy.

7. See Federal Reserve Bank of Boston (2012). The Boston Federal Reserve website reports a 2015 Diary of Consumer Choice update, but the results are not yet available as of this writing.

8. Greene and Schuh (2014, fn. 14).

9. I am grateful to Scott Schuh and David Huang of the Boston Federal Reserve, who used the consumer survey database to calculate that total consumer holdings of cash (counting all respondents) averaged 9.2% of total cash in circulation between 2008 and 2014, though the number was only 6.7% in 2014.

10. Greene and Schuh (2014).

11. The 2012 diary survey did not ask about denomination of notes held at property as opposed to on person, and it is possible that a larger share is held in $100 notes. However, accounting for $100 bills held on property can hardly go very far toward explaining where all the $100 bills are, because the total amount of cash reported is still only a small fraction of the supply, whatever the denomination of notes.

12. Bagnall et al. (2014) review recent diary studies from seven different countries: Canada (2009), Australia (2011), Austria (2011), Germany (2011), the Netherlands (2011), France (2011), and the United States (2012). The authors report making significant efforts to harmonize their approaches to gathering and

analyzing data so as to make the results as comparable as possible (understanding that there are some differences across countries in the year of the survey). Although the diary survey design is similar across countries, and the process of harmonization thoughtful, the reader must recognize that precise comparisons are still difficult, and diary surveys that require meticulous detail from participants have many limitations to begin with.

13. Purchasing power parity exchange rates aim to translate nominal quantities in different currencies into a common denominator, taking account of the different price structures in each economy. The idea here, for example, is to better be able to compare the true purchasing power consumers in different countries are carrying around in their wallets or purses.

14. The 2008 survey is documented in ECB (2011).

15. Bank vault currency was reported at 60 billion euros.

16. Bagnall et al. (2014).

17. Wang and Wolman (2014).

18. Greene and Schuh (2014, p. 29).

19. Klee (2008).

20. Federal Reserve Board (2014).

21. This point is also made by Warwick (2015).

22. Amromin and Chakravorti (2009) analyze data from 13 advanced economies over the period 1983–2003 and find that the demand for small-denomination notes decreases with greater debit card usage and retail consolidation. They also find, however, that increased debit card usage does not significantly impact demand for high-denomination notes.

CHAPTER 5: CURRENCY DEMAND IN THE UNDERGROUND ECONOMY

1. See, for example, the survey evidence and discussion in Morse, Karlinsky, and Blackman (2009).

2. Slemrod (2016).

3. For a good description of the IRS approach, see Brown and Mazur (2003). Officially, the audits began with the so-called Tax Compliance Measurement Program, which then morphed into the somewhat less intrusive National Research Program.

4. Internal Revenue Service (2012a,b).

5. Slemrod (2007, 2016).

6. See Zucman (2015) and Cebula and Feige (2012). The latter, incidentally, use econometric inference based on money demand and other factors, and arrive at a slightly higher gross noncompliance rate of 18–19%.

7. See Slemrod (2016).

8. Even with all the Internal Revenue Service's effort to estimate the tax gap, there is of course a high degree of uncertainty about the exact size of the gap; see Treasury Inspector General for Tax Administration (2013).

9. Tax Policy Center (2012). The ratios used in the text for state and local revenue relative to federal revenue are for 2010. Using 2014 ratios instead would slightly reduce the ratios, because of federal tax hikes in the interim and cyclical

variation; the ratios for 2014 are 31% for state/federal taxes and 22% for local taxes.

10. The point that even a moderate reduction in tax evasion associated with reducing cash usage can fully offset lost seigniorage costs is highlighted by Rogoff (1998a).

11. It should be noted that UK Treasury reports a tax gap figure of only 6.4% of total tax revenues for 2013/2014, far smaller than for the United States, despite likely having a larger underground economy and higher taxes. (HM Revenue and Customs 2015). It is difficult to measure tax gaps accurately without an intensive randomized auditing procedure, such as the United States has employed.

12. Treating indirect taxation and self-employment as the driving forces of tax evasion, Schneider and Buehn (2012) estimate that the average level of tax evasion relative to GDP was 3.2% across the OECD countries for the years 1999–2010.

13. The OECD is a group of 34 advanced economies with a few upper-middle-income countries mixed in. Indirect evidence is also highly suggestive of large-scale tax evasion. Pissarides and Weber (1989) find that the self-employed in the United Kingdom spend significantly more on food relative to reported income, than do non-self-employed. They conclude that the average rate of underreporting of self-employed income is about one-third.

14. See the estimates in figure 5.1. The early literature on estimating the size of the underground economy, in fact, relied heavily on the growth of cash as a measure of the growth of the underground economy (e.g., Feige 1989). There is considerable corroborating evidence, for example, with many studies finding evidence of a relationship between cash demand and tax rates; see also Rogoff (1998a). La Porta and Shleifer (2014) argue that the correlation between tax rates and the size of the underground economy is not strong for the world as a whole, of course partly because enforcement capacity differs so much across the developing world and emerging markets.

15. Schneider, Buehn, and Montenegro (2010). See also Schneider and Williams (2013), and Schneider (2016).

16. See Schneider, Buehn, and Montenegro (2010). Schneider refers to the narrower measure of the underground economy used in figure 5.1 as the "shadow economy," but to avoid a confusing plethora of terms, I will still use the term "underground economy" and just remind the reader that the discussion surrounding the estimates in figure 5.1 refers to a narrower definition that does not include illegal or nonmarket-based activity.

17. See La Porta and Shleifer (2014).

18. Recall the Dostoyevsky quote from Otmar Issing's critique of my 2014 Munich lecture, mentioned in the preface.

19. Patricia Kosmann, "Get Receipts, Win a Car: How Greece's VAT Lottery Plan Worked in Portugal," *Wall Street Journal*, March 10, 2015, available at http://blogs.wsj.com/brussels/2015/03/10/get-receipts-win-a-car-how-greeces-vat-lottery-plan-worked-in-portugal/. Slovakia has also experimented with monthly sales tax receipt lotteries. Susan Daley and Raphael Minor, "In Slovakia, the Real Prize Goes to the Tax Man," *New York Times*, April 19, 2014, available at http://www.nytimes.com/2014/04/20/world/europe/forget-the-car-in-slovakian-lottery-real-prize-goes-to-tax-man.html?_r=0.

20. Naritomi (2015).

21. Dunbar and Fu (2015).

22. Under- and over-invoicing results are reported in Reinhart and Rogoff (2002, 2004).

23. I am grateful to Juliana Rogoff for pointing out that exactly this end-around of credit card restrictions was featured on the television series *Degrassi*, season 14.

24. See Cameron (2014).

25. See Schneider (2013, 2015) for rough estimates of the share of transactions done in cash across various criminal activities, for example, the estimate for the drug trade is 80%. See also Speiser (1975).

26. Henry (1976, 1980) emphasizes the importance of cash to mob activities.

27. *Breaking Bad* is about Walter White, a high school chemistry teacher turned crystal meth drug lord. Laundering the burgeoning profits proves a huge challenge, eventually tackled by Walter's wife Skylar, who buys a car wash. An accountant, Skylar cooks the books so that it appears that the car wash is much more successful than it actually is, but eventually the drug profits become so great there is no plausible place to put the cash besides in a storage locker. This in turn creates its own vulnerabilities. Skylar and Walter are but small fictional players in a huge, and very real, domestic and international drug business.

28. I am grateful to Frederic Schneider for this example.

29. See Jost and Sandbu (2000).

30. Online searches for such key phrases as "banker caught for money laundering" result in many news stories.

31. Wealthy corporations and individuals can set up shell corporations in places like the Virgin Islands, where the identity of the true owner can be concealed, and then pair these shell companies with bank accounts in Switzerland, making payments on bogus services. As Zucman (2015) notes, they can then spend their hidden wealth by borrowing money from a US bank (perhaps a Swiss branch), using the Swiss bank account as collateral.

32. Zuo et al. (2008).

33. Kilmer et al. (2014), a RAND corporation report.

34. This estimate seems consistent with the growth of world income and the United Nations Office on Drugs and Crime (2005) estimates of drug use, but of course even the 2003 base estimate must be regarded as a rough one. More recently, the same agency estimated that the 2009 total global market for cocaine was $85 billion, and for heroin and opiates it was $68 billion (United Nations Office on Drugs and Crime 2011).

35. See discussion by Danny Kaufman in World Bank (2016).

36. Mauro (1995); Landes (1999); Acemoglu and Robinson (2013).

37. Julie Bosman, "Details about Indictment of Dennis Hastert," *New York Times*, June 9, 2015.

38. Adrian Humphreys, "The Hunt for Canada's $1,000 bills," *National Post*, November 15, 2012.

39. Dan Bilefsky and Mari-Leena Kuosa, "Finland Transfixed by Trial of Police Detective on Drug Charges," *New York Times*, August 2, 2015.

40. Charles Clover and James Anderlini, "Chinese General Caught with a Ton of Cash," *Financial Times*, November 21, 2014, available at http://www.ft.com/intl/cms/s/0/4883f674-7171-11e4-818e-00144feabdc0.html#axzz3zmCbjqjP.

41. See, for example, Transparency International (2004).

42. "Attorney General Loretta E. Lynch Announces Return of Forfeited Public Corruption Assets to Korean Minister of Justice Kim Hyun-Woong," United States Department of Justice, Office of Public Affairs, November 9, 2015, available at http://www.justice.gov/opa/pr/attorney-general-loretta-e-lynch-announces-return-forfeited-public-corruption-assets-korean.

43. "Leak of the Century: The Lesson of the Panama Papers," *Economist*, April 9, 2016. Many of the accounts unveiled were set up using shell corporations, but cash appears often to have played a role at some point, also thanks to the fact the dollar is legal tender in Panama.

44. United States Department of State (2015). United Nations Office on Drugs and Crime (2014, p. 30) discusses the issues. See also Schneider and Rudolph (2013).

45. International Labor Organization (2012).

46. United States Department of State (2015, p. 159).

47. International Labor Organization (2014, p. 16); Financial Action Tax Force and Groupe d'action Financière (2011, p. 17).

48. United States Department of State (2015, p. 38).

49. Financial Action Tax Force and Groupe d'action Financière (2011, p. 16).

50. A good illustration of many of the issues discussed in this chapter can be gleaned by examining the construction industry. Although many firms no doubt operate in full compliance with all laws and regulations, construction contractors are a routine source of problems for tax, immigration, and law enforcement authorities.

51. Pew Research Center (2014).

52. Dustman and Frattini (2012, table 2). Estimates are for the year 2009.

53. Francesco Gurarscio, "EU to Step Up Checks on Bitcoin, Prepaid Cards to Fight Terrorism," *Reuters*, February 2, 2016, available at http://uk.reuters.com/article/uk-eu-terrorism-financing-idUKKCN0VB1MK.

54. "ECB Ends Production and Issuance of €500 Banknote," European Central Bank website, May 4, 2016.

55. Financial Action Task Force (2015); Johnson (2014).

56. Federal Reserve Bank of San Francisco (2004).

57. For example, Judson and Porter (2012).

58. Stephen Mihm, "No Ordinary Counterfeit," *New York Times*, July 22, 2006. In recent years, Peru has become a central locus of counterfeiting activity.

59. In his early article on eliminating cash, James Gleick (1996) puts significant emphasis on the public health risks associated with cash. Warwick (2015) also highlights this concern.

60. Robert Lee Hotz, "You Shouldn't Put Your Money Where Your Mouth Is," *Wall Street Journal*, April 18, 2014, available at http://www.wsj.com/articles/SB10001424052702303456104579489510784385696. "NYU's Jane Carlton on Sequencing Money," *Genomeweb*, September 3, 2016, available at https://www.genomeweb.com/sequencing/nyus-jane-carlton-sequencing-money-sewage-new-york-city-and-malaria-india. See also Maron (2017).

61. See, for example, Orji et al. (2012) on parasitic infestations of both paper and polymer plastic currency in Anamber State of Nigeria.

CHAPTER 6: SEIGNIORAGE

1. Federal Reserve Board FAQs, "How much does it cost to produce currency and coin," available at http://www.federalreserve.gov/faqs/currency_12771.htm. This cost does not include many ancillary costs (e.g., counting, storage, personnel to distribute currency), but the basic point stands that the costs of printing $100 bills are trivial compared to their value. For more details on coins, see United States Mint (2014).

2. Indeed, it is quite possible that currency demand could shrink initially when interest rates eventually rise from the zero bound, and that for a few years the Federal Reserve may find itself needing to buy back dollars to prevent inflation.

3. Neumann (1992); for problems with the opportunity-cost definition of seigniorage, see Schmitt-Grohe and Uribe (1999).

4. US Treasury Direct, "Interest Rates and Prices," available at https://www.treasurydirect.gov/govt/rates/pd/avg/2016/2016_01.htm.

5. China figures are based on 2013, 2014, and 2015 seigniorage; source: People's Bank of China. Boeschoten and Hebbink (1996) represent an early attempt to estimate the loss from seigniorage in a shift to electronic money in Europe.

6. For further details on Sweden's declining currency demand since 2007, see Jochnick (2015).

7. See Jochnick (2015).

8. Calculations are based on data from the International Monetary Funds' International Financial Statistics (n.d.).

9. Board of Governors of the Federal Reserve System, "Currency in Circulation: Value," available at https://www.federalreserve.gov/paymentsystems/coin_currcircvalue.htm.

10. See Benes and Kumhoff (2012) and Kotlikoff (2011).

11. Benes and Kumhoff (2012).

12. I personally prefer the Admati and Hellwig (2013) plan, which broadly maintains existing institutions but forces financial firms to do more fund-raising in equity markets and less in debt markets.

CHAPTER 7: A PLAN FOR PHASING OUT MOST PAPER CURRENCY

1. Of course, in a coins-only world, better techniques and technologies for porting and sorting them would be available than today, when large quantities are extremely difficult to cash. For insight into the difficulties, see Alicia Tan, "Chinese Woman Drives Truck Carrying $82,000 in Coins to Deposit in Bank," *Yahoo News*, March 16, 2016, available at https://uk.news.yahoo.com/chinese-woman-drives-truck-carrying-082211877.html.

2. The technological issues surrounding how to demonstrate identity are enormously subtle and complex, with important trade-offs between privacy and security. For an excellent discussion of the evolving issues, see Birch (2014). One idea is to find ways to reveal the minimum amount of information necessary in bilateral private transactions through pseudonyms and tokens that can only be traced by the government and perhaps trusted intermediaries to underlying legal identities.

3. Federal Deposit Insurance Corporation (2014).

4. See Wright et al. (2014).

5. See Victoria Finkle, "Free Checking Isn't Cheap for Banks," *American Banker*, December 9, 2011, which reports that the average checking account costs banks between $250 and $450 per year to maintain, less any revenues.

6. The point that privacy and transaction technologies are converging problems is well known, for example, as discussed by Birch (2014).

7. The fact that digital storage costs are becoming virtually zero has led both private firms and governments to gather, store, and process increasingly vast quantities of personal information. The profound social implications of this development are emphasized in Michael Fertik's book *The Reputation Economy*, coauthored with David C. Thompson (Fertik and Thompson 2015).

8. The broad issues surrounding the need to upgrade the US payment system are detailed in Federal Reserve System of the United States (2015).

9. Woodford (2003) demonstrates that all the results of standard New Keynesian macroeconomic models still hold up when one takes an economy with money and allows the real money balances (money divided by the price level) to become very small.

10. An interesting idea somewhat related to Wallace's is the conjecture of Marimon, Nicollini, and Teles (1997), who argue that competition from electronic alternatives will put a check on the government's incentive to inflate and thereby lead to lower inflation rates.

11. "Cash Register Legislation in Sweden," *Eurofound*, June 2, 2013, available at http://www.eurofound.europa.eu/observatories/emcc/case-studies/tackling -undeclared-work-in-europe/cash-register-legislation-sweden.

12. There is a legacy 10,000-krona note last issued in 1958, but it accounts for only a trivial part of the money supply.

13. The 20% figure is from correspondence with the Riksbank.

14. See Yuka Hayashi, "Marijuana Companies Stuck Doing Business the Old-Fashioned Way, in Cash," *Wall Street Journal*, March 31, 2016, available at http://www.wsj.com/articles/marijuana-companies-stuck-doing-business-the-old -fashioned-way-in-cash-1459416605.

15. Warwick (2015) forcefully and effectively argues this point.

CHAPTER 8: THE COST OF THE ZERO BOUND CONSTRAINT

1. Although the nominal interest rate grabs all the headlines, most economic models suggest that it is the real interest rate that is most important for determining investment and consumption decisions. Nevertheless, because price and wages adjust relatively slowly and inflation expectations are sticky, short-term nominal interest rate cuts generally impact short-term real interest rates almost one for one in a low-inflation environment.

2. Bernanke (2005).

3. Reinhart, Reinhart, and Rogoff (2015) argue that heightened fear of another financial crisis or major global recession can potentially go a long way toward explaining the sharp drop in global real interest rates after 2008.

4. Gordon (2016); Reinhart and Rogoff (2009). In Rogoff (2015), I argue that the global economy is going through a debt supercycle that first began in the United

States, then moved to Europe and now to China, and that until the smoke clears, it is difficult to speculate about long-term growth trends.

5. Perhaps the most positive assessment of central banks' efforts to deal with the zero bound after the financial crisis comes from a clever literature that attempts to construct a "shadow policy interest rate" that is not constrained by the zero bound; the idea was originally due to creative genius Fischer Black (1995), famous for being one of the fathers of option pricing. The shadow rate is an indicator constructed from a wide range of macroeconomic variables and asset prices. The idea is to have an index that captures the overall stance of monetary policy and not just one measure (the interest rate). Because the shadow rate is just an artificial construct, it can perfectly well be negative. Jing Cynthia Wu and Fan Dora Xia (2014) assess the literature on the shadow policy interest rate and provide their own measures. They conclude that at the height of the financial crisis, the sum of all monetary policies (including quantitative easing and forward guidance) brought the effective policy interest rate down to −2%, even though the actual policy interest rate was between zero and 0.25%. They argue that if one looks at the shadow interest rate, the Fed managed to use monetary policy to be about as expansionary as it might have done using a Taylor rule, had negative interest rates been possible. See Hamilton and Wu (2011) for another approach to assessing the overall effect of alternative instruments of monetary policy.

6. For example, Delong and Summers (2012). Modern macroeconomics suggests that increased government spending also has a depressing effect due to higher current and expected future taxes. Keynesians tend to reject this effect as negligible. Classical economists think it is very large; the truth probably lies somewhere in between.

7. For example, see Eggertsson, Ferraro, and Raffo (2014), which builds on Eggertsson (2010). Bodenstein, Guerrieri, and Gust (2013) obtain a related result involving oil price shock.

8. See, for example, Werning (2011).

9. As nineteenth-century central banking guru Walter Bagehot stated in his seminal 1873 book *Lombard Street*: "John Bull can stand many things, but he cannot stand two per cent" (Bagehot 1873, ch. 6).

10. Hall (2013) argues forcefully that the Federal Reserve made a mistake leaving the interest rate strictly positive instead of reducing it to zero. The recent experiences of Japan and the ECB suggest that small interest rate adjustments would not have made a decisive difference.

11. Lebow (1993) anticipated many of the issues that later became central to the debate. Jeffrey Fuhrer and Brian Madigan (1997; working paper first published in 1994) make the first attempts to quantify the costs of the zero bound and show how raising the inflation target to 4% might help. Other early papers include Wolman (1998), who shows that stickiness of inflation is critical to the costs of the zero bound, and Reifschneider and Williams (2000), who make the first attempt to quantify the likely frequency and severity of zero bound episodes, a central question in assessing different policy alternatives.

12. Excellent discussions of the empirical literature on the zero bound include Williams (2009); Woodford (2012); Coibion, Gorodnichenko, and Wieland (2012); and Gavin et al. (2015). Bernanke, Reinhart, and Sack (2004) also give a useful discussion of the early literature.

13. See also the discussion of Krugman's (1998) paper in Rogoff (1998b), where earlier research on the zero bound is cited.

14. Canzoneri, Henderson, and Rogoff (1983) show that if the monetary authorities precommit to allow future interest rates to be impacted by current information (suppose that there is an adverse shock to output), monetary policy can be just as effective in stabilizing output and employment around their natural rates (essentially by manipulating inflation expectations) as it can be by manipulating the current short-term interest rate.

15. Williams (2009).

16. Reifschneider (2009). Chung et al. (2012) used a variety of models (including structural, New Keynesian, and nonstructural time series models) and found broadly similar results.

17. Reifschneider and Williams (2000) found that with a 2% inflation target, policy interest rates would be near zero about 5% of the time, and that each episode would last about four quarters. Importantly, they found that the intensity of the constraint was typically modest (meaning that, although policymakers would want to cut interest rates below zero, it would not typically be much below zero). Because under their assumptions, the zero bound does not hit often or hard, it has only a marginal effect on the variance of output around the natural rate: 3.0% with the zero bound and 2.9% without it. (Readers less familiar with standard monetary economics should understand that in most macroeconomic models, monetary policy cannot make output systematically higher, because wages and prices will rise to forestall any such attempt. Monetary policy can only stabilize output, thereby reducing its variance. If the zero bound has little impact on the variance of output, the implication is that it does not constrain monetary policy very much.)

18. Reinhart and Rogoff (2014) speculate on whether the period of relative quiescence in advanced economies may have come to an end; periods of financial market meltdowns and high volatility were certainly much more frequent before World War I. They argue that the very quiet period that followed World War II in fact reflects a long period of releveraging. As Reinhart and Rogoff (2010) note, both private debt and subnational debt had been decimated by World War II and the Great Depression, while at the same time heavy financial regulation might have helped contain financial excess and ease the burden of government debts by significantly helping to hold down interest rates. At the same time, European countries, whose capital stock had been decimated, were able to enjoy rapid growth through capital deepening and technology catch-up with the United States. As growth slowed and financial markets became more liberalized, countries may have become more vulnerable. This is speculative, but it is far from clear whether the financial crisis of 2008 was just a temporary step back from ever-continuing moderation or a return to normal.

19. The International Monetary Fund's (2013) *World Economic Outlook* argues that many of the factors that have been steadily driving down real global interest rates are likely to reverse in the coming decade.

20. In January 2015, the European Central Bank introduced a program to directly buy 60 billion euros per month in mostly public debt; the rate increased to 80 billion per month in March 2016, and the scope expanded to include corporate

debt. However, before that, it had engaged in lending programs to banks that in turn lent money to governments.

21. David Lebow (1993) recognized that with low target inflation rates, the zero bound problem that had already come to Japan might hit other advanced countries someday. Although he did not present any quantitative evidence or high theory, Lebow's simple framework did capture many key issues and options. His analysis introduces the idea of quantitative easing, including both government and private bonds, and it also considers the idea of purchasing gold. He correctly recognized that having the central bank purchase private assets is likely to have more effect than having it buy government bonds, but at the same time noted that the purchase of private assets constitutes a subsidy, blurring the line between fiscal and monetary policy. Lebow argued that it is important to analyze the effects of fiscal QE nevertheless, because it is important to know what actions the central bank can undertake on its own accord, should somehow the rest of the government be unable to act.

22. For example, Williams (2013).

23. It should be mentioned that a third alternative to purchasing private or government bonds is for the central bank to buy gold with its overnight reserves, but debt-financed purchases of gold can be very risky. The issue of gold purchases came to the fore in late 2014, when the Swiss National Bank had to fend off a referendum that would have forced it to sell a large share of its holdings of international government bonds (mostly German bunds) and invest the proceeds in gold. This strategy would have been risky, because the Swiss National Bank had issued a huge amount of short-term debt to finance its German bund purchases during a period when it was trying to peg its exchange rate to the euro. It would be risky, because a sudden drop in the price of gold would place the central bank in a weaker position to fight off a bank run or a run on its currency. (There is also a risk that German bunds lose value, but not nearly so much as gold prices.) People who have criticized the Swiss for worrying about the country's borrowing capacity have short memories. At the peak of the financial crisis in 2008, Switzerland's two megabanks, UBS and Credit Suisse, teetered on the brink of bankruptcy, and with debts equal to ten times Swiss GDP, the Swiss government might have faced great difficulties bailing them out without compromising its own solvency.

24. Wallace (1981).

25. The idea that the public might fully internalize all the risks and costs associated with future government bond debt payments is often referred to as "Ricardian equivalence." Barro (1974) launched the modern literature on the topic.

26. Krishnamurthy and Vissing-Jorgensen (2011) and Woodford (2012) point this out. Caballero and Farhi (2016) develop a theoretical framework to investigate the effects of QE. They find that QE is effective in a liquidity trap only to the extent it increases the supply of safe assets (government debt) held by the public, so although fiscal QE is effective, QE that just swaps one kind of government debt for another is far less so.

27. See David Weigel, "The Man Behind the Quantitative Easing Video Speaks," *Slate*, November 22, 2010, available at http://www.slate.com/blogs/weigel/2010/11/22/the_man_behind_the_quantitative_easing_cartoon_speaks.html.

28. Chung et al. (2012), for example, argue that unemployment in the United States at the end of 2012 would have been 1.5% higher in the absence of QE, a very powerful effect. They also find, however, that most of this came from QE during the height of the crisis and not later rounds. Wu and Xia (2016) suggest that the effects found in studies such as Chung et al. (2012) may overstate the effect of QE, because it is implicitly assumed that there is a large effect across the yield curve.

29. Krishnamurthy and Vissing-Jorgensen (2011, 2013).

30. Professor James Hamilton of the University of San Diego, whose work spans both macroeconomics and econometrics, gives an extremely insightful discussion on the difficulty of discerning any long-term effect of QE in his Econbrowser column "Evaluation of Quantitative Easing," November 2, 2014, available at http://econbrowser.com/archives/2014/11/evaluation-of-quantitative-easing.

31. I first used the golf trap analogy in op-eds in Japanese newspapers in 2003 and am cited by Kuroda (2005), who had been deputy finance minister and is now governor of the Bank of Japan.

32. The phrase "whatever it takes" was made famous by Draghi in his July 26, 2012, speech, which played a critical role in stabilizing the euro crisis.

33. The Fed has stated its intentions to let QE purchases on its balance sheet "run off" if possible, simply retiring debt as it matures.

34. Canzoneri, Henderson, and Rogoff (1983).

35. For a recent discussion of the effectiveness of data-based versus calendar-based forward guidance, see Feroli et al. (2016).

36. For further discussion of forward guidance, see Filardo and Hofmann (2014).

CHAPTER 9: HIGHER INFLATION TARGETS, NOMINAL GDP, ESCAPE CLAUSES, AND FISCAL POLICY

1. A higher general level of interest rates is the main argument in favor of a higher inflation target, but there is another, possibly important, rationale. With downwardly rigid nominal wages, it is difficult for employers to cut anyone's nominal wage, which in turn makes it difficult to change relative wages. A higher trend level of inflation makes things much easier, because then the employer can give some workers significant real wage cuts without cutting their nominal wages, and at the same time raise other workers' nominal wages well above the inflation rate. The difficulty in changing relative wages at low inflation rates can potentially lead to a higher unemployment rate, because it makes employers more reluctant to take on new workers. One prominent study, in fact, argued that with a moderate level of inflation (3%), unemployment would be significantly lower than in a world with zero inflation (Akerlof, Dickens, and Perry 1996). Of course, a society fully acclimated to low inflation might develop devices for allowing downward wage flexibility. In Japan in the 1990s, for example, bonuses constituted a significant part of workers' overall pay. This allowed firms to cut overall payments to workers by reducing bonuses without necessarily cutting nominal wages.

Some arguments go the other way. Some public finance economists have argued that higher inflation rates, even 2% inflation rates, considerably aggravate distortions in the tax system, particularly the taxation of capital income (Feldstein 1999). However, just as societies with low inflation will likely find ways to mitigate the effects of downward nominal wage rigidity, it is likely that high inflation societies would figure out ways to reduce inflation-induced distortions in the tax system.

2. Concern that the zero bound might be a problem in a world of low target inflation was raised by Lawrence Summers (1991) and also by Stanley Fischer (1996). Credit for the first serious research paper to explore the idea, though, again goes to Federal Reserve economists Jeffrey Madigan and Jeffrey Fuhrer. Already in 1994, they were experimenting to see how much having an inflation target of 4% would help resolve the problem quantitatively. The 4% target was later adopted by Paul Krugman (1998) as a way out for the deflation-challenged Bank of Japan, and he later recommended that the ECB permanently adopt a 4% target (Krugman 2014). Lawrence Ball (2013, 2014) is another leading monetary economist who has thoughtfully argued for a 4% rate. Perhaps the most prominent policy push for 4% came from International Monetary Fund chief economist Olivier Blanchard, who in 2010 coauthored a provocative paper advocating a shift to 4% across advanced countries (Blanchard, Dell'Ariccia, and Mauro 2010). Blanchard and his coauthors argued forcefully that the experience of the 2000s demonstrated beyond much doubt a profound problem with existing inflation targeting regimes, and that radical solutions needed to be considered. He took a tremendous amount of heat from some central bankers, who felt this was blasphemy and that it was inappropriate for an IMF official to espouse it. I experienced much the same pushback when I was IMF chief economist in 2003 and advocated a modest increase in inflation targets for the European Central Bank in a *Financial Times* op-ed (Rogoff 2003, available at https://www.imf.org/external/np/vc/2003/042303.htm).

3. "Inflation Rate Target Is Questioned as Fed Prepares to Meet," *New York Times*, April 28, 2015.

4. In an interesting paper, Nakamura et al. (2015) have challenged the idea that higher inflation leads to greater price dispersion, based on assessing data from the high US inflation period of the 1970s. However, the Internet and the spread of bar codes has made repricing vastly simpler today than it was 40 years ago, so even to the extent these results hold up, it is not clear how applicable they would be in today's environment.

5. Ascaria and Sbordone (2014) show that in standard New Keynesian models, the price distortion cost of higher inflation targets can be quite significant; see also Yehoue (2012) and Coibion, Gorodnichenko, and Wieland (2012).

6. Meade (1978). Jeffrey Frankel gives an excellent summary of the issues and some intellectual history of the idea in "The Death of Inflation Targeting," VoxEU.org, June 19, 2012, available at http://www.voxeu.org/article/inflation-targeting-dead-long-live-nominal-gdp-targeting.

7. Rogoff (1985).

8. On the complexities of measuring GDP in real time, see Landefeld et al. (2008), who note that the comprehensive economic census surveys needed for more precise estimates are carried out once every 5 years. Interim GDP estimates are necessarily based on statistical extrapolation from data on a subset of the economy that is often gathered for other purposes (and thus does not necessarily conform precisely to the needs of GDP accounting), and comes in at various frequencies.

9. Berkes and Williamson (2015, table 2).

10. The idea that central banks would have done well to steer for mildly elevated inflation early in the crisis is argued in Rogoff (2008).

11. The difference between proactively raising inflation targets, and price level–smoothing à la Eggertsson and Woodford (2003) and Evans (2010) is that the central bank does not wait for inflation to plummet before acting.

12. Various papers, including Christiano, Eichenbaum, and Rebelo (2011) and Eggertsson and Krugman (2012), address the theory of fiscal policy at the zero bound. Although easy to explain theoretically why fiscal multipliers should be higher at the zero bound, there is considerable debate about just how much higher they actually are. One thing that makes the multiplier difficult to estimate is that it likely shifts over time. One study by leading empirical macroeconomists, for example, finds that during the depths of the financial crisis, the fiscal multiplier was quite high, about 1.6 (implying that a dollar in government spending would stimulate private spending and raise output by more than a dollar). But by 2011, the multiplier had fallen significantly, to 0.9 (implying a small crowding out of private spending), perhaps explaining why the direst estimates of the effect of US fiscal tightening on growth did not come to pass (Christiano, Eichenbaum, and Trabandt 2014). Another reason of course is that other factors are at play, as the United Kingdom's experience illustrated.

13. See Christiano, Eichenbaum, and Rebelo (2011). A permanent fiscal stimulus is a much less effective tool for escaping the zero bound than a temporary fiscal stimulus because the drag from expected future taxes is greater, and the upward pressure on the real interest rate is smaller.

14. Turner (2015). See also Galí (2014) for quantitative estimates.

15. It is worth noting that helicopter money would do nothing at the zero bound if Ricardian equivalence holds (as mentioned in chapter 8) and the public regards the future taxes required to pay off the bonds as a full offset to the benefit being given to them. I will remind the reader again of this qualification in chapter 12. Drone money, discussed later in the current chapter, would still have an effect, because it represents a transfer from rich to poor.

16. To consider the equivalence between helicopter money and other government policies in a bit more depth, it is easiest to begin with the case of no change to the central bank's inflation-targeting regime. Let's start with Friedman's helicopter experiment of giving cash to each household directly. If the inflation-targeting central bank has not changed its stripes, it will have to sell debt to buy back any inflationary component to the money supply injection, so that in equilibrium, the currency supply rises and the quantity of government bonds held by the public also rises. (The exact outcome depends on a variety of factors, but we don't need to get into those to explain the equivalence result.)

What if instead the government issues bonds to finance transfers, with no initial cooperation from the central bank? Will the outcome be any different? No, the end result has to be exactly the same for all variables, including output, inflation, currency, and government debt held by the public. With bonds and output up, the inflation-targeting central bank will then be faced with downward pressure on prices and upward pressure on interest rates (because the supply of government bonds has increased). It will have to issue currency (bank reserves, some of which may be converted to paper currency) to mop up debt until it reaches exactly the same equilibrium as with helicopter money! Introducing the zero bound does exactly nothing to break up the equivalence between helicopter money and combinations of other government policies.

17. Feldstein (2002, p. 8).

18. Correia et al. (2013) considerably refine Feldstein's idea and try to quantify effects in a standard New Keynesian model. In some ways, Feldstein's idea is closely related to the proposal of Farhi, Gopinath, and Itskhoki (2013) to create a "fiscal devaluation" that will encourage employment by raising VATs and lowering employment taxes.

CHAPTER 10: OTHER PATHS TO NEGATIVE INTEREST RATES

1. Gesell (1916).

2. Rognlie (2016), in an interesting paper, emphasizes the subsidy to cash holders as the central trade-off. However, the practical issues surrounding externalities from a massive substitution from negative interest rate bonds to paper currency, and the potential effects on lending, are arguably more important.

3. Ashworth and Goodhart (2015) argue that the spike in the currency-deposit ratio in 2008 represented a short-lived panic.

4. If the path is prepared to have significant negative rates, banks will have to pass them on to large retail customers, though as noted in chapter 7, the central bank can move to protect small retail accounts.

5. The January 2016 Bank of Japan policy penalizes banks that converted any existing reserves into cash, by subtracting the amount from their initial quota of positive interest reserves (based on reserve holdings prior to the January announcement). Some commentators took Bank of Japan's policy as basically solving the zero bound problem by punishing any banks converting into cash, and by protecting banks' balance sheets even if interest rates go deeply negative. This interpretation, unfortunately, is deeply confused. Bank reserves are only the tip of the iceberg that central banks need to worry about if rates go negative. The real problem is that very negative rates will cause a run from short-term government debt into cash. Treasury bills are an order of magnitude larger than bank reserves, even after years of quantitative easing. In principle, the central bank can also solve the Treasury bill problem by simply charging for cash conversions, but this is basically an inferior version of the Kublai Khan–Eisler–Buiter–Kimball idea discussed later in this chapter.

6. International Monetary Fund (2016).

7. See the discussion in Alsterlind et al. (2015), a Riksbank commentary.

8. Again, see Alsterlind et al. (2015).

9. It is possible that a combination of secular (long-term trend) stagnation and elevated risk aversion could keep the real rate on overnight deposits below –2.0% for an extended period, in which case the policy interest rate would be as well, but this could be dealt with by temporarily targeting higher inflation, as discussed in chapter 9.

10. For a more detailed discussion, see Ilgmann and Menner (2011).

11. Keynes (1936, ch. 23, sec. IV, pp. 357–58).

12. See Fisher (1933), Champ (2008), and Gatch (2009).

13. See Svensson and Westermark (2015).

14. See Goodfriend (2000). Buiter (2003) and Buiter and Panigirtzoglou (2003) were also early advocates of the Gesell solution.

15. "New $100 Bill and RFID Microwave Test," available at https://www.youtube.com/watch?v=Kn5aqb-mN3Q. See also "Are You Ready for RFID Chips Built into Your Money and Documents," *Kurzweil Accelerating Intelligence*, May 7, 2013.

16. If a retail store has a camera monitoring its cash registers and time stamps bills with serial numbers attached, authorities could potentially connect bills and people.

17. Eisler (1933), Davies (2004), Buiter (2005, 2009), and Agarwal and Kimball (2015).

18. Buiter (2005, 2007).

19. Eisler (1933, p. 232).

20. Gopinath (2015) shows the remarkably high percentage of all US trade that is priced in dollars, including both exports and imports.

21. Davies (2004).

22. It is helpful that Kimball has written a formal paper with his important ideas, because there is little accountability in blog citation practices. See Agarwal and Kimball (2015).

23. I am grateful to Max Harris for this example.

24. Tullock (1957, p. 401).

CHAPTER 11: OTHER POSSIBLE DOWNSIDES TO NEGATIVE NOMINAL POLICY RATES

1. McAndrews (2015) lists some problems that might arise with negative interest rates.

2. See Bernanke and Gertler (1999) and the discussion by Rudiger Dornbusch and general discussion in the same volume. Also Bernanke and Gertler (2001), Mishkin (2007), and Svensson (2010).

3. Though most people take for granted that lower monetary policy interest rates lead to higher systemic financial risks, the theoretical case is far from black and white, as Emmanuel Farhi and Ivan Werning (2016) have shown in a rigorous theoretical model. In a nutshell, their point is that although the appetite for risky borrowing may increase as the interest rate falls, the supply of loans may shrink, so the net effect on the quantity of risky loans outstanding is not obvious. Thus the usual view that loose monetary policy is a driver of speculative bubbles might not be properly accounting for underlying factors that are simultaneously shifting both interest rates and risky borrowing.

4. See the interview of Bernanke in Rolnick (2004).

5. Reinhart and Rogoff (2009).

6. Philippon (2015) emphasizes the difficulty of measuring the contribution of the financial industry to GDP.

7. Yes, if secular stagnation turns out to imply that equilibrium real policy interest rates must remain below –2.0% for years on end (implying nominal rates

below zero), then great adaptation will be necessary, but for the moment, this is certainly not the central long-term scenario.

8. See Chris Kimball and Miles Kimball, "However Low Interest Rates Might Go, the IRS Will Never Act Like a Bank," Quartz blog, April 15, 2015, available at http://qz.com/383737/however-low-interest-rates-might-go-the-irs-will-never-act-like-a-bank/.

CHAPTER 12: NEGATIVE INTEREST RATES AS A VIOLATION OF TRUST AND A STEP AWAY FROM RULE-BASED SYSTEMS

1. If Ricardian equivalence holds (Barro 1974), the public does not respond to debt-financed transfers, because it views the future taxes as fully offsetting the benefits of the transfers. In this case, simply running money-financed budget deficits does nothing at the zero bound, because cash and bonds are the same thing when the interest rate is zero. As noted in chapter 8, although this is an extreme case, it ought to give one pause about some of the more extravagant claims one sees about the potential stimulus effects of deficits.

2. Reinhart and Rogoff (2009), *This Time Is Different* dataset (http://scholar.harvard.edu/rogoff/time-different%E2%80%94data-files). Reinhart and Rogoff (2009) show that over the longer course of history, most advanced economies have experienced bouts of extremely high inflation, if not necessarily hyperinflation.

3. See Rogoff (2004).

4. Reinhart and Rogoff (2009), *This Time Is Different* dataset (http://scholar.harvard.edu/rogoff/time-different%E2%80%94data-files).

5. Reinhart and Rogoff (2009, ch. 11, fig. 2 data).

6. International Monetary Fund (2015, p. 28). The Group of Seven (G7) is an informal group of industrialized countries.

7. Missale and Blanchard (1994) attempt to quantify the difficulty of using inflation to reduce the real value of debt in modern advanced economies. They argue that moving to shorter maturity structures is a way to commit to less inflation.

8. Reinhart and Sbrancia (2015). Financial repression is also a theme in Reinhart and Rogoff (2009).

9. Friedman and Schwartz (1963).

10. Friedman (1965, 1968, p. 193). To be fair, Friedman states his proposal with considerable nuance and emphasizes that "I do not regard this proposal as a be-all and end-all of monetary management, as a rule which is somehow to be written in tablets of stone and enshrined for all future time" (Friedman 1968, ch. 6, pp. 193–94).

11. Meltzer (2010); see also Abrams (2006).

12. Goldfeld (1976).

13. Jeff Zeleny and Jackie Calmes. "Perry Links Federal Reserve Policies and Treason," *New York Times*, August 16, 2011.

14. Andrew Jackson, Washington, DC, July 10, 1832. Source: Yale Law School Avalon Project (online repository in law, history, and diplomacy).

15. One would not necessarily want to introduce the option of negative interest rates in a low-income developing country—nor is it terribly necessary. The zero bound is not much of an issue in countries where citizens don't trust their leaders not to inflate, and where markets demand a large risk premium, even adjusting for high-inflation expectations.

CHAPTER 13: INTERNATIONAL DIMENSIONS TO PHASING OUT PAPER CURRENCY

1. The 500-euro notes are sometimes referred to as "Bin Ladens," because most people have heard of them, but few have seen one.

2. Serious Organised Crime Agency (2011).

3. Serious Organised Crime Agency (2011, p. 15).

4. As explained on the US Treasury website under "Legal Tender Status":

> The pertinent portion of law that applies to your question is the *Coinage Act of 1965*, specifically Section 31 U.S.C. 5103, entitled "Legal tender," which states: "United States coins and currency (including Federal reserve notes and circulating notes of Federal Reserve banks and national banks) are legal tender for all debts, public charges, taxes, and dues."
> This statute means that all United States money as identified above are a valid and legal offer of payment for debts when tendered to a creditor. There is, however, no Federal statute mandating that a private business, a person or an organization must accept currency or coins as for payment for goods and/or services. Private businesses are free to develop their own policies on whether or not to accept cash unless there is a State law which says otherwise. For example, a bus line may prohibit payment of fares in pennies or dollar bills. In addition, movie theaters, convenience stores and gas stations may refuse to accept large denomination currency (usually notes above $20) as a matter of policy.

5. The largest ruble note, the 5,000, is worth about $77, albeit this figure is highly sensitive to Russia's volatile exchange rate. Former head of Standard Charter Bank, Peter Sands (2015), has argued forcefully for coordinated Group of 20 action on eliminating large-denomination notes. (The Group of 20 includes governments and central bank governors from 20 major countries that hold meetings at the minister and head-of-state levels. Today it is the most important forum for major global economic issues.)

6. Colacelli and Blackburn (2009) estimate that the ability of Argentines to use dollars during the first couple years after Argentina's 2002 default might have boosted GDP by 0.6%.

7. Johnson (2013).

8. La Porta and Shleifer (2014).

9. David Segal, "Petrobras Scandal Leaves Brazilians Lamenting a Lost Dream," *New York Times*, August 7, 2015.

10. Obstfeld and Rogoff (2002).

11. See Gopinath (2015) for evidence that a significant fraction of global trade is priced in dollars.

12. See Caballero, Farhi, and Gourinchas (2015).

13. Rey (2013).

CHAPTER 14: DIGITAL CURRENCIES AND GOLD

1. For a broad-ranging discussion of the genesis of cryptocurrencies, see Vigna and Casey (2015).

2. Excellent primers on Bitcoin include Vigna and Casey (2015) and Lo and Wang (2014).

3. Per Jevons (1875), or the modern theory of money started by Kiyotaki and Wright (1989).

4. Kocherlakota (1998) emphasizes that money is a primitive form of social memory, but in principle superior devices can exist that take account of transaction history. Of course, to the extent a currency embeds transaction memory, it loses a part of its anonymity features.

5. Andolfatto (2014).

6. Buiter (2014).

7. It is curious that the standard rendition of Jevons's list of desirable qualities of money does not include anonymity, which for most modern users of currency would be near the top of the list. By and large, the academic literature on the foundations of currency also seems to overlook this issue, although see Kahn, McAndrews, and Roberds (2005).

8. World Gold Council (2015). At the end of 2014, 183,600 tons of stocks existed aboveground, roughly equal to 21 cubic meters. Residual uses of gold in electronics, dentistry, and technology account for only a modest portion of total demand. In fact gold is constantly being superseded by superior substitutes, for example, composites in dentistry.

9. The Ferengi's use of gold-encased latinum as a currency is introduced in the episode "The Gambit: Part 1" (min 2.49) of *Star Trek: The Next Generation*. Latinum and the Ferengi continued to play a role in the later series *Star Trek: Deep Space Nine*.

APPENDIX

1. See Kagin (1984).

2. Woodford (2003).

3. See Leeper (1991), Sims (1994), and Woodford (1996).

4. Taylor (1993). Dale Henderson and Warwick McKibbin (1993) appear to have introduced the same idea as Taylor's more or less simultaneously.

5. Beyond the choices discussed in the text (inflation index, potential output measure and relative weights on both), there are many other Taylor rule variants, for example, allowing for a more gradual adjustment of policy interest rates to target. In tranquil times, such as during the Great Moderation era of the late 1980s through the mid-2000s, these different variants of the rule give broadly

similar messages. But when inflation and/or output go way off target, as especially was the case for output during the financial crisis of 2008, differences that had seemed second-order suddenly become very important, and the exact choice of rule starts to matter a lot more. In a deep output recession, with output far below its full employment trend level, the Yellen interpretation of the rule would call for much deeper interest rate cuts.

6. Yellen (2012).

7. A large literature asks whether simple Taylor rules can be a close approximation to potentially much more sophisticated (and complicated) optimal rules. By and large the basic finding is that, at least during the Great Moderation period, simple rules can perform quite well.

8. Billi (2011). A sample of other papers addressing the cost of the zero bound include Reifschneider and Williams (2000); Adam and Billi (2007); Williams (2009); Chung et al. (2012); Schmidt (2013); and Christiano, Eichenbaum, and Trabandt (2014).

9. See Eggertsson and Woodford (2003). If the commitment is one sided, it would produce an inflation bias, in a manner similar to Rogoff (1985) in his analysis of the trade-off between credibility and commitment. Wolman (1998) argues that a critical issue is whether inflation expectations or price expectations are sticky. In the latter case, the costs of the zero bound are notably less.

10. Christiano, Eichenbaum, and Trabandt (2014) conclude that financial frictions are by far the most important reason for the depth and duration of the US recession of 2008, and consequently find a relatively modest effect of the zero bound in their central scenario. This is consistent with Reinhart and Rogoff's (2009) results that the aftermath of financial crises is pretty painful with and without the zero bound, presumably due to partial paralysis of the financial sector.

11. Rogoff (1985); Kydland and Prescott (1977).

12. Walsh (1995).

13. See the discussion in Obstfeld and Rogoff (1996, ch. 9).

14. See Walsh (2011) for details.

15. Inflation targeting seemed to work well in its early years, although as Rogoff (2004, 2007) noted, it had never really been stress-tested during the low-volatility, high-productivity growth period of the Great Moderation.

16. See Bernanke et al. (2001).

AFTERWORD TO THE PAPERBACK EDITION

1. Dan Joppich, "Washington's Endgame: First Your Guns, Then Your Cash," *American Thinker*, September 18, 2016.

2. Jason Horowitz, "A King in His Castle: How Donald Trump Lives, From His Long-Time Butler," *The New York Times*, March 15, 2016.

3. Damon Runyon, "Blood Pressure," *Saturday Evening Post*, April 3, 1930.

4. See annotations by Daniel Schwarz in Runyon (2008).

5. The imputed cost-of-living estimates are taken from Measuringworth.com (founded in 2006 by Lawrence Officer and Samuel H. Williamson). These are of

course very rough as it is difficult to make comparisons across long time periods when there have been large changes in the basket of consumer goods. Also, per capita real income and wealth were much lower decades ago.

6. Importantly, mega-notes were already relatively unimportant in the US currency supply in 1969 compared to the $100 bill today.

7. Per Henry (1980), "On any given Sunday, the Federal Reserve would announce that existing "big bills"—$50s and $100s—would no longer be accepted as legal tender, and would have to be exchanged at banks for new bills within a short period of time. When the tax cheats, Mafiosi, and other pillars of the criminal community rushed to their banks to exchange their precious notes, the IRS would be there to ask those with the most peculiar bundles some embarrassing questions."

8. The Greek government ran into the obstacle of printing currency in July 2015 when, following the advice of a few prominent left-leaning American economists/op-ed writers, Greece threatened to abruptly pull out of the Eurozone. This presented many problems, but one that simply was apparently not appreciated until the last moment was that creating a new physical currency overnight was nearly impossible technically. The Greeks reportedly considered a variety of radical measures including calling in and stamping existing euro notes, but ultimately retreated from the brink.

9. PTI, "Data Shows Only 1% of Population Pays Income Tax, Over 5000 Pay More Than 1 Crore," *Indian Express*, May 1, 2016.

10. In a large-scale study involving data for over 19 million people in the Indian state of Andhra Pradesh, Muralidharan, Niehaus, and Sukhtankar (2016) find that the introduction of biometrically-authenticated smart cards leads to a massive reduction in leakage between the government and the beneficiaries of government employment subsidies and pension programs.

11. For the official announcement of the European Central Bank about the 500-euro note, see (as noted in chapter 5) "ECB Ends Production and Issuance of €500 Banknote," European Central Bank, May 4, 2016.

12. Jim Brunsden and James Shotter, "Criminals' 'Currency of Choice' for Chop," *Financial Times*, February 15, 2016.

13. Joanna Mather, "Crackdown on Cash Economy Targets $100 bills and Billions for Budget," *The Australian Financial Review*, December 13, 2016.

14. *Strategies and Activities to Address the Cash and Hidden Economy*, Australian National Audit Office, April 26, 2016, (Canberra, The Australian Treasury).

15. Peter Martin, "Hoarding $100s to Ensure a Pension," *The Sunday Morning Herald*, September 25, 2012.

16. Matthew Weaver and agencies, "Venezuela Pulls 100 Bolivar Note from Circulation to 'Beat Mafia,'" *The Guardian*, December 12, 2016.

17. Christopher Ingraham, "American Gun Ownership Drops to its Lowest Level in Nearly 40 years," *Washington Post Wonkblog*, June 29, 2016.

18. Henry (1976) remarks that holdings of high notes are extremely concentrated and therefore politically more vulnerable than firearms.

19. Monetary policy is hardly a panacea, and even with effective negative interest rate policy, the economy will recover much faster with support from fiscal policy, debt restructuring and recapitalization of the banking system.

20. "Money Stock Measures," publication H.6, and "Currency in Circulation: Volume," Board of Governors of the Federal Reserve System, February, 2017.

REFERENCES

Abrams, Burton A. 2006. "How Richard Nixon Pressured Arthur Burns: Evidence from the Nixon Tapes." *Journal of Economic Perspectives* 20 (Fall): 177–88.

Acemoglu, Daron, and James Robinson. 2013. *Why Nations Fail: The Origins of Power, Prosperity and Poverty.* New York: Crown Business.

Adam, Klaus, and Roberto M. Billi. 2007. "Discretionary Monetary Policy and the Zero Lower Bound on Nominal Interest Rates." *Journal of Monetary Economics* 54 (3): 728–52.

Admati, Anat, and Martin Hellwig. 2013. *The Bankers' New Clothes: What's Wrong with Banking and What to Do About It?* Princeton, NJ: Princeton University Press.

Agarwal, Ruchir, and Miles Kimball. 2015. "Breaking Through the Zero Lower Bound." International Monetary Fund Working Paper WP 15/224, October.

Ahamed, Liaquat. 2009. *Lords of Finance: The Bankers Who Broke the World.* New York: Penguin.

Akerlof, George A., William T. Dickens, and George L. Perry. 1996. "The Macroeconomics of Low Inflation." *Brookings Papers on Economic Activity* 1: 1–59.

Alsterlind, Jan, Hanna Armelius, David Forsman, Björn Jönsson, and Anna-Lena Wretman. 2015. "How Far Can the Repo Rate Be Cut?" *Sveriges Riksbank Economic Commentaries* 11. Stockholm: Sveriges Riksbank.

Amromin, Gene, and Sujit Chakravorti. 2009. "Whither Loose Change? The Diminishing Demand for Small-Denomination Currency." *Journal of Money, Credit and Banking* 41 (2–3): 315–35.

Andolfatto, David. 2014. "Bitcoin and Beyond: The Possibilities and Pitfalls of Virtual Currencies." Federal Reserve Bank of St Louis, *Central Banker* (Fall). Slides available at http://www.stlouisfed.org/dialogue-with-the-fed/the -possibilities-and-the-pitfalls-of-virtual-currencies.

Antràs, Pol, and C. Fritz Foley. 2015. "Poultry in Motion: A Study of International Trade Finance Practices." *Journal of Political Economy* 123 (4): 809–52.

Ascaria, Guido, and Argia M. Sbordone. 2014. "The Macroeconomics of Trend Inflation." *Journal of Economic Literature* 52 (3): 679–739.

Ashworth, Jonathan, and Charles Goodhart. 2015. "Measuring Public Panic in the Great Financial Crisis." VoxEU.org, April.

Australian National Audit Office. 2016. Strategies and Activities to Address the Cash and Hidden Economy (April 26) (Canberra, The Australian Treasury).

Bagehot, Walter. 1873. *Lombard Street: A Description of the Money Market.* Reprint by Wiley in 1999. New York: Wiley.

Bagnall, John, David Bounie, Kim Huynh, Anneke Kosse, Tobias Schmidt, Scott Schuh, and Helmut Stix. 2014. "Consumer Cash Usage: A Cross-Country Comparison with Payment Diary Survey Data." European Central Bank Working Paper Series 1685. Frankfurt: European Central Bank.

Ball, Lawrence. 2014. "The Case for a Long-Run Inflation Target of Four Percent." International Monetary Fund Working Paper WP 14/92 (June). Washington, DC: International Monetary Fund.

Ball, Lawrence. 2013. "The Case for 4% Inflation." VoxEU.org, May.

Barro, Robert J. 1974. "Are Bonds Net Wealth?" *Journal of Political Economy* 82 (6): 1095–1177.

Bartzsch, Nikolaus, Gerhard Rösl, and Franz Seitz. 2011. "Foreign Demand for Euro Banknotes Issued in Germany." Deutsche Bundesbank Monthly Report (January). Frankfurt: Deutsche Bundesbank.

Benes, Jaromir, and Michael Kumhoff. 2012. "The Chicago Plan Revisited." International Monetary Fund Working Paper WP 12/202. Washington, DC: International Monetary Fund.

Bennett, Barbara, Douglas Conover, Shaun O'Brien, and Ross Advincula. 2014. "Cash Continues to Play a Key Role in Consumer Spending: Evidence from the Diary on Consumer Payment Choice" (April). FEDS Notes, Federal Reserve Bank of San Francisco.

Bennett, Paul, and Stavros Peristiani. 2002. "Are US Reserve Requirements Still Binding?" Federal Reserve Bank of New York, *Economic Policy Review* 8: (1).

Beretta, Edoardo. 2014. "The Irreplaceability of Cash and Recent Limitations on Its Use: Why Europe Is Off the Track." In *The Usage, Costs and Benefits of Cash—Revisited*. Proceedings of the International Cash Conference, September. Frankfurt: Deutsche Bundesbank.

Berkes, Enrico, and Samuel H. Williamson. 2015. "Vintage Does Matter: The Impact and Interpretation in the Official Estimates of Post War GDP for the United Kingdom." Northwestern University (February), Evanston, IL.

Bernanke, Ben S. 2005. "The Global Savings Glut and the U.S. Current Account Deficit." Paper presented at the Sandridge Lecture, Virginia Association of Economists, Richmond, March 10.

Bernanke, Ben S., and Mark Gertler. 1999. "Monetary Policy and Asset Price Volatility." In *Federal Reserve Bank of Kansas City Symposium on New Challenges for Monetary Policy*, Jackson Hole, WY, August 26–28. Federal Reserve Bank of Kansas City.

———. 2001. "Should Central Banks Respond to Asset Prices?" *American Economic Review* 91: 253–57.

Bernanke, Ben S., Thomas Laubach, Frederic S. Mishkin, and Adam S. Posen. 2001. *Inflation Targeting: Lessons from the International Experience*. Princeton, NJ: Princeton University Press.

Bernanke, Ben S., Vincent Reinhart, and Brian Sack. 2004. "Monetary Alternatives at the Zero Bound: An Empirical Assessment." *Brookings Papers on Economic Activity* 2: 1–100.

Billi, R. 2011. "Optimal Inflation for the US Economy." *American Economic Journal: Macroeconomics* 3 (3): 29–52.

Birch, David. 2014. *Identity Is the New Money*. London: London Publishing Partnership.

Black, Fischer. 1995. "Interest Rates as Options." *Journal of Finance* 50 (December): 1371–76.

Blanchard, Olivier, Giovanni Dell'Ariccia, and Paolo Mauro. 2010. "Rethinking Macroeconomic Policy." International Monetary Fund Position Note SPN/10/03. Washington, DC (February).

Bodenstein, Martin, Luca Guerrieri, and Christopher J. Gust. 2013. "Oil Shocks and the Zero Bound on Nominal Interest Rates." *Journal of International Money and Finance* 32(1): 941–967.

Boeschoten, W. C., and G. E. Hebbink. 1996. "Electronic Money, Currency Demand and Seigniorage Loss in the G10 Countries." De Nederlandsche Bank Staff Reports 1. Amsterdam.

Bordo, Michael D. 2008. "The History of Monetary Policy." In *New Palgrave Dictionary of Economics*, 2nd ed. London: Palgrave Macmillan.

Brown, Robert E., and Mark J. Mazur. 2003. "IRS's Comprehensive Approach to Compliance Measurement." Expansion of a paper presented at the May 2003 National Tax Symposium. Available at https://www.irs.gov/pub/irs-soi/mazur .pdf. See also *National Tax Journal* 56 (3): 689–700.

Buiter, Willem H. 2003. "Helicopter Money, Irredeemable Fiat Money and the Liquidity Trap." NBER Working Paper 10163 (December). Cambridge, MA: National Bureau of Economic Research.

———. 2005. "Overcoming the Zero Bound: Gesell vs. Eisler." Mimeo, European Bank for Reconstruction and Development, London.

———. 2007. "Is Numerairology the Future of Monetary Economics: Unbundling the Numeraire and Medium of Exchange through a Virtual Currency and a Shadow Exchange Rate." NBER Working Paper 12839 (January). Cambridge, MA: National Bureau of Economic Research.

———. 2009. "Negative Nominal Interest Rates: Three Ways to Overcome the Zero Lower Bound." NBER Working Paper 15118 (June). Cambridge, MA: National Bureau of Economic Research.

———. 2014. "Gold: A Six Thousand Year Bubble Revisited." Citi Economics Research Paper (November). Available at http://willembuiter.com/gold2.pdf.

Buiter, Willem H., and Nikolaos Panigirtzoglou. 2003. "Overcoming the Zero Bound on Nominal Interest Rates with Negative Interest on Currency: Gesell's Solution." *Economic Journal* 113 (490): 723–46.

Caballero, Ricardo J., and Emmanuel Farhi. 2016 "The Safety Trap" (March). Mimeo, Harvard University, Cambridge MA. Forthcoming in *Review of Economic Studies*.

Caballero, Ricardo J., Emmanuel Farhi, and Pierre-Olivier Gourinchas. 2015. "Global Imbalances and Currency Wars at the ZLB." NBER Working Paper 21670 (October). Cambridge, MA: National Bureau of Economic Research.

Cameron, Samuel. 2014. "Killing for Money and the Economic Theory of Crime." *Review of Social Economy* 72 (1): 28–41.

Canzoneri, Matthew, Dale Henderson, and Kenneth Rogoff. 1983. "The Information Content of the Interest Rate and Optimal Monetary Policy." *Quarterly Journal of Economics* 98 (November): 545–66.

Capie, Forest H., ed. 1991. *Major Inflations in History*. Aldershot, England: Elgar Publishing.

Cebula, Richard J., and Edgar L. Feige 2012. "America's Unreported Economy: Measuring the Size, Growth and Determinants of Income Tax Evasion in the U.S." *Crime, Law and Social Change* 57 (3): 265–85.

Champ, Bruce. 2008. "Stamp Scrip: Money People Paid to Use." Federal Reserve Bank of Cleveland, *Economic Commentary* (April).

Christiano, Lawrence J., Martin S. Eichenbaum, and Sergio Rebelo. 2011. "When Is the Government Spending Multiplier Large?" *Journal of Political Economy* 119 (1): 78–121.

Christiano, Lawrence J., Martin S. Eichenbaum, and Mathias Trabandt. 2014. "Understanding the Great Recession." NBER Working Paper 20040 (April). Cambridge, MA: National Bureau of Economic Research.

Chung, Hess, Jean-Philippe Laforte, David Reifschneider, and John C. Williams. 2012. "Have We Underestimated the Likelihood and Severity of Zero Lower Bound Events?" *Journal of Money, Credit and Banking* 44 (1): 47–82.

Clapham, John Harold. 1966. *The Bank of England: A History*. Cambridge: Cambridge University Press.

Coibion, Olivier, Yuriy Gorodnichenko, and Johannes Wieland. 2012. "The Optimal Inflation Rate in New Keynesian Models: Should Central Banks Raise Their Inflation Targets in Light of the Zero Lower Bound?" *Review of Economic Studies* 79 (4): 1371–1406.

Colacelli, Mariana, and David Blackburn. 2009. "Secondary Currency: An Empirical Analysis." *Journal of Monetary Economics* 56: 295–306.

Correia, Isabelle, Emmanuel Farhi, Juan Pablo Nicolini, and Pedro Teles. 2013. "Unconventional Fiscal Policy at the Zero Bound." *American Economic Review* 103 (4): 1172–1211.

Davies, Glyn. 2002. *A History of Money from Ancient Times to the Present Day*, 3rd ed. Cardiff: University of Wales Press.

Davies, Stephen. 2004. "Comment on Buiter and Panigirtzoglou." Mimeo, Research Institute for Economics and Business Administration, Kobe, Japan.

Deaton, Angus. 2013. *The Great Escape: Health, Wealth and the Origins of Inequality*. Princeton, NJ: Princeton University Press.

Delong, Bradford, and Lawrence Summers. 2012. "Fiscal Policy in a Repressed Economy." *Brookings Papers on Economic Activity* 1: 233–97.

Dostoyevsky, Fyodor. 1862. *The House of the Dead*. Unabridged replication of English translation originally published in 1851. Mineola, NY: Dover.

Doyle, Brian M. 2001. "'Here, Dollars, Dollars . . .'—Estimating Currency Demand and Worldwide Currency Substitution." Board of Governors of the Federal Reserve System, International Finance Discussion Papers, No. 657. Washington, DC.

Dunbar, Geoffrey R., and Chunling Fu. 2015. "Sheltered Income: Estimating Income Under-Reporting in Canada, 1998 and 2004." Bank of Canada Working Paper 2015–22. Toronto.

Dustman, Christian, and Tommaso Frattini. 2012. "Immigration: The European Experience." Norface Migration Discussion Paper 2012–01. London.

Eggertsson, Gauti. 2010. "The Paradox of Toil." New York Federal Reserve Staff Report 433 (February).

Eggertsson, Gauti, and Paul Krugman. 2012. "Debt, Deleveraging and the Liquidity Trap: A Fisher-Minsky-Koo Approach." *Quarterly Journal of Economics* 127 (3): 1469–1513.

Eggertsson, Gauti, and Michael Woodford. 2003. "The Zero Bound on Interest Rates and Optimal Monetary Policy." *Brookings Papers on Economic Activity* (1): 139–233.

Eggertsson, Gauti, Andrea Ferraro, and Andrea Raffo. 2014. "Can Structural Reforms Help Europe?" *Journal of Monetary Economics* 61 (C): 2–22.

Eichengreen, Barry. 1996. *Golden Fetters: The Gold Standard and the Great Depression, 1919–1939*. London: Oxford University Press.

Einzig, Paul. 1966. *Primitive Money in Its Ethnological, Historical and Economic Aspects*, 2nd ed. Oxford: Pergamon Press.

Eisler, Robert. 1933. *Stable Money: The Remedy for the Economic World Crisis. A Programme of Financial Reconstruction for the International Conference 1933: With a Preface by Vincent C. Vickers*. London: Search Publishing.

European Central Bank (ECB). 2011. "The Use of Euro Banknotes—Results of Two Surveys among Households and Firms." *European Central Bank Monthly Bulletin* (April): 79–90.

Evans, Charles. 2010. "Monetary Policy in a Low-Inflation Environment: Developing a State-Contingent Price-Level Target." Remarks before the Federal Reserve Bank of Boston's 55th Economic Conference, Boston, October 16.

Farhi, Emmanuel, Gita Gopinath, and Oleg Itskhoki. 2013. "Fiscal Devaluations." *Review of Economic Studies* 81 (2): 725–60.

Farhi, Emmanuel, and Ivan Werning. 2016. "A Theory of Macroprudential Policies in the Presence of Nominal Rigidities" (May). Mimeo, Harvard University, Cambridge, MA. Forthcoming in *Econometrica*.

Federal Deposit Insurance Corporation. 2014. "2013 FDIC National Survey of Unbanked and Underbanked Households." Washington, DC. Available at https://www.fdic.gov/householdsurvey/.

Federal Reserve Bank of Boston. 2012. "Diary of Consumer Payment Choice." Boston.

———. 2013. "Survey of Consumer Payment Choice." Boston.

Federal Reserve Bank of San Francisco. 2004. "How Much Currency Is Circulating in the Economy, and How Much of It Is Counterfeit?" (April). Available at http://www.frbsf.org/education/publications/doctor-econ/2004/april/money-supply-currency-counterfeit.

Federal Reserve Board. 2014. Annual Report. Washington, DC.

Federal Reserve System of the United States. 2015. *Strategies for Improving the U.S. Payments System* (January). Washington, DC.

Feige, Edgar L. 1989. "Currency Velocity and Cash Payments in the U.S. Economy: The Currency Enigma." Munich Personal RePEc Archive (MPRA) Paper 13807, University Library of Munich.

———. 2012a. "The Myth of the 'Cashless Society': How Much of America's Currency Is Overseas?" Munich Personal RePEc Archive (MPRA) Paper 42169, University Library of Munich.

———. 2012b. "New Estimates of U.S. Currency Abroad, the Domestic Money Supply and the Unreported Economy." *Crime, Law and Social Change* 57 (3): 239–63.

Feldstein, Martin. 1999. "The Costs and Benefits of Going from Low Inflation to Price Stability." In *The Costs and Benefits of Price Stability*, ed. Martin Feldstein. Chicago: National Bureau of Economic Research and the University of Chicago Press.

Feldstein, Martin. 2002. "The Role for Discretionary Fiscal Policy in a Low Interest Rate Environment." NBER Working Paper Series 9203 (September). Cambridge, MA: National Bureau of Economic Research.

Ferguson, Niall. 2008. *The Ascent of Money*. New York: Penguin.

Feroli, Michael, David Greenlaw, Peter Hooper, Frederic S. Mishkin, and Amir Sufi. 2016. "Language after Liftoff: Fed Communication away from the Zero Lower Bound." Paper presented at the US Monetary Policy Forum, Chicago (February 26).

Fertik, Michael, and David C. Thompson. 2015. *The Reputation Economy: How to Optimize Your Digital Footprint in a World Where Your Reputation Is Your Most Valuable Asset*. New York: Crown Business.

Filardo, Andrew, and Boris Hofmann. 2014. "Forward Guidance at the Zero Lower Bound." Bank for International Settlements, *BIS Quarterly Review* (March).

Financial Action Task Force. 2015. *Financing of the Terrorist Organisation Islamic State in Iraq and the Levant (ISIL)*. FATF Report, Paris (February). Available at http://www.fatf-gafi.org.

Financial Action Tax Force and Groupe d'action Financière. 2011. *Money Laundering Risks Arising from Trafficking in Human Beings and Smuggling of Migrants*. FATF Report (July), Paris. Available at http://www.fatf-gafi.org.

Fischer, Bjorn, Petra Köhler, and Franz Seitz. 2004. "The Demand for Euro Currencies, Past, Present and Future." European Central Bank Working Paper Series 330 (April). Frankfurt.

Fischer, Stanley. 1996. "Why Are Central Banks Pursuing Long-Run Price Stability?" In *Achieving Price Stability: A Symposium Sponsored by the Federal Reserve Bank of Kansas City*, pp. 7–34. Jackson Hole, WY, August 29–31. Federal Reserve Bank of Kansas City.

Fischer, Stanley, Ratna Sahay, and Carlos A. Végh. 2002. "Modern Hyper- and High Inflations." *Journal of Economic Literature* 40 (3): 837–80.

Fisher, Irving. 1933. *Stamp Scrip*. New York: Adelphi. Available at http://userpage.fu-berlin.de/roehrigw/fisher/.

Franklin, Benjamin. 1729. "A Modest Enquiry into the Nature and Necessity of a Paper Currency." Printed and Sold by Benjamin Franklin. Philadelphia.

———. 1786. "The Morals of Chess." Reprinted in *The Columbian Magazine* I (December 1786), 159–61.

Friedman, Milton. 1965. "A Program for Monetary Stability." In *Readings in Financial Institutions*, ed. Marshall D. Ketchum and Leon T. Kendall. Boston: Houghton Mifflin.

———. 1968. *Dollars and Deficits*. Upper Saddle River, NJ: Prentice-Hall.

Friedman, Milton, and Anna Jacobson Schwartz. 1963. *A Monetary History of the United States, 1867–1960*. Princeton, NJ: Princeton University Press.

Fuhrer, Jeffrey, and Brian Madigan. 1997. "Monetary Policy When Interest Rates Are Bounded at Zero." *Review of Economics and Statistics* 79 (December): 573–85. Earlier version published as Federal Reserve Bank of San Francisco Working Paper in Applied Economic Theory 94-06 (1994).

Galí, Jordi. 2014. "The Effects of a Money-Financed Fiscal Stimulus," CEPR Discussion Paper 10165, September.

Gatch, Loren. 2009. "The Professor and a Paper Panacea: Irving Fisher and the Stamp Scrip Movement of 1932–34." *Paper Money* 260 (March–April): 125–42.

Gavin, William T., Benjamin Keen, Alexander W. Richter, and Nathaniel A. Throckmorton. 2015. "The Zero Lower Bound, the Dual Mandate, and Unconventional Dynamics." Federal Reserve Bank of St. Louis Working Paper 2013-007F (revised May 2015).

Gesell, Silvio. 1916. *Die Natuerliche Wirtschaftsordnung*. Rudolf Zitzmann Verlag. Available in English as *The Natural Economic Order* (1958). London: Peter Owen.

Gleick, James. 1996. "The End of Cash," *New York Times Magazine*, June 16.

Goldfeld, Stephen. 1976. "The Case of the Missing Money." *Brookings Papers on Economic Activity* 3: 683–739.

Goodfriend, Marvin. 2000. "Overcoming the Zero Bound on Interest Rate Policy." *Journal of Money, Credit and Banking* 32 (4): 1007–35.

Gopinath, Gita. 2015. "The International Price System." In *Proceedings of the Kansas City Federal Reserve Bank Symposium on Inflation Dynamics and Monetary Policy*, Jackson Hole, WY, August 27–29. Federal Reserve Bank of Kansas City.

Gordon, Robert J. 2016. *The Rise and Fall of American Growth*. Princeton, NJ: Princeton University Press.

Greene, Claire, and Scott Schuh. 2014. "US Consumers' Holdings and Use of $100 Bills." Federal Reserve Bank of Boston Research Data Report 14-3 (November 25).

Grubb, Farley. 2006. "Benjamin Franklin: And the Birth of a Paper Money Economy." Paper based on a lecture presented to the Federal Reserve Bank of Philadelphia, March 30. Available at https://www.philadelphiafed.org/publications /economic-education/ben-franklin-and-paper-money-economy.pdf.

Hall, Robert E. 2013. "The Routes into and out of the Zero Lower Bound." In *Proceedings of the Kansas City Federal Reserve Bank Symposium on Global Dimensions of Unconventional Monetary Policy*, Jackson Hole, WY, August 22–24. Federal Reserve Bank of Kansas City.

Hamilton, James, and Jing Cynthia Wu. 2011. "The Effectiveness of Alternative Zero Bound Tools in a Zero Lower Bound Environment." *Journal of Money, Credit and Banking* 44, suppl. (1): 3–46.

Hellerstein, Rebecca, and William Ryan. 2011. "Cash Dollars Abroad." Federal Reserve Bank of New York, Staff Report 400.

Henderson, Dale, and Warwick McKibbin. 1993. "A Comparison of Some Basic Monetary Policy Regimes for Open Economies: Implications of Different Degrees of Instrument Adjustment and Wage Persistence." *Carnegie-Rochester Conference Series on Public Policy* 39: 221–318.

Henry, James. 1976. "Calling in the Big Bills." *The Washington Monthly* (May): 26–33.

———. 1980. "How to Make the Mob Miserable: The Cash Connection." *Washington Monthly* 12(4): 54–61.

Hicks, John R. 1969. *A Theory of Economic History*. Oxford: Clarendon Press.

HM Revenue and Customs. 2015. *Measuring Tax Gaps, 2015 Edition: Tax Gap Estimates for 2013–14*. London: Her Majesty's Revenue and Customs.

Huang, Miantang. 2008. *Summary of Historical Price in China* (in Chinese). Jinan, Shandong Province: QiLu Press.

Ilgmann, Cordelius, and Martin Menner. 2011. "Negative Nominal Interest Rates: History and Proposals." *International Economics and Economic Policy* 8 (4): 383–405.

Internal Revenue Service. 2012a. "IRS Releases 2006 Tax Gap Estimates." FS-2012-6: January. Available at http://www.irs.gov/uac/IRS-Releases-2006-Tax -Gap-Estimates.

———. 2012b. "IRS Releases New Tax Gap Estimates; Compliance Rates Remain Statistically Unchanged from Previous Study." IR-2012-4: January 6. Available at http://www.irs.gov/uac/IRS-Releases-New-Tax-Gap-Estimates ;-Compliance-Rates-Remain-Statistically-Unchanged-From-Previous-Study.

International Labor Organization. 2012. *ILO Global Estimate of Forced Labor Results and Methodology*. Geneva.

———. 2014. *Profits and Poverty: The Economics of Forced Labor*. Geneva.

International Monetary Fund. 2013. *World Economic Outlook*. April. Washington, DC.

———. 2015. *Fiscal Monitor*. October. Washington, DC.

———. 2016. *Global Financial Stability Report*. April. Washington, DC.

———. n.d. *International Financial Statistics*, various issues.

Irwin, Neil. 2013. *Three Central Bankers and a World on Fire*. New York: Penguin.

James, Harold. 2012. "Germany Should Re-read Goethe's Faust Part II." *Financial News*, October 15.

Jevons, William S. 1875. *Money and the Mechanism of Exchange*. New York: D. Appleton and Co.

Jochnick, Kerstin. 2015. "Does the Riksbank Have to Make a Profit? Challenges for the Funding of the Riksbank." Speech presented to the Swedish House of Finance, January 23. Available at http://www.riksbank.se/Documents/Tal /Jochnick/2015/tal_af_jochnick_150123_eng.pdf.

Johnson, Boris. 2013. *2020 Vision: The Greatest City on Earth: Ambitions for London* (June). City Hall, London: London Greater Authority.

Johnson, Patrick B. 2014. "Countering ISIL's Financing." The RAND Corporation Testimony Series. Testimony presented before the House Financial Services Committee on November 13. Santa Monica, CA: RAND Corporation.

Jost, Patrick M., and Harjit Singh Sandbu. 2000. "Hawala: The Hawala Alternative Remittance System and Its Role in Money Laundering." Prepared by the Financial Crimes Enforcement Network of the United States Department of Treasury in cooperation with INTERPOL/FOPAC.

Judson, Ruth. 2012. "Crisis and Calm: Demand for U.S. Currency at Home and Abroad from the Fall of the Berlin Wall to 2011." Board of Governors of the Federal Reserve, International Finance Discussion Paper 2012-1058 (November). Washington, DC.

Judson, Ruth, and Richard Porter. 2012. "Estimating the Volume of Counterfeit U.S. Currency in Circulation Worldwide: Data and Extrapolation." *Journal of Art Crime* 2012 (8): 13–29.

Kagin, Donald H. 1984. "Monetary Aspects of the Treasury Notes of the War of 1812." *Journal of Economic History* 44 (1): 69–88.

Kahn, Charles M., James J. McAndrews, and William Roberds. 2005. "Money Is Privacy." *International Economic Review* 46: 377–99.

Keynes, John Maynard. 1936. *The General Theory of Employment, Interest and Money.* London: Macmillan and Co.

Kilmer, Beau, Susan S. Everingham, Jonathan P. Caulkins, Gregory Midgette, Rosalie Liccardo Pacula, Peter H. Reuter, Rachel M. Burns, Bing Han, and Russell Lundberg. 2014. "How Big Is the U.S. Market for Illegal Drugs?" Santa Monica, CA: RAND Corporation. Available at http://www.rand.org/pubs/research_briefs/RB9770.

Kiyotaki, Nobuhiro, and Randall Wright. 1989. "On Money as a Medium of Exchange." *Journal of Political Economy* 87 (4): 927–54.

Klee, Elizabeth. 2008. "How People Pay: Evidence from Grocery Store Data." *Journal of Monetary Economics* 55 (3): 526–41.

Kocherlakota, Narayana R. 1998. "Money Is Memory." *Journal of Economic Theory* 81 (2): 232–51.

Kotlikoff, Lawrence. 2011. *Jimmy Stewart Is Dead: Ending the World's Ongoing Financial Plague with Limited Purpose Banking.* New York: John Wiley.

Krishnamurthy, Arvind, and Annette Vissing-Jorgensen. 2011. "The Effects of Quantitative Easing on Interest Rates: Channels and Implications for Policy." *Brookings Papers on Economic Activity* Fall: 215–265.

———. 2013. "The Ins and Outs of LSAPs." In *Proceedings of the Kansas City Federal Reserve Bank Symposium on Global Dimensions of Unconventional Monetary Policy*, Jackson Hole, WY, August 22–24. Federal Reserve Bank of Kansas City.

Krugman, Paul R. 1998. "It's Baaack: Japan's Slump and the Return of the Liquidity Trap." *Brookings Papers on Economic Activity* 2: 137–205.

———. 2014. "Inflation Targets Reconsidered." In *ECB Forum on Central Banking Conference Proceedings 2014: Monetary Policy in a Changing Financial Landscape.* Frankfurt: European Central Bank.

Kuroda, Haruhiko. 2005. *Zaisei-Kinyu Seisaku no Seiko* [Success and Failure in Fiscal and Monetary Policies] (in Japanese). Tokyo: Nippon-Hyoron-Sha.

Kydland, Finn, and Edward C. Prescott. 1977. "Rules Rather Than Discretion: The Inconsistency of Optimal Plans." *Journal of Political Economy* 85 (3): 473–92.

Landefeld, Steven J., Eugene F. Seskin, and Barbara M. Fraumeni. 2008. "Taking the Pulse of the Economy: Measuring GDP." *Journal of Political Economy* 22 (2): 193–216.

Landes, David. 1999. *The Wealth and Poverty of Nations: Why Some Are So Rich and Some Are So Poor.* New York: W. W. Norton and Co.

La Porta, Rafael, and Andrei Shleifer. 2014. "Informality and Development." *Journal of Economic Perspectives* 28 (3): 109–26.

Lebow, David E. 1993. "Monetary Policy at Near Zero Interest Rates." Federal Reserve Board, Division of Research and Statistics Working Paper 136 (July). Washington, DC.

Leeper, Eric. 1991. "Equilibria under Active and Passive Monetary and Fiscal Policies." *Journal of Monetary Economics* 27: 129–47.

Levenson, Thomas. 2011. *Newton and the Counterfeiter.* London: Faber and Faber.

Littlefield, Henry M. 1964. "The Wizard of Oz: Parable on Populism." *American Quarterly* 16 (Spring 1964): 47–58. Reprinted in *The American Culture: Approaches to the Study of the United States*, edited by Hennig Cohen. Boston: Houghton Mifflin, 1968.

Lo, Stephanie, and J. Christina Wang. 2014. "Bitcoin as Money." Federal Reserve Bank of Boston Current Policy Perspectives 14-4 (September). Available at http://www.bostonfed.org/economic/current-policy-perspectives/2014/cpp1404.pdf.

Lohmann, Susanne. 1992. "Optimal Commitment in Monetary Policy: Credibility versus Flexibility." *American Economic Review* 82: 273–86.

Mankiw, N. Gregory. 2009. "It May Be Time for the Fed to Go Negative." *New York Times*, April 18.

Marimon, Ramon, Juan Nicollini, and Pedro Teles. 1997. "Electronic Money: The End of Inflation?" Federal Reserve Bank of Minneapolis Discussion Paper 122 (August).

Maron, Dina Fine. 2017. "Dirty Money: The Public Health Case for a Cashless Society," *Scientific American* (January 3).

Mauro, Paolo. 1995. "Corruption and Growth." *Quarterly Journal of Economics* 110 (3): 681–712.

McAndrews, Jamie. 2015. "Negative Interest Rates: Where Is the Lower Bound?" Remarks by New York Federal Reserve executive vice president and director of research at the University of Wisconsin, Madison (May 8).

Meade, James. 1978. "The Meaning of Internal Balance." *Economic Journal* 88: 423–35.

Melitz, Jacques. 2015. "A Formal Analysis of the Beginnings of Coinage in Antiquity." Centre for Economic Policy Research (CEPR) Discussion Paper 10795 (August). London.

Meltzer, Allan H. 2010. *A History of the Federal Reserve*, vol. 2, book 2, 1970–1986. Chicago: University of Chicago Press.

Mishkin, Frederic S. 2007. "Housing and the Monetary Transmission Mechanism." In *Proceedings of Federal Reserve Bank of Kansas City Symposium on Housing, Housing Finance, and Monetary Policy*, pp. 359–413. Jackson Hole, WY, August 20–September 1.

Missale, Alessandro, and Olivier Jean Blanchard. 1994. "The Debt Burden and Debt Maturity." *American Economic Review* 84 (1): 309–19.

Morse, H. B. 1906. *Currency in China*. Shanghai: Kelley and Walsh.

Morse, Susan Cleary, Steven Karlinksy, and Joseph Bankman. 2009. "Cash Businesses and Tax Evasion." *Stanford Policy and Law Review* 20 (1): 37–68.

Nakamura, Emi, Jon Steinsson, Patrick Sun, and Daniel Villar. 2015. "The Elusive Costs of Inflation: Price Dispersion during the U.S. Great Inflation" (December). Columbia University, New York.

Naritomi, Joana. 2015. "Consumers as Tax Auditors" (April). Mimeo, London School of Economics.

Neumann, Manfred J. M. 1992. "Seigniorage in the United States: How Much Does the U.S. Government Make from Money Production?" *Federal Reserve Bank of St Louis Review* 74 (2): 29–42.

Obstfeld, Maurice, and Kenneth Rogoff. 1996. *Foundations of International Macroeconomics*. Cambridge, MA: MIT Press.

———. 2002. "Global Implications of Self-Oriented National Monetary Rules." *Quarterly Journal of Economics* 117: 503–36.

Okamura, Tadao. 1993. "The Japanese Tax System—Due Process and the Taxpayer." *Berkeley Journal of International Law* 11: 125–58.

Orji, N., E. Esiaka, L. Anyaegbunam, R. Obi, and D. Ezeagwuna. 2012. "Parasite Contamination of Nigerian Currency (Paper and Polymer Notes) in the Ihiala Local Government Area of Anamber State, Nigeria." *Internet Journal of Infectious Diseases* 10 (1).

Otani, Akira, and Takashi Suzuki. 2008. "Background to the High Level of Banknotes in Circulation and Demand Deposits." *Bank of Japan Review* (September).

Peng, Wensheng, and Joanna Y. L. Shi. 2003. "Offshore Use of Currency: Hong Kong's Experience." In *China's Capital Account Liberalisation: International Perspectives*, BIS Papers 15, part 20. Basle: Bank for International Settlements.

Peng, Xinwei. 1994. *A Monetary History of China* (in two volumes). Translated by Edward H. Kaplan. Bellingham, Washington: Western Washington University.

Pew Research Center. 2014. "As Growth Stalls, Unauthorized Immigrant Population Becomes More Settled" (September). Washington, DC: Pew Foundation.

Philippon, Thomas. 2015. "Has the US Finance Industry Become Less Efficient? On the Theory and Measurement of Financial Intermediation." *American Economic Review* 105 (4): 1408–38.

Pissarides, Christopher A., and Guglielmo Weber. 1989. "An Expenditure-Based Estimate of Britain's Black Economy." *Journal of Public Economics* 39 (1): 17–32.

Porter, Richard D. 1993. "Estimates of Foreign Holdings of U.S. Currency—An Approach Based on Relative Cross-Country Seasonal Variations." In *Nominal Income Targeting with the Monetary Base as Instrument: An Evaluation of McCallum's Rule*. Finance and Economics Discussion Series Working Study 1 (March). Board of Governors of the Federal Reserve, Washington, DC.

Porter, Richard D., and Ruth A. Judson. 1996. "The Location of US Currency: How Much Is Abroad?" Federal Reserve Bulletin, October. Washington, DC.

Reifschneider, David L., and John C. Williams. 2000. "Three Lessons for Monetary Policy in a Low-Inflation Era." *Journal of Money, Credit and Banking* 32 (4): 936–66.

Reinhart, Carmen M., Vincent Reinhart, and Kenneth S. Rogoff. 2015. "Dealing with Debt." *Journal of International Economics* 96, suppl. 1 (July): S43–S55.

Reinhart, Carmen M., and Kenneth S. Rogoff. 2002. "The Modern History of Exchange Rate Arrangements: A Reinterpretation." NBER Working Paper 8963 (June). Cambridge, MA: National Bureau of Economic Research.

———. 2004. "The Modern History of Exchange Rate Arrangements: A Reinterpretation." *Quarterly Journal of Economics* 119 (1): 1–48.

———. 2009. *This Time Is Different: Eight Centuries of Financial Folly*. Princeton, NJ: Princeton University Press.

———. 2010. "Debt and Growth Revisited," VoxEU.org, August 11, 2010.

———. 2013. "Shifting Mandates: The Federal Reserve's First Centennial." *American Economic Review* 103 (3): 48–54.

———. 2014. "Recovery from Financial Crises: Evidence from 100 Episodes." *American Economic Review* 104 (5): 50–55.

Reinhart, Carmen M., and M. Belen Sbrancia. 2015. "The Liquidation of Government Debt." *Economic Policy* 30 (82): 291–333.

Rey, Hélène. 2013. "Dilemma not Trilemma: The Global Financial Cycle and Monetary Policy Independence." In *Proceedings of the Kansas City Federal Reserve Bank Symposium on Global Dimensions of Unconventional Monetary Policy*, Jackson Hole, WY, August 21–23. Kansas City Federal Reserve Bank.

Rognlie, Matthew. 2016. "What Lower Bound? Monetary Policy with Negative Interest Rates." Cambridge, MA: Massachusetts Institute of Technology.

Rogoff, Kenneth S. 1985. "The Optimal Degree of Commitment to an Intermediate Monetary Target." *Quarterly Journal of Economics* 100 (4): 1169–89.

———. 1998a. "Foreign and Underground Demand for Euro Notes: Blessing or Curse?" *Economic Policy* 26 (April): 263–303.

———. 1998b. "Comment on Paul Krugman, 'It's Baaack: Japan's Slump and the Return of the Liquidity Trap.'" *Brookings Papers on Economic Activity* 2: 194–99.

———. 2002. "The Surprising Popularity of Paper Currency." *Finance & Development* 39 (1).

———. 2003. "The Case for Inflation Transparency." *Financial Times*, April 23.

———. 2004. "Globalization and Global Disinflation." In *Proceedings of the Kansas City Federal Reserve Bank Symposium on Monetary Policy and Uncertainty: Adapting to a Changing Economy*, Jackson Hole, WY, August 28–30, 2003. Kansas City Federal Reserve Bank.

———. 2007. "Impact of Globalization on Monetary Policy." In *Proceedings of the Kansas City Federal Reserve Bank Symposium on the New Economic Geography: Effects and Policy Implications*, Jackson Hole, WY, August 2006. Kansas City Federal Reserve Bank.

———. 2008. "Inflation Is Now the Lesser Evil." Project Syndicate, December. Available at http://www.project-syndicate.org/commentary/inflation-is-now-the-lesser-evil.

———. 2014. "Costs and Benefits to Phasing Out Paper Currency." In *NBER Macroeconomics Annual*, ed. Jonathan Parker and Michael Woodford. Chicago: University of Chicago Press.

———. 2016. "Debt Supercycle, Not Secular Stagnation." In *Progress and Confusion: The State of Macroeconomic Policy*, edited by Olivier Blanchard, Raghuram Rajan, Kenneth Rogoff, and Lawrence H. Summers. Cambridge: MIT Press, pp. 19–28.

Rolnick, Arthur J. 2004. "Interview with Ben S. Bernanke." Minneapolis Federal Reserve, *Region Magazine* (June).

Rolnick, Arthur J., François R. Velde, and Warren E. Weber. 1996. "The Debasement Puzzle: An Essay on Medieval Monetary History." *Journal of Economic History* 56 (4): 789–808.

Rothbard, Murray N. 2002. *A History of Money and Banking in the United States*. Washington, DC: Ludwig von Mises Institute.

Runyon, Damon. 1930. "Blood Pressure." *Saturday Evening Post* 202 (April 5).

———. 2008. *Guys and Dolls and Other Writings*. New York: Penguin Classics.

Sands, Peter. 2015. "Making It Harder for the Bad Guys: The Case for Eliminating High Denomination Notes." Mossavar-Rahmani Center for Business and Government Working Paper 52 (February). Cambridge, MA.

Sargent, Thomas J., and François R. Velde, 2003. *The Big Problem of Small Change*. Princeton, NJ: Princeton University Press.

Schmidt, Sebastian. 2013. "Optimal Monetary and Fiscal Policy with a Zero Bound on Nominal Interest Rates." *Journal of Money, Credit and Banking* 45 (7): 1135–1350.

Schmitt-Grohe, Stephanie, and Martin Uribe. 1999. "Dollarization and Seignorage: How Much Is at Stake?" Working Paper, University of Pennsylvania, Philadelphia (July).

Schneider, Friedrich. 2013. "The Financial Flows of Transnational Crime and Tax Fraud in OECD Countries: What Do We (Not) Know?" *Public Finance Review* 41 (3): 677–707.

———. 2015. "The Financial Flows of Transnational Crime and Tax Fraud: How Much Cash Is Used and What We Do (Not) Know." Talk presented at Johannes Kepler Universität Linz, November. Slides available at www.libinst.ch /presentationen/LI-FSchneider-Bargeldtrial.pdf.

———. 2016. "Size and Development of the Shadow Economy of 31 European and 5 Other OECD Countries" (January). Mimeo, Department of Economics, Johannes Kepler University Linz, Austria.

Schneider, Friedrich, and Andreas Buehn. 2012. "Size and Development of Tax Evasion in 38 OECD Countries: What Do We (Not) Know?" CESifo Working Paper 4004 (November). University of Munich, Germany.

Schneider, Friedrich, Andreas Buehn, and Claudio E. Montenegro. 2010. "New Estimates for the Shadow Economies All Over the World." *International Economic Journal* 24 (December): 443–61.

Schneider, Friedrich, and Alexandra Rudolph. 2013. "International Human Trafficking: Measuring Clandestinity by the Structural Equation Approach." Working Paper 1325 (December). Department of Economics, Johannes Kepler University Linz, Austria.

Schneider, Friedrich, and Colin Williams. 2013. *The Shadow Economy*. London: Profile Books and Institute for International Affairs.

Schuh, Scott, and Joanna Stavins. 2015. "The 2013 Survey of Consumer Payment Choice: Summary Results." Federal Reserve Bank of Boston Research Data Report 15-4 (July 27).

Seitz, Franz. 1995. "The Circulation of the Deutschmark Abroad." Deutsche Bank Discussion Paper 1/95. Deutsche Bundesbank, Frankfurt.

Serious Organised Crime Agency. 2011. Annual Report and Accounts, 2010/2011. London: Controller of Her Majesty's Stationery Office.

Sims, Christopher. 1994. "A Simple Model for the Determination of the Price Level and the Interaction of Monetary and Fiscal Policy." *Economic Theory* 4: 381–99.

Slemrod, Joel. 2007. "Cheating Ourselves: The Economics of Tax Evasion." *Journal of Economic Perspectives* 21 (1): 25–48.

———. 2016. "Tax Compliance and Enforcement: New Research and Its Policy Implications." University of Michigan, Ross School of Business Working Paper No. 1302 (January), Ann Arbor.

Speiser, Stuart M. 1975. "Abolish Paper Money and Eliminate Most Crime." *American Bar Association Journal* 61 (1): 47–49.

Sprenkle, Case M. 1993. "The Case of the Missing Currency." *Journal of Economic Perspectives* 7 (3): 175–84.

Summers, Lawrence. 1991. "How Should Long-Term Monetary Policy Be Determined?" *Journal of Money, Credit and Banking* 23 (part 2/August): 625–31.

Sumner, Scott. 1990. "The Transactions and Hoarding Demand for Currency." *Quarterly Review of Economics and Business* 30 (1): 75–89.

Svensson, Lars E. O. 2010. "Inflation Targeting." In *The Handbook of Monetary Economics,* vol 3b. Edited by Benjamin Friedman and Michael Woodford. Amsterdam: Elsevier.

Svensson, Roger, and Andreas Westermark. 2015. "Renovatio Monetae: Gesell Taxes in Practice" (September). Research Institute of Industrial Economics Working Paper 1083, Stockholm.

Tax Policy Center. 2012. "The Numbers: What Is the Breakdown of Revenues among Federal, State, and Local Governments?" Available at http://www.taxpolicycenter .org/briefing-book/background/numbers/revenue-breakdown.cfm.

Taylor, John B. 1993. "Discretion versus Policy Rules in Practice." *Carnegie-Rochester Conference Series on Public Policy* 39: 195–214.

Transparency International. 2004. *Global Corruption Report.* London and Sterling, VA: Pluto Press. Available at http://www.transparency.org/whatwedo /publication/global_corruption_report_2004_political_corruption.

Treasury Inspector General for Tax Administration. 2013. "The Internal Revenue Service Needs to Improve the Comprehensiveness, Accuracy, Reliability, and Timeliness of the Tax Gap Estimate." Reference Number: 2013-IE-R008, August 21. Washington, DC: Department of the Treasury.

Tullock, Gordon. 1957. "Paper Money—A Cycle in Cathay." *Economic History Review* 9 (3): 393–407.

Turner, Adair. 2015. *Between Debt and the Devil.* Princeton, NJ: Princeton University Press.

United Nations Office on Drugs and Crime. 2005. *World Drug Report 2005.* Geneva.

———. 2011. *World Drug Report 2011.* Geneva.

———. 2014. *Global Report on Trafficking in Persons.* Geneva: United Nations.

United States Department of State. 2015. *Trafficking in Persons Report, 2015.* Washington, DC: Government Printing Office.

United States Mint. 2014. *Biennial Report to Congress.* Washington, DC: U.S. Department of the Treasury.

United States Treasury. 2006. "The Use and Counterfeiting of United States Currency Abroad, Part 3." Final Report to Congress by the Secretary of the Treasury (written in cooperation with the Board of Governors of the Federal Reserve System and the United States Secret Service). Available at http://www .federalreserve.gov/boarddocs/rptcongress/counterfeit/default.htm.

Vigna, Paul, and Michael Casey. 2015. *The Age of Cryptocurrency: How Bitcoin and Digital Money Are Challenging the Global Economy.* New York: St. Martin's Press.

Von Glahn, Richard. 1996. *Fountain of Fortune: Money and Monetary Policy in China, 1000–1700.* Berkeley: University of California Press.

Wallace, Neil. 1981. "A Modigliani Miller Theorem for Open Market Operations." *American Economic Review* 71 (3): 267–75.

Walsh, Carl. 1995. "Optimal Contracts for Central Bankers." *American Economic Review* 85 (1): 150–67.

————. 2011. "The Future of Inflation Targeting." *Economic Record* 87: 23–36.

Wang, Zhu, and Alexander L. Wolman. 2014. "Payment Choice and the Future of Currency: Insights from Two Billion Retail Transactions." Federal Reserve Bank of Richmond Working Paper 14-09 (April), Richmond, VA.

Warwick, David. 2015. *The Abolition of Cash: America's $660 Billion Problem*. Santa Rosa, CA: David Warwick.

Werning, Ivan. 2011. "Managing a Liquidity Trap: Monetary and Fiscal Policy." NBER Working Paper 17344 (August). Cambridge, MA: National Bureau of Economic Research.

Williams, John C. 2009. "Heeding Daedalus: Optimal Inflation and the Zero Lower Bound." *Brookings Papers on Economic Activity* Fall: 1–37.

————. 2013. "Lessons from the Financial Crisis for Unconventional Monetary Policy." Panel Discussion at NBER conference, October 18. Available at http://www.frbsf.org/our-district/press/presidents-speeches/williams-speeches/2013/october/research-unconventional-monetary-policy-financial-crisis/.

Wolman, Alexander. 1998. "Staggered Price Setting and the Zero Bound on Nominal Rates." Federal Reserve Bank of Richmond. *Economic Quarterly* 84 (4): 1–24.

Wolman, David. 2012. *The End of Money: Counterfeiters, Preachers, Techies, Dreamers—and the Coming Cashless Society*. Philadelphia: Da Capo Press.

Woodford, Michael. 1996. "Control of the Public Debt: A Requirement for Price Level Stability?" NBER Working Paper 5684 (July). Cambridge, MA: National Bureau of Economic Research.

————. 2003. *Interest and Prices: Foundations of a Theory of Monetary Policy*. Princeton, NJ: Princeton University Press.

————. 2012. "Methods of Monetary Accommodation at the Zero Bound." In *Proceedings of the Federal Reserve Bank of Kansas City Symposium on Economic Policy*, Jackson Hole, WY, August 30–September 1. Federal Reserve Bank of Kansas City.

World Bank. 2016. "Six Questions on the Cost of Corruption with World Bank Institute Global Governance Director Daniel Kaufmann." Available online at http://web.worldbank.org/.

World Gold Council. 2015. "Gold Demand Trends: Second Quarter 2015." London: World Gold Council. Available online at http://www.gold.org/supply-and-demand/gold-demand-trends.

Wright, Richard, Erdal Tekin, Volkan Topalli, Chandler McClellan, Timothy Dickinson, and Richard Rosenfeld. 2014. "Less Cash, Less Crime: Evidence from the Electronic Benefit Transfer Program." NBER Working Paper 19996 (March). Cambridge, MA: National Bureau of Economic Research.

Wu, Jing Cynthia, and Fan Dora Xia. 2016. "Measuring the Macroeconomic Impact of Monetary Policy at the Zero Lower Bound." *Journal of Money, Credit, and Banking* 48 (2–3): 253–91.

Yehoue, Etienne B. 2012. "On Price Stability and Welfare." International Monetary Fund Working Paper 12/189. Washington, DC.

Yellen, Janet. 2012. "Perspectives on Monetary Policy." Remarks at the Boston Economic Club Dinner, Federal Reserve Bank of Boston, June 6. Available at http://www.federalreserve.gov/newsevents/speech/yellen20120606a.htm.

Zucman, Gabriel. 2015. *The Hidden Wealth of Nations: The Scourge of Tax Havens*. Chicago: University of Chicago Press.

Zuo, Yuegang, Kai Zhang, Jingpin Wuo, Christopher Rego, and John Fritz. 2008. "An Accurate and Nondestructive GC Method for Determination of Cocaine on US Paper Currency." *Journal of Separation Science* 31 (13): 2444–50.

INDEX

Abacha, Sani, 71
ABSCAM, 70–71
Acemoglu, Daron, 70
Admati, Anat, 262n12
Agarwal, Ruchir, 167, 171–74
Ahamed, Liaquat, 29
Alexander the Great, 18–19
"All About the Benjamins," 253n5
alternative payment mechanisms: for
  corrupt and criminal activities, 72;
  proliferation of, 32; for use as paper
  currency is phased out, 100. *See also*
  Bitcoin; cryptocurrencies
American Hustle (Russell), 71
Amromin, Gene, 258n22
Andolfatto, David, 213
Antràs, Pol, 256n12
Argentina, 44, 82
Ascaria, Guido, 268n5
Australia, 52, 132
Australian National Audit Office, 228,
  276n14
Austria: cash, per capita holdings of,
  33; cash used for different kinds of
  purchases, percentage of, 55–56;
  coinage debasement in, 20; currency
  held by consumers in, 51–52; deutsche
  mark currency demand, as a control
  for estimating, 45; stamp currency
  experiment in, 164–65
Automated Clearing House system, 103

Bagehot, Walter, 264n9
Bank Act of 1844 (Peel's Act), 255n25
Bank of England: inflation target, choice
  of, 153; interest rate hike prior to 2008,
  impact of, 177–78; nominal policy
  interest rates, 2000–2015, 130; notes
  convertible to specie, early issue of, 26;
  quantitative easing by, 135–36
Bank of Japan: inflationary expectations,
  challenges faced in lifting, 124;
  inflation target, choice of, 153; January
  2016 policy of, 270n5; museum of,
  understanding coinage debasement in,
  20; negative interest rates, experience
  with, 1, 161; quantitative easing by,

135–36, 143; zero-bound problem
  of, lack of international coordination
  regarding, 206
Bartzsch, Nikolaus, 256n23
Baum, Frank (author of *The Wonderful
  Wizard of Oz*), 192
Belgium: cash used for different kinds of
  purchases, percentage of, 55; currency/
  GDP ratio, 1995, 46–47; restrictions on
  the use of cash, 64
Bennett, Paul, 257n4
Bernanke, Ben: financial stability, limits to
  concern regarding, 176; "global savings
  glut," 122; "Helicoper Ben," advice for
  Japan from, 155; inflation targeting
  adopted under, 232; macroprudential
  regulation, argument for, 177; Perry's
  attack on, 191; small interest hikes,
  limited impact of, 177; "taper tantrum"
  set off by, 126, 141
Billi, Roberto, 229
biometric method for estimating foreign
  holdings of currency, 43–44
Birch, David, 262n2, 263n6
Bitcoin/bitcoins: "Bencoin" as governmental
  version of, 209–10, 213–14; blockchain
  technology pioneered by, 112; as a
  currency, possibility of, 211; as encrypted
  digital technology, 208; inflation and,
  213; market price of, 212; as payment
  mechanism for criminal activities, 72;
  security of using, 67
Black, Fischer, 264n5
Blackburn, David, 273n6
Blanchard, Olivier Jean, 268n2, 272n7
blockchain technology, 112, 210, 213–14
border control, issue of, 75–76
Bordo, Michael D., 254n6
Brazil, 65, 183–84, 191, 205
Breaking Bad (TV series), 68, 260n27
Bretton Woods regime, 30
bribes, 70
Britain. *See* United Kingdom
Bryan, William Jennings (US politician), 192
Buehn, Andreas, 259n12
Buiter, Willem, 167–74
Burns, Arthur, 189

Rösl, Gerhard, 256n23
Rubin, Robert, 2
Runyon, Damon, 222, 275n3–4
Russell, David O., 71 (director, *American Hustle*)
Russia, 44, 83–84, 191, 203

Sands, Peter, 273n5
Sargent, Thomas J., 19
Sbordone, Argia M., 268n5
Schneider, Friedrich, 62, 259n12, 259n16
Schwartz, Anna, 188
Secret Service: foreign holdings of currency, estimate of, 44–45; founding of to fight counterfeiting, 77
security concerns, 111–14
seigniorage, 80–81; cost of substituting interest-bearing debt for paper currency, 86–90; measures of, 81–85; political economy importance of, central bank independence and, 90–91, 106; revenue as a percentage of GDP, 2006–2015, 84; shrinkage of revenues if currency were phased out, 85–86, 202–4
Seitz, Franz, 45, 256n23
Serious Organised Crime Agency (SOCA), 200
sexual exploitation in the United States, 74
shadow policy interest rate, 264n5
Shi, Joanna Y. L., 256n13
Shleifer, Andrei, 64, 259n14
short-stick lotteries to pay negative interest rate on currency, 165
Silk Road, 214
Simon, Henry, 86
Sims, Christopher, 227
Singapore: discount rate cuts in response to recent crises, 132; foreign demand for paper currency of, 34; large-denomination notes of, 33, 37; phaseout of large-denomination paper currency in, 95, 255n4; revenue as a percentage of GDP, 2006–2015, 83–84
Skolimowski, Jerzy (director, *Moonlighting*), 74
Slemrod, Joel, 61
smartphones. *See* cell phones/smartphones
Snowden, Edward, 101
Spain: cash used for different kinds of purchases, percentage of, 55–56; currency/GDP ratio, 1995, 46; pieces of eight, 26; restrictions on the use of

cash, 64; underground economy, estimated size of, 62–63
Speiser, Stuart M., 260n25
Sprenkle, Case M., 256n10
Stein, Jeremy, 177
Stockholms Banco, 25
subsidized debit cards, 48, 99–100, 204, 218
substituting interest-bearing debt for paper currency, cost of, 86–90
Suharto, 71
Summers, Lawrence, 122
Suzuki, Takashi, 255n6
Svennson, Lars, 231
Sweden: banknotes and coins in circulation, 108; cashless society, movement to, 107–9; currency/GDP ratio, 1995, 46–47; currency/GDP ratio, 2015, 36–37; decline in use of notes and coins, 84; declining total demand for large notes, 108; discount rate cuts in response to recent crises, 132; early private notes issued in, 25; financial stability concerns, negative interest rates and, 178; interest rates near the zero bound, 131; low-income individuals, accommodations for, 3; negative interest rates, payment on bonds and, 163; negative interest rates in, 5, 123; phaseout of large-denomination paper currency in, 95, 107, 109; revenue as a percentage of GDP, 2006–2015, 84
Swiss National Bank, 160–61, 266n23
Switzerland: borrowing capacity and debt-financed gold purchases, 266n23; currency/GDP ratio, 2015, 36; currency per capita, 37, 40; discount rate cuts in response to recent crises, 132; financial stability concerns, negative interest rates and, 178; foreign demand for paper currency of, 34; foreign holdings of currency, 41; interest rates near the zero bound, 131; large-denomination notes of, 31, 37; negative interest rates in, 5, 123; revenue as a percentage of GDP, 2006–2015, 83–84; as tax haven, 66; underground economy, estimated size of, 62–63

"taper tantrum" of May 2014, 126, 141
Tax Equity and Fiscal Responsibility Act of 1982, 253n6